Classic Christianity

*A Year of Timeless Devotions
Volume I Winter and Spring*

Based on the Writings of The Reverend L.A. Meade,
Revised and Edited by
Patricia Ediger and Cara Shelton

Artumitze Publishing

Artumitze Publishing, a division of Classic Christianity, 09/01/2015
Springville, CA
Printed by CreateSpace, An Amazon.com Company

©2015 Patricia Ediger and Cara Shelton. All rights reserved.

No part of this book may be reproduced, stored in a retrieval system, or transmitted by any means without the written permission of the author.

First edition published by Crossbooks, 10/26/2011

ISBN : (sc) 978-1-944023-00-3
ISBN: (e) 978-1-944023-01-0

Library of Congress Control Number: 2015913867

Printed in the United States of America

This book is printed on acid-free paper.

Any people depicted in stock imagery provided by Thinkstock are models, and such images are being used for illustrative purposes only.

Certain stock imagery © Thinkstock.

Because of the dynamic nature of the Internet, any web addresses or links contained in this book may have changed since publication and may no longer be valid.

Scripture taken from the New King James Version. Copyright © 1982 by Thomas Nelson, Inc. Used by permission. All rights reserved.

All rights reserved. Reproduction or use of the editorial or pictorial content of this material in any manner is prohibited by law without the express permission of the author.

Table of Contents

Preface ix

Winter
Introduction to the Author xi
Daily Devotions for January, February, March.................... 1
Devotions for the week between Palm Sunday and Easter 183

Spring
Introduction to the Author 201
Daily Devotions for April, May, June............................... 203

Preface

Several years ago, as we helped our elderly mother move, we discovered a treasure in the rafters above her garage.

Our grandfather, the Reverend Lawrence A. Meade, was an internationally known evangelist and ordained minister who preached all over this nation for more than fifty years. We had known he spoke and taught with passion and fervor, sincerity and integrity to the Word. What we hadn't realized was that he wrote with the same power and honesty.

When we lifted the lids on the dusty boxes in the attic, we discovered words so fraught with meaning for today's world and for today's Christian that we were amazed. Could words this fresh really be over ninety years old? It seems impossible, but it is so.

This treasure was a stewardship from God to us. We have felt deeply the responsibility to share these insights that others might benefit. And now, this stewardship passes to you, the reader. These devotions are not a fast-food meal, dear friend. They are a full course dinner to be savored and enjoyed over time. They are not flashy. The light that shines through them, however, is steady and unwavering. This is a book for those of us who want "more" of God. God bless you as you follow Him.

Patricia and Cara

Classic Christianity

A Year of Timeless Devotions

WINTER

*Daily Devotions for January,
February, and March*

*With an Appendix containing
A Passion Week Supplement*

Based on the Writings of
The Reverend L.A. Meade

Revised and Edited by
Patricia Ediger and Cara Shelton

Samuel Meade, surrounded by his five sons.
L.A. is on the far right.

Introduction to the Author

Over a hundred years ago, in the small town of Brockville, Ontario, Canada, yet another son made his appearance in the household of Samuel and Rhoda Meade. Samuel was the pastor of a small local church, Rhoda the mother of now five sons and one daughter. Little did they realize then that each of their sons would someday feel the tug of God on his heart to full-time Christian ministry.

This youngest Meade son, Lawrence Adelbert, would someday preach before crowds filling a 3,000 person capacity tent. Beginning in 1914, he preached God's word faithfully for over 50 years, first as a traveling evangelist and then as a pastor of local churches. During his years of travel, he was commended by pastors across denominational lines as having the highest scriptural and personal integrity, as well as teaching that was compelling, inspired, sincere, and produced enduring spiritual growth.

In the days when the Rev. Meade preached, people were worried about impending war, financial problems, cultural changes, and the uncertain future. The same things concern people today. People then were confused about whether God really loved them, and if they could ever be forgiven. They wondered if God was to be trusted, and if He could heal their situation. The same things concern us today. People then were seeking assurance of God's protection, a strong shelter for their loved ones and themselves. We seek the same things today. The Reverend Meade's messages addressed these issues. His heart ached to see souls saved, and lives mended. But, even further, his passion was to see Christians fulfilling their place in God's plan.

Lawrence A. Meade was our "Papa." He was born on September 11, 1892 and died Sept 10, 1971. His life spanned the changes of both world wars and Vietnam, yet he shook the hands of Civil War veterans. He was a witness to the changes industry brought, yet he stood fast on the timeless truths of Scripture. His words are as much for today as they were for yesterday, and they will be as much for tomorrow as they are for today.

January 1   The Untrodden Path

Scripture Reading: Joshua Chapter 3

Key Verses: "... you have not passed this way before.... Sanctify yourselves, for tomorrow the Lord will do wonders among you." Joshua 3:4b-5

No matter what tomorrow holds, God's people are prepared for it if they draw near to Him. Whether the untried paths are those of a new land, as for the Children of Israel, or those of a New Year, we can trust in Him.

There will be new experiences to face, new problems to solve, new trials to endure and new temptations to meet. There will also be new opportunities to grasp, new tasks to perform, and new blessings to enjoy. Yes, the new way may hold all of this, and more.

After forty years of wilderness wandering, the Children of Israel stood at the border of the new country which they had left Egypt to possess. Only the Jordan River separated them from it. Through the parting waters of the Red Sea they left the land of bondage and through the parting waters of the Jordan they would enter fair Canaan, the land "flowing with milk and honey." Tomorrow they would tread new and untried paths in which God would do wonders among them; and Joshua calls upon the people to sanctify themselves for this new experience which awaits them.

For the Children of Israel, this would be a way of testing. Not only was the river swollen, obliterating all fords, but there were Jericho's towering walls to consider. In the new land there were giants to fight, and cities to conquer. But the Lord has never promised His people an easy time in this world. And, as for them, so for us; faith will overcome every difficulty.

As soon as the feet of the priests who carried the Ark of the Covenant touched the waters, they were parted. And so it is with us, for, "If God is for us, who can be against us?"

While there are sure to be difficulties this New Year, we need not have fear because the One who goes before us knows them and is equal to them all. We need the testing of our faith for the greater experiences to be enjoyed and the greater work to be done.

The swollen Jordan challenged the progress of the Children of Israel, yet divine provision for their crossing was at hand. God is saying to us today, as He said to His people of old, "This is the way, walk in it, whenever you turn to the right hand or whenever you turn to the left." (Is. 30:21). For every challenge, there is always ample provision for those who have the faith to obey.

When you are discouraged or blue this year, read Hebrews 11. What a catalog of the victories of faith! It gives eloquent testimony that where God leads there is provision for those who faithfully follow. While we are constantly surrounded by life's uncertainties, we rejoice that we have heavenly certainties. Life is uncertain. Wealth is uncertain. Friendships are uncertain. But thank God, God is a certainty. His presence in your life is assured.

This New Year will have much to offer. It presents an untrodden path, and the feet of faith falter not upon entering it. Because of the One who goes before us, we walk with assurance. The treasures of this path await those who have the courage to follow on and possess them. Trust God, for we are under His care and in His keeping.

Dear Lord, thank You for allowing me the privilege of this New Year. I ask, as I enter it, that You help me to remember that I do not need to understand where each day will take me. I must only remember to follow You. Please help me to be faithful in that walk this year, Lord, that I might bring glory to Your precious name. Amen.

January 2   What is That in Your Hand?

Scripture Reading: Exodus 4:1-17

Key Verse: "So the Lord said to him, 'What is that in your hand?' He said, 'A rod.'" Exodus 4:2

Moses was simply keeping sheep in Midian, when God told him to go and deliver Israel out of bondage. He shrank from such an undertaking, for he was without training in warfare. He had nothing but his shepherd's rod, cut out of the thicket, the mere crab-stick with which he guided his sheep. Any day he might throw it away and get a better one.

But God said, "What is that in your hand?" And Moses said, "A rod." God told him that with that rod, that mere stick, he should save Israel. And, so it was. The rod constituted his visible means. God made it sufficient. So it is today, as God calls us to tasks for Him. We should use the little things we have, the present means we possess, for God, and not wait for wealth, ability, influence, or power. Use what is in your hand. This is the method by which all great works for God have been accomplished.

It is encouraging to see examples in Scripture of how God used little things to accomplish great things. "What is in your hand, David?" It was only a sling. A little weapon he made for pleasure, or to keep the wolves away from his sheep. Yet with that sling, he slew Goliath whom the whole army of Israel did not dare meet. Some of us have accomplishments we have never thought of more seriously than as a source of some slight pleasure. Have we ever thought of using that talent for God?

"What is in your hand, young follower of Christ?" "Oh, nothing but five barley loaves and two small fishes." "Bring them to me." Obedience led to the boy having the reward of seeing a multitude fed. You, too, may be young. You may say, "I can't do much." Let God use the things you have, and be blessed!

"What is in your hand, poor widow?" Only two mites? Give them to God and behold how the fame of your riches fills the world. As a result of your giving, streams of wealth from the rich and poor have flowed into the Lord's treasury for the extension of His kingdom in the world. Give Him what you have. Learn the joy of stewardship and partnership.

"What is that in your hand, weeping woman?" "Oh, it is a small alabaster box of fragrant ointment." Give it up to God. Break it and pour it upon the Savior's head and its sweet perfume is the fragrance in the church, filling the world more and more with its grateful aroma. Have you not some ornament you have stowed away, something you can bring out and use for the Master's sake? To give it to Him is the best way to save it. To break your alabaster box is the only way to let the fragrance out.

"What is in your hand, diligent Dorcas?" "I only have my needle, Lord." Use it; use it for God, and those coats and garments keep multiplying, giving warmth to those who are cold and needy and naked in this world. There is no end to the supplies that have fallen from hands that plied a needle like Dorcas.

God wants us to serve Him, where we are and with the things we happen to have just now. Moses, David, the young lad, the poor widow, the weeping woman, and Dorcas all accomplished great things for God. But, they would not have done so, had they failed to use the things they had at the moment. We must be willing to let God use us as we are. There is no such word as "only" about human life. God invests every part of it with grandeur and possibility.

Dear Lord, Use me! Use me where I am, and use what I have in my hand. Use it for Your eternal Kingdom and Your glory. What an honor, Lord, to be used by You! Thank You for the privilege, Lord. Amen.

January 3   The Gospel of Grace

Scripture Reading: Acts 20:17-32

Key Verse: "But none of these things move me; nor do I count my life dear to myself, so that I may finish my race with joy, and the ministry which I received from the Lord Jesus, to testify to the gospel of the grace of God." Acts 20:24

S. Campbell Morgan says there is no word in the New Testament that more baffles the expositor than this word, "grace." If you gathered up the occasions in which it is found in the New Testament and read them in their context, you would sit down and wonder, and worship. Another has said, "Grace is more than pity with tearful eye, more than mercy with outstretched hand, it is an omnipotent arm made bare for a mighty task." Yes, grace is something that has its origin in God's great heart of love and is bestowed upon undeserving sinners. Dr. Griffith Thomas, in his book *Grace and Power* says, "It is God's mercy pitying, it is God's wisdom planning, it is God's power preparing, it is God's love providing."

Grace is in contrast with the law. The law makes demands, grace bestows favors. The law says, "Do this;" grace says, "Take this." The law offers men something to be kept; grace offers something to keep them. The law is the expression of divine righteousness; grace is the expression of divine love. Law says, "Give the man what he deserves"; grace says, "Have mercy on the man." The law shows men their sins; grace shows a remedy for sin. The law reveals to men condemnation; grace reveals to men redemption. The law says, "Pay the debt"; grace says, "Christ has paid the debt."

The supreme manifestation of the grace of God is the gift of His Son. But, grace not only brought Jesus to the world, it led Him to Calvary. In I Peter 4:10, we read of the manifold grace of God, literally it says the many-colored grace of God. As light falls on a prism and sheds many colors, so grace shining through Jesus Christ manifests itself in many ways.

Make a study of grace, and your soul will overflow with joy until it dances with a sense of satisfaction in the assurance of God. There is no perfect synonym for grace. You say it is love, and it is, yet that is not all. You say it is mercy, and it is, but that is still not all. You say it is like longsuffering, yes, but still that is not all. You say it is tenderness, yes, but that is not yet all. Put all these words together and there is still an eternity between them and grace. Would you like to know the measure of grace?

Ascend to heaven and put your ear against the beating heart of God, then come down, down, down to Golgotha's hill and watch Jesus die for your sin. Hear the drip of His precious blood flowing for our salvation, but don't stop there. Turn your back on Calvary and go down, deeper, deeper, until the waves of that lake of fire and brimstone rage at your feet. Hear the groaning and moaning of the lost and damned. Tell me the distance between the heart of God and the bottomless pit of hell by way of Calvary's cross, and then I can give you a definition of grace itself.

Paul says, "For you know the grace of our Lord Jesus Christ, that though He was rich, yet for your sakes He became poor, that you through His poverty might become rich." This One who was rich in station, in surroundings, in sovereignty, became poor in person and position, that through His poverty we might be rich in forgiveness of sin, in fellowship with God, and in the glories of Heaven. Praise His holy name!

Dear, Holy, Wonderful, Marvelous God—thank You. Thank you for this wonderful thing called "grace." Praise Your name, Who planned and paid for it. Praise Your name, Who suffered, and then gave it freely. Thank You, God, that You love me this much. Amen.

January 4

Finding Mercy at the Bottom of the Sea

Scripture Reading: Jonah Chapter 2
Key Verse: "Then Jonah prayed to the Lord his God from the fish's belly." Jonah 2:1

When a man runs away from God, he can hardly expect smooth sailing. This particular vessel had hardly cleared the harbor when a wind, then a storm, then a gale, cast that ship about in the sea. When a hardened sea captain throws the wares overboard, and goes about calling upon every man to pray to his god, it is some storm indeed.

One can picture the surprise of the captain as he stumbles about in the hold of the ship and falls over the form of Jonah, fast asleep. The captain wastes no time in shaking Jonah out of his slumber, crying to him to call on God to save them. This period of sleeping marked the greatest danger for Jonah. As the space of water grew between him and shore, a kind of deadly calm came upon him. Jonah had fully made up his mind to rebel against God. He was without God, and satisfied to be so. No greater danger can come to any man than that.

As long as the thought of your sin breaks your heart, and you have sleepless nights, tears and sorrow, there is hope near at hand for you. But, when you become content with your sin, that it is the best possible for you, that it is good enough, then you are in danger indeed. Now, hear me beloved! Jonah's danger is the danger of many both in and out of the church today. So many out of the church are trying to make themselves content without Christ, and so many in the church are asleep to their own condition of contentment with sin.

Praise God, He did not leave Jonah undisturbed, to perish in his sin. God had his minister, in the shipmaster, take Jonah by the nape of the neck and shake him out of his slumber to face the great crisis of that hour. Praise God, He will not leave us to our own way, either.

We must notice that to slumber in sin does not keep one's sin secret, however, for the lot fell on Jonah. Yes, when the sailors cast lots to determine whose fault the storm was, the lot of the judgment exposed the guilt of the runaway prophet. Sin is often exposed to the world in unpleasant and unexpected ways. God does not want us to become comfortable in our sin. Judgment fell on Jonah, and that seemed to be the end of him. But God was not finished with Jonah quite yet.

Jonah's experience in the stomach of the fish was certainly a symbol, a type if you will, of Christ's burial and resurrection. Jonah's experience also illustrates God's purpose in judgment. God's affliction was for Jonah's reform. And the stomach of a fish, instead of being a burial place, became a place of prayer. He prayed from the bottom of the sea, pledging fulfillment of his vow. Through the mercy of God, Jonah is given a second chance, and is re-appointed by the Lord.

What a wonderful God we have. He is continually seeking us. He opened His revelation calling to man, "Adam, where are you?" and closes it with that immortal invitation, "The Spirit and the Bride say 'Come!' And let him who hears say, 'Come!' And let him who thirsts come. Whoever desires, let him take of the water of life freely." God is continually seeking that one sheep.

It is a good thing for every one of us, from time to time, to take a spiritual inventory. Where do you stand with God? Is there some sin with which you have become content? Go to Him now, He is merciful.

Dear Lord, I confess there are sins in my life that seem to be a lifelong struggle. I am tired of living my life with this sin between us. Please forgive me Lord, for_____. I repent, and humbly seek Your aid in walking in Your way. Amen.

January 5   The Song of the Lord

Scripture Reading: II Chronicles 29:20-36

Key Verse: "Then Hezekiah commanded them to offer the burnt offering on the altar. And when the burnt offering began, the song of the Lord also began, with the trumpets and with the instruments of David king of Israel." II Chronicles 29:27

For sixteen years, there had been no song in the temple of Israel, and then one day early in the morning, the king and the rulers of the city went up to the temple. The Levites came with their harps, and the priests with their trumpets. The House of God was filled with music, and sixteen songless years came to an end.

The Israelites had been accustomed to song. They went into battle with it. They celebrated their victories with it. And whenever the Lord was with them, there was singing all the time. My, but it must have been a sad, long time when there was no song in Israel's heart and no voice of musical praise on their lips.

It would be good for us to ask why Israel lost her song. It seems that Ahaz the king had no use for the worship of God. He drove out the temple singers. He cut the gold and silver vessels into pieces. He hewed down the altars. He put out the lights, locked the doors of the temple, and the house of God filled with dust and dirt and became the abode only of birds and vermin.

Yes, it was closing the doors of the house of the Lord that robbed Israel of her song, and if the song has gone out of your life it is exactly for the same reason: the temple of your heart has been closed against its rightful Lord. Of course, you didn't close it with a bang. So many things became important. Soon the door of your life opened to other things, and closed to God.

The question for today is how can we get the song back? After King Ahaz died, the first thing Hezekiah did was to open the temple doors and start services. Well, we are the temple of the Holy Spirit, and we need to open wide the doors of our heart to Him.

The next thing that happened when Israel's song for the Lord returned was that the temple was cleansed. You could not worship in such a temple, and you cannot worship with your whole heart while there is anything contrary to Him found within it. Yield to God; destroy the idols behind the door, and give God every key. The song of the Lord will return.

Then, you will notice that they restored the holy vessels that had been taken away. Just so, perhaps there are things in our life that need to be restored before the song of the Lord begins. What about the place of the Word in your life? Begin to study and read His Word. What about prayer? That is another vessel that might need to be restored.

And finally, the sin offering and the burnt offering were given again in the temple, the sin offering for repentance, and the burnt offering for consecration. For the Christian today, what do these things mean? That the Lamb of God has been slain for our sins. We may go to God for forgiveness, because our debt has been paid.

The last words of this account are that the thing came about suddenly. At this moment, if you are tired of an empty present and long for the joyous song of the Lord to return to your life, you do not have to wait. Open the door of your heart. Examine your life for anything that must be turned from, and for the things that should be restored to your life. Finally, pray and ask forgiveness for your sin. Then, sing praises to His holy name! Let the Song of the Lord begin again within your heart!

Let all that is within me praise Your name, Father God! Please fill me with Your Spirit that I may serve those around me with joy, with patience, and with constant praise for You. Amen.

January 6 — Winning the One

Scripture Reading: Luke 15:1-7

Key Verses: "What man of you, having a hundred sheep, if he loses one of them, does not leave the ninety-nine in the wilderness, and go after the one which is lost until he finds it? And when he has found it, he lays it on his shoulders, rejoicing. And when he comes home, he calls together his friends and neighbors, saying to them, 'Rejoice with me, for I have found my sheep which was lost!'" Luke 15:4-6

One of the central truths in Christianity is God's conception of the worth of one human soul. With Jesus, it is never the ninety and nine, but always the one. We count up to millions, but Christ never counts beyond one. We talk about the masses, but He is concerned about the man. We are suffering in this generation from the tyranny of numbers. We have the idea that we cannot do anything without a crowd.

But Jesus did not seek the crowds. He sought the individuals and crowds came to Him. He began His ministry not by trying to change the civil powers, or by challenging the temple, but by laying siege to the hearts of obscure men as He met them in the marts of toil and trade. As Dr. Buttrick said, "His aim was not to give millions a whitewash of religion, but to make twelve men alive with it."

Yes, Jesus might have headed up a social crusade, but rather He chose to begin with a few obscure individuals to establish His new church. On these twelve, Jesus lavished the wealth of the gospel. They were only average men. They quarreled. They were not always brave. Often they were childish in their understanding. Jesus might have found scores like them. Yet, in Jesus they were made immensely useful. Doesn't that bring hope to your heart?

Our Lord consistently dealt with one apart. With Nicodemus, for example, with the Samaritan Woman, and with so many others, Jesus went after the one sheep until He found it. He was truly the champion of the individual. And that is the need of this hour, not for the ninety and nine, but the one lost one, crying alone in the dark. Out of a love for people, with a heart warmed by God through prayer, we need to search for the one.

If we are truly willing to search for the one, as Jesus did, then we need to imitate our Lord in three things. First, we must show an intense love for people evidenced in our care, concern, and service for them. I know of a woman who came to the Lord not because she was brought to service by a friend, but because that Christian friend stayed home with the woman's sick children so she could go to service. Secondly, if we are to win the one for Christ, we must make use of the tool of intercession. The source of spiritual power for all ministry is found in prayer. And finally, we must by our lives shine forth the presence of the living Christ. Your best witness will be what you live.

In our age, secular pressure has reduced the individual to a mere digit. It is up to the disciples of Christ today to recall to the individual his rightful destiny. It is up to us to deliver the message that God still values the individual. God still cares for the one. Our best offering to any person is the gift of God's presence without which men still raise hungry hands. For that, the world is starving.

Dear Lord, help me to see the world through Your eyes, through Your love, and through Your sense of mission. I know there must be one near me who is seeking, who is crying out. Please make me a divine appointment with that one today, Lord. And help me to be able to show that one that God cares especially for them. In Jesus's name, amen.

January 7   Running After The Corn

Scripture Reading: I Thessalonians 5:12-28
Key Verse: "In everything give thanks...." I Thessalonians 5:18

Some translations of this verse tell us to give thanks in all circumstances. How can we possibly obey this command? First, we need to cultivate the habit of looking at what we have instead of what we have missed. Some people get their gaze so fixed on what they have missed that they fail to see what they have. It has happened to me, has it ever happened to you?

I worked on the farm as a boy and one of my tasks was to feed the hogs. I have carried a basket full of corn, possibly 100 ears, and poured it all together out on the ground. Each hog could have at least four ears of corn for his very own. But instead of acting as if that were the case, one silly pig would grab a single ear and dart off up the hill as if death were at his heels. What was more amazing was that often three or four other pigs, squealing and grunting, weeping and wailing, would run after him as if he had the only ear of corn worth eating. How like us.

Some people can't go window-shopping without coming home miserable. If we are going to be grateful we must look at what we have instead of at what we have missed. That was Paul's way and he commended it to us. He said, "If there is anything praiseworthy, meditate on these things."

After all, if we face the facts, all we have has been a gift from God. God put us here in the world. He gave us the health and strength we have, the brains to study, and the opportunity to work. All that we have in the last analysis has come to us as gifts from God. If we are to be grateful we must see something special in the gifts that have been put into our hands and into our hearts.

There are few words uglier than the words "of course" when wrongly used. When someone told the poet Heine that God would forgive him, he gave this devilish answer, "Of course, that is His business." He saw nothing special in the greatest gift ever given.

If we are going to be grateful, we must give expression to our gratitude. I know how hard it is for some of us to do that. We tell ourselves, "She knows how much I appreciate her. He knows how much I appreciate him." But how do they know unless we tell them? Besides, even those who know like to hear it, and God is no exception.

Across the years it has been my lot to hold many a funeral. Not once have I had a desperate soul grasp my hand and look at me with dry eyes that could not weep and say, "I was too thoughtful and too appreciative of this dear one who has passed." But how many funerals I have held when I knew that the greatest sorrow was the fact that the one who mourned was trying to say to the dead what he knew he ought to have said to the living.

If we give expression to our gratitude, it will grow from more to more. If we shut it up in our hearts, it will die. Paul refused to run this risk. He constantly cultivated the fine art of appreciation by giving it expression. So persistent was he in saying thanks to both God and man that it became a habit.

It was as spontaneous as the gushing of a spring, as the song of a bird, as the laughter of a happy child. Paul's Master has a right to call us to this high duty and privilege. Give thanks in all circumstances as the Scriptures and the fathers of the faith teach us to do.

Father, how I thank You for the gifts You've given me. Open my eyes to see them clearly and with gratitude instead of chasing up the hill after what I imagine to be better. Amen

January 8 — Remember Jesus Christ

Scripture Reading: II Timothy 2:1-13

Key Verse: "Remember that Jesus Christ, of the seed of David, was raised from the dead according to my gospel."
II Timothy 2:8

Despite the fact that Jesus never organized a revolt, wrote a book, or championed a political party, never initiated a reform or commanded an army, captained a ship, or governed a commonwealth; despite the fact that His relatives thought he was a fool, and His enemies thought Him a liar, He stands today as the most misunderstood and misinterpreted, most cussed and discussed man that ever lived.

Was it merely the son of Joseph and Mary who crossed the world's horizon 2,000 years ago? Was it merely human blood that spilled on Calvary's hill? What thinking man can keep from exclaiming "My Lord and my God"? Remember Jesus Christ.

He is imbedded in the world's history. "It were easier" said Bushnell "to untwist the beams of light in the sky and to separate and expunge one of the primary colors than to get the character of Jesus, which is truth, out of the world." History without Christ is like astronomy without the stars, like geology without rocks, or like botany without flowers.

He is everywhere in nature. Every bush is afire with God to the man whose heart is aflame with Christ. It is a poor astronomer who fails to locate the Star of Bethlehem, a poor biologist who misses Life, and a poor horticulturist who has not found "the True Vine."

He cannot be forgotten while art remains. Bare indeed would be the walls of the world's art galleries without *The Annunciation*, *The Transfiguration*, *The Last Supper*, *The Descent from the Cross*, *The Resurrection* and *The Ascension*. Remove the Michelangelos, Da Vincis, Raphaels, Durers, Rubens and Titians and the finest galleries would contain only dust-covered walls.

The world, its politics, its life and its destiny stand before the person of Jesus Christ. Upon their attitude toward Christ nations have risen and fallen, kingdoms have been established and uprooted, philosophies created and discarded, reforms agitated and created, kings exalted and dethroned. Remember Jesus Christ.

Paul, as an old minister facing martyrdom, writes to young Timothy to remember three great central facts about this Jesus of Bethlehem. Remember His incarnation. He was the Son of Man, for He was the son of Mary, and He was the Son of God for He had no human father. Remember His death on the cross, for there you find the heart of God. Finally, remember the resurrection, the crowning revelation of His power.

And now, who is the Jesus Christ whom the text admonishes us to remember and whom we worship today? What is to be our answer? Shall we say as some of the false teachers say that Jesus is the spirit of self-sacrifice and unselfishness? Shall we say as some psychologists are saying that Jesus was a Palestinian idealist with the soft touch of a woman, ever unwilling to hurt the feelings of anybody? Or shall we say with some religionists today that Jesus was simply an ethical teacher, a mild fanatic, dying for a mistaken cause? No, let us proclaim the truth, that Jesus is the Son of God, the Redeemer of men, the King of willing subjects, the Lord and Master of all believers and the coming King over all the earth. He is the living Christ of the manger, the cross, the resurrection, and the throne. Remember Jesus Christ.

Almighty Christ and God incarnate, how I worship You today. I lift up Your Holy name and recognize Your authority in the universe. I submit myself to You, so grateful that with all Your power and majesty, You reach out to me with pure, perfect love. Amen

January 9 — A Man With A Grudge

Scripture Reading: Hosea 6:1-3

Key Verse: "...pursue the knowledge of the Lord....He will come to us like the rain." Hosea 6:3

Rain is a page of the book of nature which some of us would like to tear out. If it would only come when we want it, we would feel kindlier, but no, rain is notorious for its perverse propensity to butt in just when it chooses. If there's a picnic in sight, rain starts for it. If there's a day on the program that demands a blue sky, the rain clouds all hear about it and gather for action. Rain often acts like a man with a grudge.

And so, rain has a damaged reputation. It turns the roads into mud, makes the walks slippery, dampens our clothes, wets our feet, and brings the whole town down with the sniffles at once. It affects our heart, our feelings get dripping wet, mud puddles form in the soul, and the spirit droops under a gray sky as the world fills with melancholy.

But rain is not an affliction to children. They love to be rained on, delight in rubber boots and rubber coats; they like even better wet shirts and bare feet. To a lively boy, a bathtub is nothing compared to a sloppy street. They are not afraid of losing their health; they have so much of it. Rain brings to them blessings, one of the most precious: the mud puddle. Mud comes out of rain, so blessed be the rain.

Those of us too old to play in it, should look to see what we are missing.

If you get tired of looking at the rain, close your eyes and listen to it. It makes music. Go to the country where you can hear it falling on the surfaces not made by man, on the bushes, the flowers, the grass, or the lake. It is music played in many keys and tempos. Some are easy-going leisurely rains, in no hurry, plodding all day long at the same pace. The monotony of its quiet breathing lulls the heart into a state of peace. There are rains which are gentle and rains which are furious, rains which are noisy and rains which are quiet.

Some rains leave the world jubilant. The sun comes out, the rainbow laughs, and under that rainbow the world glows with hope. The face of nature is clean and everything looks bright.

But it is more than a scrubwoman. It is a chemist of renown. We cannot drink seawater. It must be distilled in the clouds and returned to us in rain. We all drink rainwater no matter what we call it. No spring, fountain or reservoir has anything to offer except rain. God uses the sun as a ladle and dips water from the sea to pour it out on lands which wait for it. God delivers distilled water at every door.

In the Old Testament God and rain are frequently linked together, for a great problem for the Hebrews was lack of water. In the life of Israel rain played a great part, for it meant their very life. There was a gratitude for rain shown by them that might seem foreign to us, but then, we can sometimes overlook the greatest blessings wrapped in the simplest package.

So, when we are looking around us for proof that God is indeed good, we blunder if we overlook the rain. It is proof of great compassion. Jesus said that God sends the rain on the just and unjust alike. What proof of God's all-embracing love. It is a miracle of His power, an evidence of His wisdom, and a token of His love. In the words of Hosea, "Let us pursue the knowledge of the Lord… He will come to us like the rain."

Almighty God, who holds the clouds and the sun in Your hands, thank You that You feed us and give us drink. You meet our needs as water poured on thirsty dust. You are the life-giver, now and for life eternal. Amen.

January 10   The Telephone Booth

Scripture Reading: Proverbs 1:20-33
Key Verse: "Whoever listens to me will dwell safely, and will be secure, without fear of evil." Proverbs 1:33

The other day I had occasion to call a friend from one of those little telephone booths. You all know those fascinating little houses? When you step inside, it all lights up. Well, I had not quite closed the door, and as a result I could not hear the voice of my friend on the other end of the line. The booth was filled with the noise of passing trucks and trains, the whistling of engines and the voices of the people outside. I just could not make out his voice, however hard I tried.

Well, at last I realized what was wrong, and I pulled shut the door. I was still in the midst of the bustle. In fact, I could see all the movements through the glass quite clearly, but I was shut off from it by invisible barriers. I was still in the same place, yet my whole perception had changed. I could hear every word my friend said. It reminded me of the verse that speaks of us being in the world, but not of it. If you want to hear, you must close the door. And if we want to hear the voice of the dearest Friend we have, we must shut the door on the constant clamoring of the world.

Now, that is true even in church service, is it not? You must shut out the outside noises that come, the temptation to whisper to a neighbor, or write notes. You must give God the right of way. If you want to hear, you must shut the door on distraction.

In the Scriptures, we see little Samuel sleeping in the temple. He heard God's voice quite clearly, while Eli the High Priest did not. Why was that, do you suppose? Well, the old priest had allowed the noises of this world, even in the temple, to break in upon him and drown out the voice of God.

In our text, we are told of the call of wisdom on our lives. We are told in verse seven that "The fear of the Lord is the beginning of knowledge," and then in verse 28-29 that "...They will seek me diligently, but they will not find me. Because they hated knowledge and did not choose the fear of the Lord." The text goes on to describe the foolishness of those who would not listen to the Lord, and then, in the last verse, we are told, "But whoever listens to me will dwell safely, and will be secure, without fear of evil."

Beloved, in our lives it is as it was for me in that little telephone booth. We want to listen to the voice of the Lord. We have the handset to our ear. And yet, somehow the noises of this world, the distractions of the day, overwhelm and drown out the voice of our Beloved Friend. When you enter into your closet for prayer, dear one, close the door on the world. Our text makes it quite clear that we can choose to listen, that we can choose the reverence of the Lord.

And when you leave your prayer closet, remember that you are still separated from the world by an invisible barrier. The fact of your relationship with Christ sets you apart from the world. You are still in the same place; you can see the bustle of the world around you. But you are separate. You may be in this old, chaotic, sin-saddened world, but you are not of it. The distractions of the world do not rule your life. Listen to Him, dwell safely, be secure, and fear not.

Dear Lord, I want You to have the right of way in my heart, in my life, and in my worship. Today, Lord, I praise You for Your holiness, for Your patience with me, and for Your loving persistence. Lord, I am simply listening to You. Amen.

January 11   When God Forgets

Scripture Reading: Jeremiah 31:31-40

Key Verse: "...I will forgive their iniquity, and their sin I will remember no more." Jeremiah 31:34

    The thought of forgetfulness on the part of God is at first a bit jarring. We are not accustomed to associating forgetfulness with God and hence to speak of His forgetting seems almost irreverent.

    We think of forgetfulness as peculiar to ourselves. It is human, not divine. We forget each other's names, our promises and responsibilities. One preacher I know recently forgot a funeral. Again and again we are humiliated by our forgetfulness.

    A boy was sent home from the hospital. The train had stopped at a little depot and out of the passenger car they saw this chap, very pale and frail, being lifted onto the platform, with his crutches, for he had lost a leg. They leaned him back against the station and put the crutches under his arms and there he stood looking this way and that way wistfully as if he was expecting someone. The train pulled away and left the little fellow there alone. No one had come to meet him. Do you suppose those who loved him had forgotten him?

    Oh, you say, I would not forget my loved ones, and yet, your mother has looked for a letter from you for months and it has not come. Your husband's heart is aching for a bit of appreciation, all because you forgot.

    Not only do we forget one another, but we forget God. We forget Him in whose hands our breath is. We forget the Christ of the manger and the cross. He knows how we are, how we forget. He gave us the beautiful communion service so we would remember the sacrifice of His son. He gave us the rainbow so we would remember His promises. In fact, He knows there is absolutely nothing that we do not tend to forget.

    But does God also forget? Yes, we read in His book that He does. But, His forgetfulness is of such a nature that it is the mother of hope and not despair. It is a truth as fragrant as violets. It is the sweetest story I could tell, not alone because He forgets, but because of what He forgets.

Now, He does not forget everything as we do. Oh no. God never forgets His universe, He never forgets a single child of His. He promises when mother and father forget, He will pick you up. He never forgets to clothe the lily and feed the sparrows. He remembers every kind word we speak, every kind deed, unselfish gift, visit to the sick, every prayer offered, every tear shed in penitence. Yes, Jesus remembers when the world forgets.

Then, what does He forget? He forgets only one thing. Lay hold on this truth and your soul will have a resurrection. Believe this message and it will serenade your life with music. Accept this truth and you shall live eternally. Listen. "Their sin will I remember no more." If we confess our sin and come to Christ, He who was wounded for our transgression and bruised for our iniquities will forgive our sins and remember them no more—forever!

What a wonderful Savior! He stands ready to forgive and forget, ready to take you back into fellowship and confidence as if you had never failed Him. Make this promise your own. "I will forgive their iniquity and their sin I remember no more."

Dear Father Who loves me, thank You for forgetting all the ways I've failed You. How wonderful that You are probably now saying—"What ways?" because You choose to forget my mistakes. Lord, on this new day, help me to forgive and forget the cruelty and mistakes of others and choose to be like You and "Remember their sin no more." Amen.

January 12   Confessions of a Prodigal

Scripture Reading: Luke 15:11-31

Key Verses: "...I perish with hunger! ...Father, I have sinned against heaven and before you." Luke 15:17b-18.

This confession has sobbed its way through the centuries. Often our confessions of sin are mechanical and lifeless, rather than the spontaneous outcries of a wounded and tortured spirit. Not so this confession.

The one who made this confession long ago is generally called "the prodigal," and his story has something to say to every one of us, regardless of the stage we have reached in our spiritual pilgrimage.

This young fellow set out to go into the country. Now, he did not wake one morning with the sudden, desperate conclusion that he should go out and wreck himself. No, he was no monstrosity. He had no more thought, when he set out on this adventure, of landing in the hog pen by the swill-trough than you or I have.

Nobody makes up his mind in advance that he is going to fling himself into the garbage can of worthless and wasted things. No train ever leaves the station with the intention of going into the ditch. No boat ever leaves the harbor with the intention to go on the rocks. And no lad ever goes out from his father's house with his mind made up that he is going to damn himself.

Nor did the boy go out to the country to purposefully pain someone's heart. He had no desire to spite his parents. No, there was only one reason for his going. He was seeking to please himself. He thought he would be free, and he thought this freedom would bring him a larger joy and a better time generally. He was simply bent on living his own life, unhampered by the restraints that authority put upon him. Self-pleasing is the very fountainhead of all sin.

Self-pleasing is expensive. He who is bent on pleasing himself is doomed to pay a terrible price. Nor is he the only one who pays. The moment that self-will becomes the goal of any soul, that soul breaks with God and loses all sense of His fellowship. To go from God is to go from the heart's true home. Nothing but disappointment and homesickness await us, until we sing with the psalmist, "Lord, You have been our dwelling place in all generations."

The prodigal's sin also cost him his freedom. What a tragic irony, for it was his freedom that he went out to seek. The road by which he sought freedom, sin, led him into slavery instead. What humiliation for a Jew to be forced to feed the swine. But, in the end we note that his sin cost him "all." When he was morally, spiritually, and financially bankrupt, having bought with his father's money a pinched face and an empty stomach, he came to himself. It was bad enough to be in the swine-pen, but to be there when he might have been at home in his father's house was tragic. And it was enough.

The prodigal regained his senses, and faced the facts about himself. Note that he did not say, "I will arise and reform myself." No, that is not the answer. The prodigal knows he must face his father, and there is something fine and universal about his confession. Every one of us is in the truest sense a prodigal who is living away from God until we too say, "make me your servant." And every prodigal we see, in the end, lacks only God to make his life right.

Dearest Lord, I have not always followed You as I ought. I did not set out to hurt my family, friends, or You, Lord. I understand that anytime I choose pleasure or self- will over obedience to You, I am in sin. I don't want to pay the price of seeking my own way anymore, dear Father. Please keep me right in the center of Your will. Amen.

January 13   The Christian's Anchors

Scripture Reading: Acts 27:27-32

Key Verse: "They dropped four anchors from the stern and prayed for day to come." Acts 27:29

Here is an account of an epic shipwreck in maritime literature. Paul was on his way to Jerusalem when he was advised that bonds and imprisonment awaited him. He appealed and was placed in the custody of Captain Julius, a centurion on a ship. Along with other prisoners he was soon on his way to Rome.

On the journey they were swept by the Euroclydon, the dreaded storm that strikes the Mediterranean at that season. We read that they dropped four anchors off the stern and prayed for morning. Those anchors were their safety. Now, God has equipped the Christian with four anchors, anchors that never drag no matter how rough or angry the billows.

The first anchor is God's blessed Book. The Bible is not a book. It is the Book. It is the indestructible, ever living, ever-enduring Word of God. Oh beloved, the Bible is a lion. Let it out and it will defend itself against its enemies. God's Word says it is a two-edged sword, piercing and dividing the soul and spirit and is a discerner of the thoughts and intents of the heart of man.

Are you anchored to the Word of God? If you are, you are anchored to the saving, guiding, assuring knowledge of God. Cast out this anchor and let the ship rock and the storm rage. The morning comes.

The second anchor is the cross of our Lord Jesus Christ. If you are anchored to the cross, you are anchored to God's saving grace. "For by grace you have been saved through faith." If you are anchored to the cross you are anchored to His cleansing blood. "And the blood of Jesus Christ His Son cleanses us from all sin." If you are anchored to the cross you are anchored to His keeping power. He has sworn that no man shall pluck you out of His hand. No matter how dark the night, it will soon be morning.

The third anchor is the empty tomb. If you are anchored to Christ's resurrection you are anchored to faith's foundation. If He has not risen, Heaven's doors are closed, hell's doors are open, and hope is forever dead. But faith takes its stand by the empty tomb and shouts "O death, where is your sting? O grave, where is your victory?" And there comes from glory the voice of Him who lived, died, and is alive forever more these words, "Because I live, you will live."

If you are anchored to Christ's resurrection you are anchored to immortality. Do you have this anchor? Be of good cheer, though the ship may rock and the storm may rage, day will soon be dawning, the morn is near.

The fourth anchor is the promise of His coming again. Anchored to His coming you are anchored to the comforting hope of His people. We believe that Jesus died and rose again and that all who sleep in Jesus He will bring with Him. What a glorious reunion awaits those who are His. You are loosed from the world if you are anchored to His unfailing promise "For yet a little while and He who is coming will come and will not tarry."

These are the anchors that safely hold. They never drag and no storm can sweep them away. Are they yours? Then let your soul rest in sweet confidence. Euroclydons will cease. Storms will give way to calm. The morning will dawn with the sunrise of eternal day. They are glorious anchors, unfailing and eternal; cast them out my friend in this night of storm, and wait for the day.

Dear Lord, thank You for Your Holy Word, the cross, the resurrection of Your Son, and the promise of His return. These are solid anchors for my soul. Amen.

January 14   A Man Who Refused to be Fired

Scripture Reading: I Samuel Chapter 12
Key Verse: "...Far be it from me that I should sin against the Lord in ceasing to pray for you...." I Samuel 12:23

These are the words of Samuel, who was told by Saul that his services were no longer desired. This great man was the first mountainous personality to appear after Moses, who had died some three centuries before. Not only did Samuel become a prophet, but he became a judge, going over his district and holding court in various centers. He was a great and inspired leader especially fitted to serve his people in a difficult day. Yet, the people did not realize how well off they were and, they demanded a change. Longing for a more colorful ruler; longing to be like the nations round about them; they fired Samuel in order to put a king in his place.

Samuel understood that the people had rejected God, not himself. This did not lighten his grief, but rather sharpened it. Samuel really cared for the people of Israel. He longed to serve them. And just because he could not serve them in his chosen way, did not mean he would not serve them in some way. If other doors were shut, there was still one door open, the door of intercessory prayer.

When you pray for others, the first result is that it helps you. Of all the forms of prayer, intercessory prayer brings us into divine fellowship and enables us to share the passion of our Lord like none other. Prayer opens doors of opportunity.

Now, it so happened that as Samuel prayed in deep sincerity, he found that God was opening up for him other ways of serving the people. Samuel saw a need for what amounted to a theological seminary. Through this school for prophets, it is possible that Samuel made an even greater contribution to the spiritual nurturing of Israel than he had before.

Earnest prayer receives answers. The Bible abounds in victories wrought through such prayer, such as when Simon Peter was in prison in Jerusalem. Humanly speaking, he did not have a chance in a million. But in spite of prison walls, chains, and iron gates, Peter walked free. How? Scripture tells us, "But earnest prayer was made for him to God by the Church."

Years ago, I was conducting a revival in Marked Tree, Arkansas. There I met a godly woman whose husband was a notorious gambler. She had gathered two or three trusting, praying souls and together they began intercessory prayer for this husband. She determined to fast and pray until her husband was saved. It was several nights into the meeting that, as I gave the invitation, a man came down the aisle as fast as his feet could carry him, he cried, "Pray for me, pray for me. I'm lost, I'm lost, I'm lost!" And as he threw himself at the altar, his wife recognized him and jumped up, "Thank God, thank God! He has answered my prayers!" This man broke up all his gambling paraphernalia, piled it up in the street, and set fire to it. So great was the stir in the town that the mayor, who had been much opposed to the revival meetings, came to God.

Prayer offered in sincerity makes it possible for God to do for us, and in us, and through us, what He would not do in another way. Because this is true, let us each say with Samuel, "Far be it from me that I should sin against the Lord in ceasing to pray."

Father God, I come before You humbly to confess that I have not prayed as I should. Too often I do not see prayer as the important ministry that it is. Please forgive me, Lord, and stir my heart to remember in prayer those in authority, those who need to know You, and those who are ministering for You. Thank You, Father. Amen.

January 15   Delightful Uplift of a Morning Uplook

Scripture Reading: Psalm 5

Key Verse: "My voice you shall hear in the morning, O Lord; in the morning I will direct it to You and I will look up." Psalm 5:3

A great deal depends upon the way in which one begins day. Certainly the Psalmist has discovered the right way in which to begin the year, and each day therein. He said to God, "My voice you shall hear in the morning." The mood of the morning molds the day. He had found the delightful uplift of a morning uplook.

Now man was made to look up. That which distinguishes man from other earthly creatures is his yearning for something higher than either sense or reason can provide. Yet despite the fact that man was made to look up, many have an antipathy for the uplook. Their minds are so completely filled with material things and earthly pleasures that they have nothing more than a horizontal view. For them, life has no verticals. It does not reach up to God.

There are others who refuse to look up because they deny that there is anyone to whom they may look. They are like the ancient Professor of Padua who, when Galileo discovered the moons of Jupiter in the blue above Florence, refused to look through the telescope, lest he might see that which he refused to believe was there. His disbelief did not blot out the moons of Jupiter, or any other satellite in the heavens. Nor has man's disbelief blotted God out of His universe.

The early morning uplook affords us a helpful inlook. We get a glimpse of the status of our sinful selves as we behold the holiness of God. The helpful effect of this morning uplook is well illustrated by the experience of Isaiah, who on going into the temple with a burdened heart and seeing the Lord high and lifted up exclaimed, "Woe is me for I am undone! Because I am a man of unclean lips... for my eyes have seen the King, the Lord of Hosts." So you see, as he looked up to

God, he became painfully aware of the fact that he was a sinner. That is one of the blessed ministries of this early uplook of the morning. With simply a look around on our own level, we shall rather take comfort in measuring ourselves by others. But the minute you compare yourself to Him who was tempted in all things like as we are, yet was without sin, there comes a deep sense of repentance.

Also, the morning uplook provides a wholesome outlook. We get a better perspective on life. We realize what, with heaven's help, we may become. And God enables us to rise on the stepping stones of our dead selves to higher things. One cannot practice the morning uplook and spend the day on a low moral level. It lifts us out of the mire of self-content and indifference, to joyous participation in the things of God.

Time spent with God each day allows us to push back the low-hanging horizon of life and make for ourselves a large place in which to dwell. Even Abraham once sat in his tent brooding until God brought him forth saying, "Look now toward heaven, and count the stars."

Oh, beloved, how we need to hear God say to us, "Look now toward heaven." Yes, so many of us sit so close to the fire of everyday life that we cannot see the stars. How we need to have the larger outlook that comes only by the consistent morning uplook.

Yes, Lord, I commit to look up to You this year. As I raise my voice in praise and prayer, as I seek You out in Your word, and as I wait upon You, please reveal Yourself to me. Convict me of sin, inspire me to live largely for You, and use me this year, Lord, in new, exciting adventures for Your glory. For Christ's sake, amen.

January 16   Two Men I Know

Scripture Reading: Genesis Chapter 13

Key Verse: "Abram dwelt in the land of Canaan, and Lot dwelt in the cities of the plain and pitched his tent even as far as Sodom." Genesis 13:12

Three times over Abraham is called the "friend of God," and for this reason he is worth knowing. As is often the case, however, we can get a clearer view of Abraham by looking at him as he stands beside another man, his kinsman, Lot.

These men had much in common, yet they present a sharp contrast. They were both religious men, both builders of altars. They were of the same family and each was wealthy in the money of their day, livestock. The New Testament calls Lot a "righteous man." Yet, in spite of Lot's religion, he was a tragic failure.

Abraham, on the other hand, presents faith at its radiant best. In spite of the fact that the years handed him many disappointments, he never gave up. He believed God, and God brought blessing to him and to the world through him.

Now, why this sharp contrast between these two men? The biggest fact about Abraham was his relationship with God. Since he was constantly walking in the direction that God was going, their roads ran together, and they became friends. With Lot, however, when there was the necessity of a choice between his own interests and those of the Lord, his own interests won. Lot's religion never seemed to make a very big difference in his life.

A crisis, of course, never makes character. It only reveals it. And into the life of Abraham and Lot came a crisis. They were both stockmen, and their large flocks and herds make it necessary for them to part ways. Abraham generously gives Lot first choice, and Lot looks over all the land. To the right is a wild, rugged country where his herds and flocks can find sustenance only if he is diligent. To the left is a beautiful country, well-watered and looking like the Garden of Eden itself, with the cities of the plain in the midst.

Lot chose the more favored land. In fact, Scripture says, "Lot chose for himself." That is, Lot made his choice asking only what he could get out of it, not consulting God. We see him making his choice with his eyes fixed on his own material interests. Therefore, we are not surprised to read next that, "Lot…pitched his tent even as far as Sodom." While Abraham remained in the hill country, confident that God would provide, Lot moved his tent toward Sodom. Well, in the next chapter we read that he lived there. And by chapter nineteen, Lot is sitting in the gate, having become a city elder.

And how did their choices work out? Lot's choice placed his family in close contact with the worst people in Canaan. Scripture tells us, "The men of Sodom were exceedingly wicked and sinful against the Lord." As a result of this choice, Lot lost his family, and his home. Far worse, the descendants of Lot did not serve the Lord.

Abraham, on the other hand, continued to trust God. He was not perfect, in any sense of the word. But his fellowship with God continued, and God blessed Abraham. Abraham's descendants were the children of Israel, God's own chosen people. Yes, Abraham was blessed, and in turn, Abraham became a blessing to many. We can all be a blessing, but only if we walk with the Lord.

Dear Lord, I desire to be known as "the friend of God." I desire that kind of constant, abiding, faithful relationship with You. Please draw me nearer, Lord, to You. Help me to relinquish my own selfish motives, and to live instead for Your sake, on Your terms, following where You lead. Amen.

January 17   In Training

Scripture Reading: Exodus 2:11-25

Key Verse: "...the children of Israel groaned because of the bondage, and they cried out; and their cry came up to God because of the bondage." Exodus 2:23

He was just a baby born on the banks of the Nile, a child of slaves. But, God knew better. God was preparing this child for a great destiny.

Moses was a child of faithful parents. By faith, we read, Moses was hidden three months by his parents. In spite of the order of Pharaoh, these faithful parents believed that God had a purpose in the life of their boy. So, Moses's sister was set guard to watch him as he floated in his little basket sealed with pitch along the reedy banks of the Nile. But, it is impossible to hide a lively baby boy for long; and soon he was discovered by the daughter of Pharaoh.

This Egyptian Princess has never been rightly honored for making three decisions of great importance. She decided that the baby would live. She decided to adopt him as her own. And lastly she unwittingly decided that his own mother should be his nurse. This last decision was of tremendous importance. But for this, Moses would have had loyalty only to the gods of Egypt, rather than to the God of Israel.

Soon, he would be taken to live in the great court of Pharaohs, but he was to be with his mother Jochebed for a while. What she would do, she must do quickly. There in that humble home, Moses received his first and most important course of training.

And when he left the hut on the Nile for Pharaoh's palace, his second course of training began. Through this adoption into the family of the king of Egypt, he came to know the courteous and gracious life of the palace, and the best schools and tutors of the day were opened to him. The record of Scripture tells us that he was learned in all the wisdom of the Egyptians, and was mighty in word and deed.

But God had yet a third school for Moses to attend. He did not go to this wilderness school by his choice, nor was it part of his own plan.

Moses came upon an Egyptian striking one of his fellow Hebrews and in hot anger, Moses struck the Egyptian dead, and hid his body in the sand. But he soon discovered that his act was known, and both his own people and Pharaoh were set against him. Moses fled in disillusionment. In Midian, he married the daughter of a priest and became shepherd of his flocks. What a terrible come-down for one who had lived in the court of Pharaoh. Yet, those forty years were not just Moses's best days slipping through his fingers. They were the best years of training for the task before him

God was allowing him to get better acquainted with the wilderness he would one day lead his people through. Year by year, Moses died more and more to his own importance. This gifted man started his task with too much pride and self-confidence. He had to be brought to realize that true strength is found in God.

Oh, beloved, this great leader was no accident. This amazing man did not just happen. Moses was trained up by God for his task. God used his believing parents, and their faithful home. God used the pagan courts of Pharaoh. And, God used the wilderness and a scrubby bush. God can use anything in our lives to shape us for the work He has prepared for us, if we by faith are willing to submit to His leading and His teaching.

Father God, it brings me such comfort to know that You are not just aware of my circumstances, but are working through them to my benefit and the benefit of Your kingdom. I submit to Your training in my life, Lord, today and every day. For Your glory, amen.

January 18   Convict Number 1

Scripture Reading: Genesis 4:1-15

Key Verse: "Then the Lord said to Cain, 'Where is Abel your brother?' He said, 'I do not know. Am I my brother's keeper?'" Genesis 4:9

This question God poses to Cain is one of the first questions to man. Now, everybody is acquainted with Cain. He has a branded brow, the world's first murderer, convict number one.

And, because he was a murderer, we feel no kinship with him at all; we like to think of him as made of altogether different clay from ourselves. But we are wrong. Cain is a blood brother to us. If we do not realize this, it is because we only see the one view of him, that of a man with a club in his hand. But, Cain was not only a murderer.

I doubt that any mother was ever any happier than Eve at Cain's birth. How glad and rapturous was that mother's heart. A baby's hand was never softer or more dimpled, a small body never more tender and warm. And she named him what? She named him Cain, meaning, "I've gotten a man from the Lord." Oh yes, he was a child of hope. But, as he grew older, sin became part of his life.

Cain became a wrongdoer. Eventually, he became so brutally and viciously sinful that he actually stained himself with his brother's blood. But, mark you; he did not descend to that awful depth all at once. The first time we glimpse Cain the wrongdoer is at the altar of sacrifice. The world's first quarrel was at an altar. A man does reveal himself by his religion, doesn't he? He reveals himself by his conception of God.

Well, we read that Cain and Abel went together to offer sacrifice and that God had respect unto Abel and his offering, but to Cain and his offering, He had no respect. Cain's offering was rejected because Cain himself was rejected. Then God made this reasonable appeal, "If you do well, will you not be accepted? And if you do not do well, sin lies at the door." Now, what was the sin of Cain? Oh, you say, it was murder! No, no, that was the outcome of his sin. Cain's sin was, at the beginning, envy. He became angry with his brother and hated him.

He murdered his brother, not because he had been harmed by him, but because he envied him.

Envy is an old sin with a club in its hand. It was envy that made Saul seek David's life. It was envy that sought to feed Daniel to the lions, and it was envy that drove nails into the feet and hands of Christ.

Cain was envious, and anyone of us who has never envied anybody may throw a stone at him. I confess the thought palsies my arm. Does it pain you to hear another complimented? Does it grieve you to have another given an assignment, or publicly thanked, and not you? Then, beware, for you have envy in your heart.

Cain, when envy mastered him, committed the fatal crime that ruined his life. And yet God did not give up on him. God came seeking Cain, asking, "Where is your brother?" God knew what Cain had done, and He knew what had happened. But Cain only answered insolently, "Am I my brother's keeper?" Abel is nothing to me, he might as well have said. Every fellow for himself was Cain's doctrine. But it can't be ours.

Oh, beloved, look around you. Is there one toward whom your attitude has been envious? God only asks that we realize our sin and repent. Make it right. Go to Him, now, won't you?

Oh, Dear Heavenly Father, I ask that You would stir my heart that envy might not reside there. I am willing, but weak. Please, Lord, replace the envy in my heart with compassion; replace the selfishness with love. In Christ's name, amen.

January 19   Woman at the Well

Scripture Reading: John 4:1-10
Key Verse: "...If you knew the gift of God..." John 4:10

Our Lord has been on a trip from Judea to Galilee and He had to pass through Samaria. He came with His disciples to a little village named Sychar, which means "purchased." It was a place of death until Jesus came, and then it became a place of life.

Just out of Sychar, a road led back through a valley to the city nestled in the hills for protection. All the inhabitants had to come down the rocky road, out of the city to the Well of Jacob. It is an ancient well that still flows today; from which men still drink.

Here is one of those little touches which shows the humanity of Jesus. He was tired. As Jesus sat down to rest beside the well, a woman came from the village with a water pot on her shoulder. He was alone and she was alone. He was weary and she was weary. He was thirsty and she was thirsty. Beyond this they are opposites.

As she proceeds to draw water, she is suddenly surprised by the voice of Jesus asking her to give Him a drink, surprised because the Jews looked down on Samaritans and usually had no dealings with them. They were outside the law, and did not recognize the altar of the temple and that sacrifices were to be offered only at Jerusalem. So, Samaria was alienated from God and from Israel, but Jesus stepped into the breach. With a love that knew no bounds of race, color or creed, He asked the favor of a drink of water.

So, when the woman expressed amazement that He, being a Jew, would ask her, an outcast Samaritan, for a drink, Jesus answered that it was because of who He was. "If you knew the gift of God and who it is who says to you, 'Give me a drink,' you would have asked Him and He would have given you living water."

"If you knew," these words come to us today with unparalleled force. There are people that you love who do not know. No matter what our condition, Jesus wants us to know. He wants us, and those we love, to know that if we only knew all He is willing to do for us, we would give Him a chance. He wants to give us living water, not stagnant pools, not muddy puddles, but water that is living, dynamic and satisfying.

What a promise, an artesian well, not a poor, dried up creek experience! Not serving the Lord in my weak way. Not dependence on religious externals, but a glorious, victorious, satisfying, dynamic experience of an overflowing, effervescent, relationship with God. Rushing, living water can light New York City, and rushing, living water from Christ Jesus can fill us with power, strength, purpose, and deep joy that is everlasting.

Yet, look at the broken cisterns and muddy wells people have been drinking from, and have continued to thirst, for they do not satisfy. Some have drained their cup at the well of riches; others have drawn water from the well of fame, honor, and pleasure. Some have sought satisfaction from the wells of lust or exciting waters of crime. But no man has ever been satisfied with the product of earth's tantalizing streams.

One is almost overwhelmed with the sense of the need of the human race. Jesus has the answer. Jesus is the answer. He gives the living water by which we will never thirst again. Share it, dear believer. Share Jesus with thirsty souls in this desert world that they too may never thirst again.

Lord, You offered life to a simple, sinful, discarded woman out of Your great love. I thank You that You offer the same to me. I accept. Please let me share Your love with others today. I will watch for a divine appointment and know it came from You. Amen.

January 20　　　　　　The Great Alternative

Scripture Reading: John 6:41-69

Key Verses: "Then Jesus said to the twelve, 'Do you also want to go away?' But Simon Peter answered Him, 'Lord, to whom shall we go?'" John 6:67-68

You know, Jesus never made the terms of discipleship easy. He never coaxed anyone to join His Church. When He had spoken plain words to the multitude and plain words to those who had called themselves "Disciples," from that time, said John, many of His disciples went back and walked with Him no more. Jesus watched in silence as those who had lost their faith and zeal departed, and turning to the twelve He said, "Do you also want to go away?" Peter's beautiful and loyal answer was "Lord, to whom shall we go?"

Now the test of value of any given thing is whether or not a substitute can be secured for it. If some other thing will serve just as well, then its value is limited. But if there is no substitute for it, it is of the highest value. This is what Peter was saying with his question. Who would take your place? Who can offer us what you do? Who can speak to us words of Eternal Life?

Christ alone died for sinners. He's the sinner's only substitute and for Him there is no substitute. On the cross He offered to God His sacrifice of perfect obedience and holiness. No other could make that sinless offering. You remember that in the garden of Gethsemane in the midst of His agony he cried, "Father, if it is possible let this cup pass from Me." But it was not possible. He had to drink the cup and bear the burden of our sins. Do you think, therefore, that where Almighty God could find no substitute for Christ your Savior and His death on the cross, you will be able to find a substitute?

You'll remember how the children of Israel, after they had finished forty years of wanderings and trials, temptations and enemies, still had to face the most difficult and final trial at the end of their pilgrimage, the River Jordan. So too, at the end of our pilgrimage, there flows the cold, dark river of death. And I care not what success you have had with your other foes; here is one you have not conquered. Now, how shall we meet and conquer death? Who will help us over that river? Only Jesus, who has gone down into the River of Death and emerged out of it victorious, can help us. He said, "I am the resurrection and the life," and proved it by His own death and resurrection. If you reject Christ, then on the shores of death, where will you go?

There are some sins that wither and blight life in a flash, but they are not the common sins. There are some trees that are overthrown in one great blast of a winter's gale, but the real cause of its overthrow, if you examine the trunk, is a slow process of decay. The storm only revealed what had been going on for a long time. So it can be with us. One can drift away from Christ so gradually that your friends and fellow Church members do not detect it. But there comes a crisis of sorrow, or loss, or testing, something that shakes to the very foundation, then the destructive processes of the past are all unveiled and discovered in the overthrow.

"Willie," said Mother after he had fallen out of bed, "Did you sleep too near where you got in?" "No mother," he said, "I slept too near where I fell out." Let us get in the middle of Christ and His Church and stay there. Have you fallen out? Then arise and say, "Jesus, I'm coming home." Or are you too near the place where you may fall out? Get back to Him, to enjoy the warmth and safety and security of the very center of His will.

Dear Lord, I don't want to be on the edge of truth. I want to be in the very midst of it, where blessings and a fruitful life are produced. Since only You are the "Way, the Truth and the Life," I choose You. Amen.

January 21 Eating Soup with a Hatchet

Scripture Reading: Luke 14:15-24

Key Verse: "But they all with one accord began to make excuses." Luke 14:18

The story is told of an old farmer, whose boy ran into the house shouting, "Pa, Neighbor Brown wants to borrow the hatchet again." Now, Neighbor Brown had borrowed the hatchet before, and he always seemed to forget to return it. So, the farmer replied, "Son, tell Neighbor Brown I would gladly lend it to him, but we just can't, 'cause I'm going to eat soup with it." In amazement, the boy's eyes almost popped out of his head, but he obediently carried his father's message to Neighbor Brown. That night, they did have soup for supper, but Pa did not use the hatchet. When his son mentioned it, the old man replied, "Son, I had to give Neighbor Brown some kind of excuse, so I thought as long as I was tellin' a lie, I had just as well tell a big one."

Now in our text today, you can see these excuses are lies. For who would purchase land without first seeing it? Or who would buy a horse or a yoke of oxen without first trying them out? No, these men did not want to accept the Master's invitation, so they offered excuses. There isn't a person on earth who can offer even one genuine reason why he should not serve Christ. All they have are "hatchet lies."

There is the young man who says, "Oh, there are a few more things I want to do, a few more wild oats I want to sow, then I'll settle down and join the Church and work for the Lord." Well, he is making two fatal mistakes. First, he doesn't know that the joy and peace that will come to him in the service of Christ will be infinitely greater than all the thrills in a life of sin. Nor does he realize that the longer he continues in sin's grasp, the harder it will be to break away from it. A jeweler would not hesitate for one moment to exchange a trunk full of tin for a shoe box full of gold, so why should we hesitate to bring our handful of sand and pebbles to God, who will give us abundant life in exchange?

Then, there is the one who complains about not joining with a

Church because of the hypocrites in it. Is that a reason or an excuse? If that is a reason, then will that person refuse to join other clubs or organizations? Will he refuse to vote? Because I hear politics is full of hypocrites. Will he refuse to associate with his neighbors, among whom there might be a hypocrite? No, this excuse is like eating soup with a hatchet.

Saddest of all, perhaps, is the person who doesn't feel he needs Christ at all. He says, "I'm not such an awful fellow." What does he mean? He is thinking about thieves and murderers, liars and wife-beaters, and just because he does not do these things, he considers himself worthy of heaven. Deep down in his heart, he feels that he is good enough already. The truth is that the man does not live today who really does the best that he knows how to do, every day, all the time. There is none among mankind who does not descend from Adam, and share in his sinful nature.

We all know those who make excuses, who have their own version of the hatchet-lie. Maybe some of us even find ourselves making excuses to God sometimes. If offered the deed to a house in exchange for an act of service, we wouldn't hesitate. Yet, Jesus offers more than this. He offers a life of peace and joy and a blessed relationship with the best friend in the entire world. What could be worth more than that?

Dear Lord, as Isaiah said, "Here I am, send me." I truly desire to be available to be used by You as an instrument for Your glory. I gladly bring You my pebbles, in exchange for the gold of Your provision. Amen.

January 22   The Tongue

Scripture Reading: James 3:1-12
Key Verse: "And the tongue is a fire...." James 3:6a

The tongue is a part of our body that is tiny. It is not so large as a hand or a foot. It is not at all beautiful and it is not intended to be looked at. It is carefully hidden away in the mouth with two rows of teeth set in front of it. Over the teeth are drawn curtains of flesh to make sure the tongue shall not be seen. The physician is the only one in town who asks the privilege of looking at it.

But it is wonderfully important and we could not get on well without it. While the feet do a rather mechanical drudgery, and the hands do more difficult and artistic work, it is the work of the tongue which is the most delicate and noble of all, for it works with words. Words are the coins with which we carry on our intellectual business. The tongue deals with thoughts, feelings, ideas and ideals, mental pictures, and heart melodies. Man is the only creature who is blessed with mastery of articulate speech.

James compares it to a bridle of a horse, or the rudder of a ship, and points out how amazing it is that such a little thing as this can move about such great objects. When he speaks of its power, he likens it to fire, one of the mightiest forces in nature. When it gets going it is difficult to check. A big fire comes from a little one, as a forest fire comes from a camper's fire. Just so, the tongue is capable of enormous good or enormous evil. It can speak the kindest words or blister, blight and blast. Therefore the apostle comes to the conclusion that one of the first things and most important tasks to which a person gives himself is the management of the tongue.

He begins his letter with an earnest exhortation. Be "slow to speak." Let us ask ourselves how we are using our own tongue. There is the "loose tongue" wherein the tongue runs away with the person. Have you ever seen a horse run away with a rider? It is frightening. It is the rider who is to be in control. There is the "idle tongue" which is not a tongue that says nothing, but rather a tongue that chatters about trifles and petty subjects, wasting the intellect on babble and prattle.

There is the mischievous tongue that exalts in bearing tales, repeating gossip, and rehearsing stories which hurt and sting. These tongues are usually owned by people who feel it is their duty to pass out the mouth everything that comes in the ears. There is an unkind tongue, which is what the apostle had in mind when he compared it to a fire. For one unkind tongue can set a community ablaze, and burn up the peace of a household, the sacred ties of friendship, or the mutual confidence of neighbors.

Words are deeds. You do things with your tongue more than you do things with your hands. You are responsible for your words and therefore must tend to its education. Prayerfully ask God to help you with this task. Ask forgiveness, offer restitution, and think before you speak. It is with your tongue that you can do your finest work for God. You can teach, admonish, encourage, and console. With your words you can put out fires, which may consume the happiness of homes. You can turn away wrath, reconcile enemies, and extend the kingdom of God with your tongue. You can strengthen faith, brighten hope, and deepen love.

Jesus of Nazareth went about doing good with His tongue. He cheered, instructed, and strengthened. The world was made better by the things He said. Now I ask, how so us?

Dear Father, help me to remember that my tongue can burn and blister those I love. Help me to make it an instrument of peace, consolation, and reconciliation. Amen.

January 23   Getting the Best of Trouble

Scripture Reading: Psalm 4

Key Verses: "...You have relieved me in my distress..."
Psalm 4:1

"It is good for me that I have been afflicted, that I may learn Your statutes." Psalm 119:71

To get the best of trouble is an important victory in life, for trouble is sure to come. Trouble is as universal as human nature, for "man is born to trouble as the sparks fly upward." Trouble is no respecter of persons. It knocks at the door of the millionaire and peasant, philosopher and illiterate, believer and unbeliever. There are all kinds of trouble: troubles of the body, troubles of the mind, and troubles of the soul. There are troubles we bring upon ourselves and the troubles others bring upon us. No man is exempted.

The barometer lets us know when a storm is coming, the warning siren tells us of an approaching air raid, and the train whistle warns of an oncoming train. But, trouble comes without a trumpet, unheralded and unexpected.

Trouble is, after all, a divine appointment. One way to get the best of trouble is to realize that it is permitted by God. There are no accidents, no chances in God's providential rule of my life. He makes no mistakes. In His eternal plan, there are no errors. And trouble comes for a purpose, though it is not necessary for us to know that purpose.

Since trouble does not come without God's permission and appointment, we can call upon God to give us strength and hope in the midst of it. The Psalmist said, "It is good for me to draw near to God. I have put my trust in the Lord God, that I may declare all Your works." Hezekiah called upon the Lord for help when he got that blasphemous letter from Sennacherib's lieutenant threatening destruction to Jerusalem and all the people of God. He took the letter into the temple, the place of prayer, and placed it before the Lord. God heard him and delivered Israel.

And David, too, called upon the Lord in his distress. That is also what Paul did. Prayer is to the soul in time of trouble what a life jacket is to the shipwrecked passenger.

Now since trouble comes by divine appointment, we can have faith that there is good to be derived from it, "It is good for me that I have been afflicted," said the psalmist. We need to meet trouble as did Jacob of old, when after the Angel had pushed out his thigh bone, Jacob cried, "I will not let You go unless You bless me."

And then, in trouble there is found good for others also. That is, there is good for others through us. Our own troubles increase our sympathy, and our desire to help our fellow traveler on life's journey. There is no one who can offer comfort to the afflicted like one who has survived just such an affliction.

On the shores of the Pacific in Oregon, there is a place called Agate Beach. After the fierce storms that rage against those shores pass, agate hunters come early to seek precious agates, moonstones, and jasper. The storms bring treasures in along with the raging waves. So it is with life's fierce storms. If we go out after the storms and billows have passed over us and gather up the heavenly agates and jaspers which they have strewn upon the shores of life, our lives will be richer, more blessed, and more beautiful because of the storms that come.

Dear Heavenly Father, today I ask that You would teach me to trust You more completely. When trials come, I ask that You would prompt me to look for You in the midst of my trouble. Help me to learn from the trials that come my way. And in everything, thank You. Amen.

January 24   An Old-Time Mother

Scripture Reading: I Samuel Chapter 1
Key Verses: "For this child I prayed... therefore I also have lent him to the Lord; as long as he lives he shall be lent to the Lord..." *I Samuel 1:27-28.*

    We lean across the centuries to get a look at Hannah's winsome face. She is glad with the glorious gladness of motherhood as she looks into the face of her first-born baby boy. We are interested in her not because of her cleverness; though I am sure she was quite clever. We are interested in her not because she was a leader in society. No, we are interested in her because she was a mother, a successful mother.

    Now I am aware of the fact that Hannah lived a long time ago, and that in that far-off day there were not many honorable vocations open to women. Of course things are different now, and to this I make no objection. A woman's sphere is no longer circumscribed, and she may succeed in business, medicine, literature, or politics. But, I do say this; Hannah's vocation was, and is, the highest. Women exercise a tremendous influence in various vocations outside the home, but her place of greatest power ever will be in the home.

    We owe much to the gifted and brilliant women who from platform and printed page have made their contribution to the world, but we owe still more to those hidden toilers who were the mothers of the great contributors of history. While "Mrs. Wesley" would have shone anywhere, she rendered her finest service in giving, through her boys, the mightiest influence for the spread of the gospel since the days of the Apostles. The calling of motherhood is noble.

    Hannah was a praying mother. She could say, "For this child I prayed," and you feel confident that prayer was one of the fixed habits of her life. She was a woman of genuine piety, and real consecration. She put God first in her own heart. And there is no influence more dominant in the shaping of the life of a child than prayer.

    Many of us who are active in Christian life today would say we were brought up in a home where prayer was the vital atmosphere. The influence of a Christian home cannot be overstated, and I can attest to that influence. The recollections of the oldest of my brothers and sister do not go back beyond the family altar. Every child reared in my parent's home became an active Christian, the oldest of whom at past 84 years of age was still preaching after more than 58 years of ministry. All five sons of us became ordained ministers, and our sister became a pastor's dear wife and helpmate.

Hannah was a wise mother, also. She recognized that her child was really God's child, and believed that God was interested in him. She believed that God loved him and had a place for him. Therefore, she dedicated him to God. Some parents even today are afraid to do that. How many of us urge our children to consider the pastorate, or missionary service as their vocation? How many of us are willing to trust that much?

You will miss the whole point of the record if you look upon Samuel as an abnormal boy. He did not become a prophet by accident, you see. Hannah put God first in her own life, she put God first in her own home, and she prayed. Whether there are children in our home, grown out of our home, or within our sphere of contact, let us do this for them as well.

Father in heaven, I know in my heart that You must love these children even more than I do, although it hardly seems possible. I trust You to work in their lives, and I am honored to be one of the tools You have chosen to use to do so. Please fill me with Your Spirit, and fill my house with Your presence. In Jesus's name, amen.

January 25   The Choice of Faithfulness

Scripture Reading: Ruth Chapter 1

Key Verse: "But Ruth said, 'Entreat me not to leave you, or to turn back from following after you; for wherever you go, I will go; and wherever you lodge, I will lodge. Your people shall be my people, and your God, my God.'" Ruth 1:16

The Book of Ruth is one of the briefest books of the Bible, but the portrait it gives of this Moabite woman, who came as a young widow to Bethlehem with Naomi, is unforgettable. When Benjamin Franklin was abroad as our representative in Europe, he would sometimes gather together a fashionable company and, telling them he had come upon a most remarkable piece of oriental literature, he would read to them the Book of Ruth. When he had finished, all would express their great delight and ask him how he came upon such a gem of literature. Only then would he tell them it was in the Bible.

Ruth is a sweet interlude of peace and love between the fierce chorus of war found in Judges and Samuel. In this book, there is not a single wicked, cruel, or licentious person making their appearance. In Ruth, we behold the attractiveness of virtue, the beauty of sacrifice, and the winsomeness of simple trust in God.

This famous story yields two great and timeless truths. First, we see the fact of God's providence in our life. Every one of the characters of the Book of Ruth reverently owns the presence of God in life and human affairs. Naomi saw the hand of God in her sorrow and adversity, Boaz recognized the hand of God in the good fortune that gave him Ruth for a wife, and Ruth herself put her trust under the wings of the Lord God of Israel. The whole Book of Ruth turns upon that which might seem just a happenstance. But there is no happenstance with God. He guided Ruth's footsteps.

Faith recognizes God's hand not only in the obviously pleasant things of life, but as well in what we call the hard things of life. As Shakespeare wrote, "There's a divinity that shapes our ends, rough-hew them how we will."

The second great truth so dramatically illustrated here is the power of choice and decision. Ruth chose, definitely and forever, the people of God as her people and the Lord God of Israel as her God. Orpah yielded to the entreaties of Naomi to return to her people, and her idols, in Moab. She did not have a desire to break with the world. But Ruth truly turned to the Lord. She did not even have a backward look toward Moab, the land of her birth and her family. There Ruth stood on the bank of the River Jordan, with her back to Moab, and on her lips that grand decision. And once she decided, there was no turning back.

Many people we meet today are like Orpah. They seem to have some desire to go with Christ along the way. They seem to want to be with His people. But they never bring themselves to the point of breaking with the world. Their hearts are in Moab, and eventually back to Moab they go. How sad, for they never truly get to experience the riches that following Christ brings.

How much better an example is Ruth who, once decided, never turned back. Her decision was no different from decisions many of us will have to make in our lifetime. Great things hung on Ruth's choice, and great things today hang upon our decision to follow Christ, and to obey God today and every day.

Dear Father God, I have put my hand to the plow to work for You. Yet, each and every day I must work to follow and not turn aside. There is so much in the world to distract or tempt me. Please help me today to resist temptation, to resist distraction, and to set my eyes firmly on you. In Jesus's name and for His sake, amen.

January 26   The Patience of Christ

Scripture Reading: II Thessalonians 3:1-5
Key Verse: "Now may the Lord direct your hearts into the love of God and into the patience of Christ."
II Thessalonians 3:5

The patience of Christ is perfect. Let's look to Him as our example as well as our Savior and Lord. We are to walk in His steps and be imitators of Him.

See Christ's patience in dealing with His own disciples. Once, two of the disciples selfishly and ambitiously insisted they be allowed to sit, one on His right and one on His left side in His kingdom. How slow they were to comprehend the spiritual nature of His kingdom, yet how patient he was with His selfish disciples.

Think of His patience with His foes. He prayed for His murderers, gave the softest answers to their wrath, and after being reviled and scourged, He climbed up the lonely hill and upon that cruel cross died for us all.

There was only one thing with which Jesus was impatient and that was evil. "For this purpose the Son of God was manifested, that He might destroy the works of the devil." Where would the cause of liberty be in America if not for her heroic impatience against tyranny? Where would the cause of missions have gone but for William Carey? We are called to be aggressively impatient against wrong and for the right throughout the social order everywhere.

Not only do we need patience with ourselves, but also we need it in all the relations of life. We need it in the home where we should live at our highest and best, but do we? Parents need this grace in the training of growing children. Husband and wife need it with each other. We need it with our aging parents and they with us. And then, we need patience in our work with our fellow Christians in the church. Not all persons are reasonable and congenial in the Lord's work. Some are exacting, faultfinding and critical. Surprised? Then remember we are all a work in progress. You may be someone's thorn tomorrow, be patient today.

Unless we have a right measure and proper use of patience, we shall sorely misunderstand and misjudge others. Once in the days of slow trains, when nightfall came the tired passengers hastened to find rest after the day's hot and dusty ordeal. At one end of the Pullman car a man was seen with a tiny baby in his arms trying vainly to quiet it. The more he strove to quiet the fretting child the louder were its cries. Tired people turned uneasily in their berths. Presently a big, brawny, impatient fellow called out to the man trying to quiet the child, "Why don't you take that baby to its mother?" There was a moments' pause and then came back the reply, "The baby's mother is in her casket in the baggage car ahead."

Again there was an awful silence, and then the big, burly man who asked the cruel question dressed himself and hurried to the man with the motherless child to make his worthiest apology. The father of the child was then entreated to get some sleep while the thoughtless questioner gave himself for hours to the task of quieting and caring for the little child.

Why is Christ our example of patience? For this simple reason, He loves best. What makes a mother patient with her exacting and endless duties in her home? It is love. What was it made Jacob toil seven arduous years and then for seven more? His love for Rachel. What is the heart of the glorious gospel of Christ? "The life I now live in the flesh I live by the faith of the Son of God who loved me and gave Himself for me."

Lord God, thank You for Your patience with me. Thank You for understanding my faults and imperfections and loving me anyway. Amen

January 27   A Whole-Hearted Saint

Scripture Reading: Joshua Chapter 14
Key Verse: "...but I wholly followed the Lord my God."
Joshua 14:8

Here is a young man with a life experience worth telling. He has had a grand yesterday, he has a noble present, and he is looking out expectantly upon tomorrow. Mark it well; Caleb is not swollen with conceit. He is not boasting; he is testifying. He is no swaggerer. So, we rejoice in his testimony. We rejoice also in the quiet confidence with which he tells his story. His life has been an open book. It has been a living epistle known and read of all men. When he declares that he has been a follower of God, he is stating a truth borne out before witnesses.

There is solid joy and satisfaction in a testimony like this. He is not wringing his hands in vain regret over ill-spent years. He is rather rejoicing over all his radiant yesterdays. He looks back upon them with grateful and humble heart. Men have regretted their loyalty to other gods, and deplored their devotion to all other masters. But let me say, beloved, no single soul has ever found regret in a life of service to God.

Not only does Caleb claim that he is a follower of the Lord, but he uses a word to describe that following that most of us dare not use. He says, "I <u>wholly</u> followed the Lord my God." I have given Him my undivided allegiance. I have served Him with whole-hearted devotion. I have not been a straddler. I have not been lukewarm. I have given Him the loyalty of my whole soul. I have placed God in my affections where He ought always to be, first.

Of course, it was by faith that Caleb came to know God, but it was through loyalty to God that he found a larger and ever-growing faith. If you don't follow the gleam you will find your light becoming dark. If you don't obey the voice of God in your conscience or by His spirit, you will find that voice becoming quiet. It is in the wholehearted loyalty that we find a larger faith.

Remember when we first met Caleb? He had just returned with the other spies from exploring the land of Canaan. All the spies are not of one mind. The majority report is that while the land is rich, the job of getting possession is futile. Then Caleb comes forward, just Caleb and Joshua, and with conviction they said let us go up at once and possess it…God has given us the land and victory is certain if we only dare to claim it.

Oh, what an asset is a man possessed of valiant, victorious faith. It is ever the person of faith who subdues kingdoms, works righteousness; turn violence to flight and out of weakness is made strong. Courage is the natural outcome of faith. Faith is ever the mother of courage.

Caleb was a man who never grew old. We meet him some fifty years later at Kadesh Barnea, eighty-five years old but still young and winsome. At this late date in his life, he came to Joshua and requested the hardest task in the kingdom. He was burningly eager at this late date to undertake the most difficult job he had ever undertaken. Though he had accomplished much for the Lord, he was not content to enter a spiritual retirement.

Caleb left the grand legacy of a life lived in unswerving loyalty to God. So, we rejoice in his testimony. We rejoice also in the knowledge that God stands ready to use us, if only we will serve Him wholeheartedly.

Oh, Father, how I want my life to count for You. I eagerly desire to bring glory to Your name. I want to be able to say with Caleb that I have wholly followed You all my life. I want my life to bring praise to Your name. Please lead me, Lord, and help me to walk faithfully in the paths You have laid out for me on this earth. Amen.

January 28   That Magnificent Minority

Scripture Reading: Luke 17:11-19

Key Verses: "... when he saw he was healed, returned and with a loud voice gloriied God, and fell down on his face at His feet, giving Him thanks and he was a Samaritan. So Jesus answered and said, 'Were there not ten cleansed? But where are the nine?'" Luke 17:15-16

When we first meet this engaging, grateful fellow, there is nothing to distinguish him from his colleagues. He is part of a group of ten men bound by a wretched tragedy. They stagger under the weight of the common woe of leprosy. They are facing the same ghastly death. They are outcasts, abandoned bits of human wreckage.

They are all also alike in their desperate determination to live. When they heard that Jesus was coming, they all went out to meet Him. When they had come as close as they dared, their faith was evidenced by their cry for help, and the supreme proof of their faith is their obedience. Jesus laid upon them a bewildering command, "Go, show yourselves to the priests." They were still loathsome with the disease, yet they obeyed.

Finally, they were alike in their healing. The path of obedience is always the path of healing, and the path of discovery. That was true of all ten.

With feet made nimble with joy, the nine departed to their families, to their friends, and to their business to share the good news of their healing. Nine have gone, and one man was left. There is tender joy on his face, mixed with bewilderment. He too has loved ones he hasn't seen for many months. He too has business to attend. But there is something more pressing.

So, he turned back, even though he turned back alone. He made his way to Jesus and in abandonment of joy fell at His feet, giving Him thanks. Ten go to plead, one returns to praise. A small minority of gratitude we must confess, but what a magnificent minority. He had an appreciative heart.

But, why was only one grateful, while the nine were not? Well, you may say, surely they were grateful, but were not as demonstrative as the one. We hear of such gratitude daily. "He knows I am grateful," we say glibly, or, "She knows how thankful I am." Undoubtedly, if you met these nine on their way home and asked them, "Did you go back and thank the Master?" they would have replied something like this, "Oh, no, but He knows how much we appreciate it."

That kind of gratitude is cheap. It lifts no load, brings no joy, and dries no tears. Scripture says, "Let the redeemed of the Lord say so," and "Forget not all His benefits." The kind of gratitude in a heart that never expresses its thanks, soon finds it has no thanks to give. It gets so absorbed in the gift, that it forgets the giver.

It was not so with the one. When he thought of his blessings, he gave Him thanks. Thanking follows thinking as naturally as night follows day.

Now, whether we have read their motives aright or not, this is yet true: the Master was deeply conscious of it all. "Were there not ten…?" By their failure to give thanks, they grieved the loving heart that gave them healing. It is a good thing to give thanks unto the Lord. May we ever be found with the magnificent minority, at the feet of our Lord, giving thanks with hearts of gratitude.

Dear Heavenly Father, thank You for the blessings You have given me. Everything I have or am has come from You. With the Psalmist, I cry, "Bless the Lord, oh my soul, let all that is within me bless His holy name!" I am so truly, endlessly grateful, Lord. Thank You. Amen.

January 29   That Bewildering Mixture

Scripture Reading: Matthew 13:24-30
Key Verse: "Let both grow together until the harvest..."
Matthew 13:30

Here we see a proprietor at work in His own field. He has sown good seed, because he desires to gather in a good harvest. But something has gone wrong. The field is sown with tares, which in the first stages of growth will be impossible to distinguish from the good seed. That difference will only be manifested later.

The thing which arrests our attention is that the tares are maliciously sown by the enemy of the owner of the field. This second sowing is done by a trespasser. He has no right there. He came by stealth, while the man of the field slept. Notice that he could gain nothing by the sowing. The tares were as worthless to one man as to the other. This is an act of pure malice, an act of hatred toward the owner. The world and all that is in it belong to Jesus Christ, but our adversary the devil has come to sow in His field. The devil has no right on the ground; he is simply trespassing on Jesus' land.

The seeds are scattered, mingling counterfeit with real. And in this world we sometimes discern the imitation in every realm, do we not? Turn where you may in the world, the church, or the human heart and you will find tares growing with the wheat.

And how long will this go on, this coexistence of wheat and tare in the field, of evil and good in the world? Is this not the perplexing question that has been asked down through the centuries? The Master of the field has spoken. Both the good grain and the tares will be allowed to mature to their final manifestation. The evil nature of the tare seed will produce evil fruit; and the sons of the kingdom will produce kingdom fruit. Christ is certainly on a mission against evil; it is His plan and purpose to destroy the works of the devil, but not by the method the servant suggested.

"Pull them up!" may sound practical. But, sometimes discerning the difference between tares and wheat requires more wisdom than you or I ever could possess. Remember, there were sincere, devout Jews who felt Jesus was a tare in the wheat field. Secondly, you cannot practice tare pulling without disturbing the roots of the wheat as well.

"Let them grow together until the harvest," Jesus' method, is far better. Rather than focusing on the negative, He focuses on the good. After all, no man is a Christian by virtue of what he does not do. No tare pulling will ever bring in the kingdom of God. It will only bring about a desert. No matter how many tares we pull up, there is no increase in the wheat.

While Jesus was among men, this was also His method. Rather than bombarding the evil in men, Christ won them through His love. And so should we seek to show people the love of Jesus until they see something satisfying to their hunger.

Does evil seem more diabolical? Well, yes it does. But has the gospel of Jesus Christ spread further than ever before, reaching more people than ever before? Well, yes it has. The seed in the field is maturing.

The tares of this world? Oh, He will not always leave them alone. The tares will be gathered and burned, and the wheat will be gathered for the sake of the Owner. In the meantime, beloved, take joy. We know Who owns the field.

Dear Father, thank You for the comfort that this marvelous word picture brings. The evil in the world that so alarms me is neither a surprise, nor an unplanned eventuality to You. You are just waiting for the harvest. Help me to work in the field for good as I wait. Amen.

January 30

The Conquest of Discouragement

Scripture Reading: I Kings 19:1-18

Key Verse: "And he prayed that he might die, and said, 'It is enough! Now, Lord, take my life, for I am no better than my fathers!'" I Kings 19: 4

Discouragement is a terrible thing. It results from many causes and brings various reactions. It results in the obscuring of faith and the prostitution of strength. It leads us into the blind alley of despair and drives us into the wilderness of depression. We see nothing of God and we see everything of evil and foreboding surrounding us.

Elijah was a man of meteoric nature. He acted first and meditated afterwards. This is why we find him in the wilderness where many of us have sat, beneath the juniper tree of discouragement. However, when Elijah found a juniper tree and prayed to die, God gave him strength to live. He then left the tree for a cave. Under the tree Elijah met the angel of encouragement. In the cave, he met the God who encourages. Here the word of the Lord came to Elijah. "What are you doing here, Elijah?"

He had no business there. His place was among his people. Here he was pitying himself and lamenting his lonesomeness. He cried out to God with a hopeless and discouraged cry. What a place for a prophet, hiding in a cave! Yet, many of us have been in caves, the caves of despondency, worry, hopelessness, and fretfulness. If you are there now, God is saying to you, "What are you doing here, Elijah?" A cave of despair is no place for any child of God. He belongs on the mount. He belongs in the surging stream, not in a cave.

In essence, God was asking him why he was not working. Elijah said sulkily, that he had no one to help him and what's the use of one man trying to change the world? And God told him to get right back to work.

Beloved, have you ever been blue, disgruntled, or discouraged? Have you ever thought you were carrying all the load and what was the use? Have you ever been about to quit and give up the whole business?

Remember the story of King Robert Bruce of Scotland? He took refuge from his enemies in a little cabin and there God sent a spider to spin a powerful lesson to the king. His wife had been captured, his brother executed, and he was in despair. But as he lay there, about to give up, his eye was attracted to the spider hanging from a long thread endeavoring to throw a line to another beam and secure its web. Six times it tried and failed, just as six times the king had fought against the British and failed.

The seventh time the spider gave itself with all its might as it swung toward the beam. This time it succeeded. Bruce arose to go out on the field of battle and this time he went on to glorious victory. Not unlike this are some of the lessons God teaches us by one means or another as we lie in our caves of despair.

Elijah was asked to go up to Mount Horeb and there to stand before the Lord. There, the glory of the Lord passed by. Neither he, nor you or I, will never see the glory of the Lord so long as we remain in the cave of despondency. We must go out and stand on the mount.

Just as Elijah on Mount Horeb learned that in God was his strength, and never again sought the juniper tree or the cave, so you too my friend, can find in the Savior the one who will take your discouraged life and fill it with the glory of His presence. He will transform your life into one of usefulness and service and delight.

Dearest Lord, I so often am like Elijah in that I act, and then meditate. Thank You for loving me even with my moods and lack of faith. Please help me now to come out of the cave and get back to work. Amen.

January 31   The Provision of God

Scripture Reading: Job 38:4-41

Key Verse: "Who provides food for the raven, when its young ones cry to God, and wander about for lack of food?"
Job 38:41

When the President of the United States plans to travel, the most elaborate and extensive preparations are undertaken to secure his well-being and safety. Well, God's preparations for us are no less elaborate and extensive. We find countless illustrations of this truth in the Bible. We read of waters gushing forth from rocks, manna coming down from Heaven, and honey stored in the carcass of a lion. We read about a prophet fed by ravens, the widow's oil that continued to flow, meal in a barrel that was exhaustless, a well of water found in a desert and more than 5,000 fed with a child's lunch.

And what preparations did our Father make for us before we were called to take our place in this world? He created this earth for us. He saw to it that minerals were in the mountains, fish in the waters, cattle on the plains, grain in the fields, fruit in the orchards, nuts on the trees, berries on the bushes and timber on the slopes. Our nature-earth-cupboard was filled to overflowing.

And what a marvelous house He constructed for our spirit to live in. There is the eye by which we enjoy the colors of the rainbow, the daily miracle of the sunset and the indescribable pageantry of a summer garden. There is the ear, a gateway through which enters the music of the waterfall, the anthem of the sea, the whispers of the trees, the warbling of the birds, and the cry of a child.

Our hands and feet are in themselves an incredible chest of tools to master the earth. Our memory appropriates the knowledge of the yesterdays while imagination anticipates the possibilities of tomorrow. And for our immortal spirit God's ministries have spoken to us by stars and sunbeams, mountain and mist, flower and firmament, coronation, and crucifixion. Truth has exhorted us by day and conscience has counseled us by night.

Are we anxious about yesterday? God provided the blood of Christ to pay our debts of yesterday, today, and tomorrow. Tomorrow? Whatever it brings, whether sickness, health, gladness or grief, summer sun or killing frost, it will be well.

What a glorious promise for this New Year ahead, with all its mysteries, joys and sorrows. No one knows when the journey will end. One day our pulsing hearts will cease, but as God knows our life, so also He knows our death. He is providing for our future even now. He said in Scripture, "In my Father's House are many mansions… I go to prepare a place for you."

Your yesterdays are paid for, whatever comes today will be well since it will be God's will, and tomorrow is already prepared for you by the all-loving Father. So, here is my word for the New Year, time will not stand still. The days, the weeks, and months will pass on in solemn parade each with its face looking onward.

God's work demands your loyalty, your love, and your service. Your soul cries out for growth. You must go on. But sad to state, how many fail to go on? The largest class in college is always the freshmen class. Only two out of 600,000 went on into Canaan. No, beloved, we must go on. We must go on in prayer, in Bible study, in a deeper sense of the fellowship of God, and a richer companionship of God's saints. We must go on, yielded to the leadership of His Spirit saying "Not my will, but Yours." Lead us on, Lord, we will follow all the way.

Almighty Father who loves and cares for me, may I be faithful this New Year to finish the race You've put before me, knowing that You have already provided all I need. Amen.

February 1   Mind Your Own Business

Scripture Reading: I Thessalonians 4:1-12

Key Verse: "That you also aspire to lead a quiet life, to mind your own business, and to work with your own hands, as we commanded you." I Thessalonians 4:11

"Leave us alone," people cry. "Mind your own business." Well, after all, what is my business?

As an individual I may not be master of my fate, but how I manage it, what I make of it, is my business. It is my business to make my life all that it can and ought to be. It is my business to be honest and fair, to see that I am kept from all that is sordid, low, and mean. If I can find a way to escape evil of any or every kind it is my business to find that way. If there is a source of power and redemption from both wrong and weakness it is my business to turn to that source and accept all possible aid. It is my business to make my mind, my heart, my life, and my character all they ought to be. These are individual responsibilities. They are sacredly personal.

As a member of society, I have obligations to the many and I cannot evade these any more than I can evade my personal obligations. We have civic duties as citizens of a great republic. To do one's duty whether in the home, at the office, at the polls or in the President's chair is an important matter. If there is poverty, injustice, or evil, it is my duty to help change it.

Yet, beyond these narrow limits I must go. I am a member of a world society. Read the books of the prophets of old. They were primarily citizens, not preachers. They had a world vision and deep interest in international affairs because they saw their duty. "A fire burns in my bones," said one. "I have to speak." We have important business as a citizen of the world.

Spiritually, there is no one who can do my business but me. We need to remember that four times in the trial of Jesus, the Master was handed over to someone else on the plea that "He was their affair." The High Priests handed the prisoner to Pilate. Pilate handed Him over to

Herod. Herod sent him back to Pilate. Pilate finally handed Jesus over to the Roman soldiers to be crucified whimpering that it was not his business and he was innocent of this man's blood.

But every time one of these men said, "That's your affair," he uttered a lie. Jesus was Pilate's affair. Jesus was Herod's affair. Jesus is everyone's affair. People try to evade all personal responsibility by insisting "He's your affair." But He is the affair of every one of us and what you do with Jesus is your business.

I ask, why did Whitfield and Asbury come to America? Why did Livingstone go to Africa, Morrison to China and Carey to India? They went to attend to their business as Christians in this world. And if the Spirit controls and leads us, we shall desire to help in this business no matter the color or caste or the cost.

We are not all Moodys or Careys or Livingstones. Our ways of doing God's work are many and varied. But even as a boy Jesus knew that His first priority was to be "about His Father's business." And here is the key. Jesus' business was the Father's business, and so is ours. Let us mind our own business and be about the Father's business. Let us help not hinder, lift up not pull down, be selfless not selfish, put God first not ourselves first, and befriend, and not belittle. Let us follow Christ's example and feed the hungry, heal the sick, live out the gospel in our lives and lead others to God. This, beloved, is our business.

Holy Father God, I think I have priorities in the wrong order and they need re-arranging. Help me to examine my life to be sure that I am minding my own business by minding Yours. Amen

February 2   The Reconciliation

Suggested Reading: I Corinthians 15:1-11

Key Verses: "...Christ died for our sins according to the Scriptures, and that He was buried, and that He rose again the third day according to the Scriptures." 1 Corinthians 15:3-4

We are told by some that Jesus was a great moral teacher, and so He was, but the apostles never gloried in that fact. We are constantly reminded that He was a great reformer, and so He was, but Peter, John, and Paul didn't know it. It is asserted that He was a great philanthropist, caring for the lives of common men, and so He was, but the New Testament does not seem to care about that. No, the Bible never sees Him from any of these standpoints. According to apostolic writers, Jesus was manifested as "the Lamb of God that takes away the sin of the world." And the awful fact that broke the Apostle's hearts and sent them out to baptize the nations into His name was that "Christ died for our sins."

No one can read the New Testament without seeing that its central and most conspicuous theme is the death of Jesus. Look at the Gospels. Why, one quarter of their pages is given up to the account of His death. Take the Epistles; there is scarcely a quotation from the lips of Jesus. Wouldn't that be strange if He was only the Greatest Teacher, and nothing more? Every letter is laden with the pathos of His death.

Listen to Jesus Himself. The thought of his death is wrapped up inside all He said. When He spoke to Nicodemus, He said, "As Moses lifted up the serpent in the wilderness, even so must the Son of Man be lifted up..." In the temple, He declared, "Destroy this temple, and in three days I will raise it up." While visiting Jerusalem, He said, "I am the Good Shepherd. The Good Shepherd gives His life for the sheep." They did not understand these words, but we do. Again and again, Jesus revealed that He came to die for our sins.

Whatever men may think of Jesus, there is no question concerning what the men who wrote the New Testament thought of Him. To those men, Jesus was not a Socrates, a Seneca, or an Abraham Lincoln. His life was not an incident in the process of evolution. His death was not an episode in the dark and dreadful tragedy of human history. No, His life is God's greatest gift to men. His death is the climax and the crowning revelation of the heart of the Eternal God. "Christ died for our Sins," is the theme that set the apostles afire and turned the world upside down! This is a mighty love, that the Father spared not the Son, but delivered Him up for us.

A noted missionary, who came to speak to Native American Indians early in the history of our country, began to teach them of God. He spoke of a God of grandeur and glory, telling of the heavens and the stars, and they laughed. He told of the God of nature, who formed the streams, the mountains. They did not respond. Baffled, he began to picture to them how God came down to earth as the man Christ. He told them of the cross, of Christ's pierced hands and feet. And he told them that Christ had come out of love, to pay for the sins of man. Then they cried aloud, "Was it for me He died?"

Christianity's distinction is in the life, death, and resurrection of our Lord Jesus Christ. This is its claim. This is its power. We dare not lose sight of that.

Oh, dear Lord God, break my heart today with the realization of Christ's death for me. Forgive me for the times I have taken Your sacrifice for granted. And now, set me on fire with the burning purpose of sharing so great a love that would pay a debt it didn't owe. Let me hold onto the fact of Christ's death, burial and resurrection like a torch, lifting it aloft in this dark world that all may see the light, and come to Him. Amen.

February 3   God and Company, Builders

Scripture Reading: I Corinthians 3:5-17
Key Verse: "For we are God's fellow workers..."
I Corinthians 3:9

The Creator God is not only busy, He is busy working. Did you ever watch God transform dust and moisture and sunlight into a glorious sunset? Did you ever watch Him as He transforms a dirty, homely bulb into a beautiful hyacinth or a spotless lily? Did you ever watch Him in springtime as He runs the sap up into the arteries of the trees and fashions buds and leaves and blossoms?

He is building civilizations, the universe, and through Christ, the Church militant. In all these you and I are working with the Master Builder. We ask for bread, He gives us a handful of seed and points to the soil. We ask for fish, He points to the brook. We ask for a mast, He points to the forest.

If we are lazy, and we are as lazy as we dare be, He sends necessity as a prod. The coal would still be in the hills of Pennsylvania if December winds and snow did not chill us. Only fever and aches made man discover the medicine in bark. Only pain in the vitals made man discover the knife and explore the human body. In all these things God created the raw material for man before He put him to work as a fellow-craftsman.

If God is our partner, we can make our plans large. Human soil is marked with divine footprints. We simply follow the trail. So it was that Moses was a herdsman at Mt. Horeb, Paul a tentmaker in Arabia, Peter a fisherman on Galilee. Man is not a thistle-seed blown by the wind of time and circumstance. Man is a star held in its course. He who makes the stars and calls them by name, knows man and calls him. "Abraham!" "Moses!" "Samuel!" And they work together from that hour.

We speak of a minister being "called" to preach. Yet, isn't the blacksmith called to the forge, the carpenter to the bench, and the weaver to the loom? "Let each one," says Paul, "remain in the same calling in which he was called." All business is our Father's business. The tailor is called to help God clothe His human children. The grocer helps God by distributing sugar, rice, and other foods from God's hand. The doctor helps Him bring health, and the missionary helps God disseminate the Gospel to the ends of the earth. We are workers together with Him. What an honor.

I often pass by a shop that has three golden balls hanging over it, called a "Pawn Shop." Sure enough, the window is full of tools. I see the sign that reads "Unredeemed," for workmen have lost their tools of life. But, Brother Workman, we have a Redeemer who will buy things back. He will buy you back and give you a new start, a new heart, a new life, and a new desire to work. That is the reason for the church, the business of the Christian, and the joy of every Christian life.

Before Jesus went away He left us a little memorial. He showed us what kind of God He was when He girded himself with a towel. It might have been a robe, a crown, a scepter, a kingdom, but it was a towel. And in beautiful humility He washed the disciples' feet and said that this was the true spirit of service. Oh my friend, have you taken the towel? Are you working in the name of Christ at whatever He has called you to? Are you building for eternity? Have you made your plans big? The name of your firm? Oh yes, it's God and Company, Builders. We are all workers together with God.

Holy Father, Creator and King, I want to do my best for You in whatever You call me to do. I know I may plant a seed, but it is You who ignites the spark of life in it. In what I do today, ignite the life in it and make it great for eternity and for Your glory. Amen.

February 4   Messages from Heaven

Scripture Reading: Hebrews 11:1 to 12:1

Key Verse: "...Since we are surrounded by so great a cloud of witnesses, let us lay aside every weight, and the sin which so easily ensnares us, and let us run with endurance the race that is set before us." Hebrews 12:1

Years ago in my hometown in Canada a great marathon was run to decide the champion long-distance runner of Canada and Great Britain. Among the runners was a hometown boy, a Christian lad and a member of my father's church. Thousands of people lined the road for miles to greet and encourage their favorite entrant. But I shall never forget when the news was flashed that our boy, Ellard White, was in the lead. When his form flashed over the hill and down the grade to the finish line I can still imagine the shouts, the cheers that actually lifted him along the way, and when a great burst of speed broke all existing records and gave to him and our city the honors of the hour, those faces filled with joy. Truly that day a great cloud of witnesses surrounded him, filling his heart with hope and strength.

Well, here in chapter twelve of Hebrews, the writer shows us that we are also surrounded with a great cloud of witnesses. Sometimes we need to hear those cheers and those words of instruction by those who understand and have gone before.

Abel says to us, "Do not be afraid to worship God with your best, and do not be afraid of your brother's anger." To those of you who faithfully bring your offering, and with love and purpose lay it upon the altar of the Lord with prayers that God will bless it and you, be encouraged. Despite the criticism of others, God sees and blesses.

I hear brother Enoch say, "Do not be afraid to walk with the Lord." So many of us are afraid to come out on the Lord's side, but Enoch was not afraid and what fellowship, spiritual progress, and light were his. By walking with the Lord he did not even feel the sting of death. This is a true picture of God's plans for the human family. Some are to die and some are to be caught up to meet the Lord.

Noah says, "Do not be afraid to work for the Lord though it is discouraging, even seemingly hopeless, at times." Some of you have worked thirty years. Well, Noah worked 120 years for God on that old ark. Noah saved his household and he warned the world. Is your house saved? Are you warning men and women? That's a hard job but it is your job and mine.

Abraham, the father of the faithful, says, "Do not be afraid to be a pilgrim." We are strangers here below and our motives and our mission are misunderstood. Keep up your pilgrimage. God will lead you to Canaan. As we gaze at the happy face of Sarah, she calls, "Don't be afraid to wait on God. Wait on the Lord." Our God is a miracle-working God; wait patiently for Him.

Moses says, "Don't be afraid to wrestle with the Lord in prayer. You have a prayer-hearing and a prayer-answering God. When I saw the golden calf I was never so discouraged, but I climbed back up to the top of the mountain and I prayed. Prayer changes things; it will change a nation, a church, a home, or a life."

Rahab reminds us, "Do not be afraid to watch for God." In Jericho the scarlet cord that Rahab tied from her window said," this home is protected by the blood." In obedience to God's will, Rahab trusted and waited for her deliverance.

God grant that these voices from heaven inspire and encourage us on our way to eternity.

Dear Father, It is true that each thing that tests and tries me has befallen someone else. Thank You that I can learn and be uplifted by their example. Amen.

February 5   A Quartet That Raised the Roof

Scripture Reading: Mark 2:1-12

Key Verse: "Then they came to Him, bringing a paralytic who was carried by four men." Mark 2:3

As Christ returns to Capernaum He stops at Peter's house. Mark paints the crowd flocking to the humble home, overflowing its modest capacity, blocking the doorway and clustering round it outside as far as they could hear Christ's voice. So here is a church service in progress, not in a cathedral but in a house. It is a glorious service, for Christ is there. He is the source of our power and conviction and without Him what does all our music and preaching, and outward show amount to?

Yes, when Christ is in the house good men will be attracted, bad men will be benefited, lost men will be saved, weak men will be strengthened, sick men will be healed, and Christian men will be energized to serve. The world is tired of philosophy and psychology, book reviews, current events, politics and man's opinions, but the world hungers for the Gospel of the Son of God.

I wish we knew more about the four men in our verse. They might have been neighbors, men of business who were willing to take time off to get this man into the presence of Jesus. I imagine they had a short meeting and said "Now, Jesus is here and our poor brother down the street can be healed if we get him to where Jesus is. Let's just team up and get him to Peter's house today." And so, each man took a corner of his responsibility and they finally arrived at the place where Jesus was. Here is the test of our love for our fellow man.

There was a big crowd around Jesus, but these men didn't say, "Sorry brother, we did our best, but we can't get in." I see co-operation. Each man took his corner of the sheet. I see labor. It was no easy task to carry a man and his bed to the roof. I see faith, risking, extraordinary faith that met and conquered difficulties. Their faith never faltered until their burden was in the presence of Jesus. This was perseverance and earnestness. They removed the tile, the moss, the mud, and reeds. They continued until every obstacle was gone and they had opened a hole in the roof big enough to lower the man to Jesus. There is no easy way to lead men to Jesus.

What was the outcome of all this? When Jesus saw their faith He said "Rise, take up your bed and walk." Rise? How could he rise? But he did walk in obedience to the author of Eternal Life. "Take up your bed!" Lug it away. You have no further need of it. "Walk!" That's the cost of the cure. For if you don't walk you will have paralysis again.

And so, here is our task. We must join our brother and our sister in taking our corner of the sheet to carry men to Christ. Let's pray, but don't stop there. Put feet to our prayer. Let's plan together with God. Let's, with Him, meet and conquer every obstacle. Let's carry our friends to the presence of Christ. He will do the rest.

There was a great procession in New York, with bands and soldiers, floats and horses. But then came a number of big buses and trucks filled with people. Behind these buses walked a goodly number of New York City Firemen. Before the vehicles, there was carried a large sign that read "These people saved from death by New York City Firemen."

What about you? When you pass the reviewing stand of God in heaven, will there be souls you've snatched from the cinders and carried into the presence of Christ? Take your corner of the sheet beloved. Our neighbor counts on us.

Dear Great Physician, who heals our bodies and our souls, help me to love my neighbor as myself. Help me as I take up my corner of the sheet. Amen.

February 6   The Science and Art of Prayer

Scripture Reading: James 4:1-10
Key Verse: "...you do not have because you do not ask." James 4:2

James is absolutely sure of the efficacy of prayer. He stands looking in amazement upon our spiritual poverty and declares with conviction, "You do not have because you do not ask. You ask and do not receive, because you ask amiss, that you may spend it upon your pleasures." Real prayer, assures James, would meet all our needs.

This business of prayer has its rules. God edited them, and He abides by them. He plays no favorites. God's rules on prayer begin with an admonition, "And when you pray, you shall not be like the hypocrites. For they love to pray standing in the synagogues and on the corners of the streets, that they may be seen by men." Does that word 'hypocrite' surprise you? It really is just reminding us to pray to God. At the dedication of a Bunker Hill monument, one of New England's finest orators prayed. A Boston newspaper reported the next day that, "It was one of the finest prayers ever delivered to a Boston audience." Prayers that are delivered to an audience do not rise higher than the roof of the church. So, Rule #1 is—Pray to God. Whether other folks hear or not is incidental.

Rule #2 says, "When you pray, go into your room, (some translations say "closet") and when you have shut your door, pray." This is for concentration, you see. The Eastern closet in their stone buildings was an inner room, untouched by the sun yet ventilated. It was a storehouse for keeping food in those hot climates. So this passage might read, 'go into the storehouse.' Who has the right to the storehouse? Why, members of the household have that right, of course. So we have a right to take from the storehouse of God, if we are children of the household of faith.

Rule #3 begins, "according to your faith let it be to you." Think of the audacity of faith. Faith's daring is equaled only by its simplicity.

God's reservoirs are full and overflowing. But the size of your pitcher determines how much you will carry. You must ask simply believing.

Rule #4 states, "If you abide in Me, and My words abide in you, you will ask what you desire, and it shall be done for you." The word 'abide' speaks volumes. It means living in Him. So if we want God to answer our requests, we must live in Him. We must study the desires, purposes, and aims of God. Remember one of the kindest things a parent can do for a child is to refuse a request that would hurt that little one. One of God's kindest mercies is to refuse us some things. A study of Bible prayers will show you adoration, confession, thanksgiving, forgiveness, unity, faith, supplication, submission, confidence, and persistence. But one notable thing is absent, selfish motive.

And so, Rule #5 is that we may accept whatever God in His infinite goodness and wisdom may send for our welfare. "…not My will, but Yours, be done." In other words, we must come into harmony with the will and mind of God if we want to pray aright, and then no matter what may come we shall be able to say, "All things work together for good to those who love God, to those who are the called according to His purpose." And this is the secret of the whole matter. God's answer to your petition may be "yes," "no,," or "wait awhile." But, your prayer is essentially answered if you rise from your knees quiet and confident in your Lord.

My dear and loving Father in Heaven, I praise Your Name. Help me to draw near to You, to abide in You. Help me to see the world through Your eyes that I might ask aright. Thank You, dear Lord. Amen.

February 7   The Secret of Victory

Scripture Reading: Revelation 12:7-12

Key Verse: "And they overcame him by the blood of the Lamb and by the word of their testimony, and they did not love their lives to the death." Revelation 12:11

    Are you in the midst of a battle? If you are a vital Christian you are. It is the one who makes a difference for the kingdom of God that the devil battles. So, how do we win the war?

    In the book of Revelation we see two groups of people, the overcomers and those who have been overcome. They are those who have won and those who have been defeated. And keep in mind; you cannot be an overcomer without a battle.

    Here in the twelfth chapter of Revelation, two truths stand out. First, the Lord Jesus Christ defeated Satan in the wilderness, and so have God's followers defeated him since. Secondly, in verse eleven the secrets of their victory are revealed; the blood of the Lamb, their testimony, and their courage.

    Divine blood means divine life, for the life is in the blood. There was a pale child who was brought to the hospital frail, weak, and helpless. The doctor prescribed food, treatment, and a transfusion of blood that the big brother gladly gave. In a week the child improved and was soon back to school. She had overcome by the blood of her brother.

    We are weak and frail against the tempests of life until the blood of Jesus is a part of us. The blood must be first, and without it all else is without power. The transfusion comes when we accept Him as our Lord and Savior. We are filled with His power, His life, and His victory.

    Then, they overcame by their testimony. They had seen Christ, had been changed by Him, and were busy telling others what the Lord had done for them and through them. John the Baptist was there telling his story of redeeming love. Stephen was there telling how he faced death for the Lord and how Christ stood by him in death. And the thief on the cross was there telling of his last minute salvation. They did not win because of their great numbers, or great influence, but they, through faith, subdued kingdoms, wrought righteousness, obtained promises, and escaped the edge of the sword. They overcame by their faith and their testimony.

Then, they overcame by their daring courage. Queen Esther was not a coward, "If I perish, I perish," she said as she dared to stand before the king. Stephen was not a coward "You stiff-necked and uncircumcised in heart and ears!" he preached. As Christ was not a coward when He rolled up His sleeves and turned over the tables of the moneychangers, driving them out of the temple, so the disciples went right on preaching after being imprisoned and whipped for the Gospel.

So what was the secret of their success? The blood of the Lamb had cleansed their hearts and had united them. They were not ashamed of the Gospel of Christ. They took the offensive. They dared to face and fight the devil. Too long Christians have retreated and fought a rear guard action against the evil one. Let us rise up in the strength of the Lord and drive the enemy back. We have the power, we have the weapons, and we have all we need for victory because of Christ. Let us never, ever retreat. Take up the armor and fight to victory!

Almighty Lord, I've given up in a couple of areas and ceded territory to the evil one that was never meant to be his. In the name and power of Jesus I appeal for the soul of that lost loved one. Please help me as I battle in the area of my health. I appeal to you for aid in the battle I face of _____. Pleading victory by the blood of Our Lord Jesus, amen.

February 8   A Call to Praise

Scripture Reading: Psalm 103

Key Verses: "Bless the Lord, O my soul; and all that is within me, bless His holy name! Bless the Lord, O my soul, and forget not all His benefits." Psalm 103:1-2

There is not a single sad note in this entire Psalm. It is all joy. There is not a sentence of supplication, it is all praise. And have you noticed in the Bible how many more calls to praise there are, than even calls to prayer? Prayer is a great essential of the Christian faith, the very breath of our soul. There are many words about prayer, yet it is important to note that praise is pressed as a duty even more repeatedly than prayer.

The book of Psalms is full of calls to praise. All creatures are called to praise God. The last word in the book of Psalms sums up in one sentence the burden of all 150 Psalms, "Let everything that has breath praise the Lord. Praise the Lord!"

Praise is the highest function of life, and we can never reach the best possibilities of our nature until all that is within us unites in praising God. Just think of the reasons enumerated in the Psalm for praising Him! After all, who forgave all our iniquities? Who redeems our life from destruction? Who crowns us with loving kindness and tender mercies? These are only a few of the praiseworthy attributes of our dear and loving heavenly Father.

Think of the revelation of our God in the Christ of the New Testament. His nature is love. He loved us even to the point of forfeiting His own life for our eternity. Can we help praising a God to whom we owe such blessing?

Some people are like the elder brother in the parable of the prodigal son. They forget all of God's wonderful benefits to them. A moment's pain blots out a year's health and happiness. There are some who have yet to develop a contented spirit, a thankful spirit, a praising spirit. They find fault in everyone and everything. What these people need is not better circumstances, no, what they need is the only thing that will cure them of their miserable grumbling and unhappiness, to allow the love of Jesus to overwhelm their heart.

We will never grow to be very fine workmen in any department of life, never amount to much among men, or reach much beauty of character, until we get this quality of praise into our heart and life. No one can do his best work with a sad heart. Nehemiah said to the despondent people building the wall, "The joy of the Lord is your strength." And so it is in every walk of life. Pessimistic people make it harder for others to live. They sap the strength of others. On the other hand, he who lives with the joy of the Lord evident in his life is a blessing to everyone he meets. No matter your sphere, you are a better man, a better teacher, a better lawyer, a better merchant if you have the joy of Christ in your heart.

Christ said, "You are the light of the world." Can you imagine a pessimistic, sad sort of light? No! Light naturally brings joy, praise and beauty in its wake. And, as we go out in Christ's name, we exude those qualities.

Does all that is within you bless the Lord? Is every channel of your heart full of praise? Is there a song rising continually from your lips unto Him? In the great struggles of life, bless God. In the hard moments, praise His holy name. What comes easily from our lips in the joyful, happy, moments is no less deserved by Him every moment of every day. Truly, "Let everything that has breath praise the Lord. Praise the Lord!"

Praise Your name, O Mighty God! Praise Your name, O God who paid my debt for sin! You are ever merciful and just; compassionate and holy. I will never forget the mercies You shower down on me, and the blessing of being Your child. In Christ's name, amen.

February 9   John and Us

Scripture Reading: John 1:6-34

Key Verse: "There was a man sent from God, whose name was John." John 1:6

Oh, it is a great thing when God lays hold of a man and says, "I want you to go on my errand." As John the Baptist came to bear witness of the light in the dark world, so may we. He was the herald, running ahead of the Christ with the shout, "The King, The King!" He came witnessing to the drowsy ears of a self-satisfied. Self-righteous leaders had reduced religion to petty precepts. In the false sense of their own superiority, they were too enlightened to have much belief in anything, and too comfortable in their self-approval to be disturbed by fanatics such as he.

It was a wilderness situation and demanded a voice like a trumpet blast to awaken deaf ears. John cried, "I am the voice of one crying in the wilderness. Prepare ye the way of the Lord." Oh people, in a very real sense we face this situation today. There is much religion but little room for Christ.

We talk much about methods. But men are God's method. When God wants something done, He looks for a man or a woman. In some cases they aren't even at first faithful or willing. When He wanted to warn Nineveh, He called Jonah, much to his initial dismay. When He would move His people out of slavery He called Moses, who tried every excuse to escape the assignment. When He needed a judge, He called Deborah; needing an escape for His servants, He called Rahab. When He wanted to save a nation to be His peculiar people, He called Abraham. Christian men and women with strong faith and sturdy arms must care for the Lord's husbandry.

We must be people of purpose. What the magnetic pole is to the compass, a great Christian purpose is to life. Purpose keeps you set in the right direction. It overcomes difficulties and makes them stepping-stones to success. To purpose for holy service is the soil out of which great movements have grown, whose streams of influence flow out to bless the world.

We must be men and women of zeal. With many, zeal in religion is bad form, but it is okay everywhere else. A man may shout himself hoarse at a ballgame, go to any length for a candidate in office, be beside himself over a pet hobby, but if this same love, belief, and enthusiasm is about His God, he is considered a fanatic. What of Jesus, of whom it was prophesied, "Zeal for Your house has eaten me up."

Zeal is not empty noise. It is directed energy. Wisely it has been said, "Every great and commanding movement has been the triumph of enthusiasm firmly founded and sanely directed." It requires firm faith in God and passionate devotion to Christ and expresses itself in steady and consistent service. It is not strange that Christians should be zealous. The vast fields of ripened harvest demand consecrated zeal.

You will be given as many excuses as you need by Satan. But remember, your excuses are but the skin of a reason stuffed with a lie. The One who calls you has first rights. First rights to what? To everything, including your "yes." Consecrate yourself to His cause today.

Holy Father, I see it is a matter of will, Yours or mine. You have a wonderful plan for my life that completes me and fulfills me, uses all the talents and graces You have given me and designed me for. Just as John the Baptist was chosen and sent by You, I submit with joy and eagerness to Your plan for my life. Help me to be strong and offer no excuses. Send me, Lord. In the name of Jesus, amen.

February 10   The Blessed Man

Scripture Reading: Psalm 1

Key Verses: "Blessed is the man who walks not in the counsel of the ungodly, nor stands in the path of sinners, nor sits in the seat of the scornful; but his delight is in the law of the Lord, and in His law he meditates day and night. He shall be like a tree planted by the rivers of water, that brings forth its fruit in its season, whose leaf also shall not wither; and whatever he does shall prosper." Psalm 1:1-3

The first thing we see about a man who wishes to be blessed is rather startling. We find that like every good thing, blessedness must be sought. Three kinds of peril threaten this man. The blessed man, we are told, will guard his direction, his leisure, and his company. This man will not just drift with the current. He has a goal in mind, and he fixedly stays the course he set.

Then we read that "In His law he meditates day and night." To meditate about a thing is to have one's thoughts come back to it, to have them play about it during the leisure moments of the day, and the quiet watches of the night. So, to meditate in God's Word brings blessedness. Meditation and blessedness are interdependent, you see. There is a natural connection.

Now, all meditation is thinking, but all thinking is not meditation. To meditate is to mutter a subject over to oneself, to brood over it, muse over it in one's thoughts. In the blessed life described in this Psalm, meditation is the starting point. And, it is so necessary today. In our lives there is so much noise. There is so much to crowd out thoughts of God. If God is crowded out of the life of a believer, his life has no beauty and no strength; he needs excitement at every turn. He knows nothing of this blessed life which comes by meditation on God's Holy Word. This should never be.

Meditation on God's Word is not only a foundation for blessedness, but it carries the purifying, repairing forces of the Word throughout one's whole nature. The Word of God cleanses the thoughts, heart, emotions, habits, and imaginations. Meditation is not dreaming; it is thinking about God, communing with Him, searching for Him in His Word.

What is the picture we are given of this blessed man? "He shall be like a tree planted by the rivers of water." The tree was planted; it did not plant itself. Behind it all, God the husbandman directs and provides and nurtures. The tree's roots grasp the underlying ribs of the earth and it reaches up with its branches and leaves, drinking in sunshine and rain. So the man of God must be, rising to communions with his roots twisted around the Rock of Ages. He knows no shifting or change. He is planted, rooted fast. A tree is the most steadfast and enduring of all living things.

Isn't this a marvelous picture of a righteous man? See him as a tree with its head in the scorching sunshine and its feet bathed by a perpetual stream that has its source way up in the snowy mountains. This is like the man of God, flourishing in the withering atmosphere of this world, enduring fiery trials of life, because his wellsprings are in God and the source of his human steadfastness and hope are high in the heavens. He is independent of the supplies of the world as he stands, defying wind, sun, heat, and storm, and bringing forth fruit to the glory of God.

Dear Father God, You are truly my source, and Your Word is a perfect revelation from You. I want to find my delight within its pages. Please help me to grasp hold of it, to love it, to delight in it. Help me to grow, as a tree, planted deep within the principles of Your Word, and to bring forth fruit to Your glory. Amen.

February 11   Things Not Shaken

Scripture Reading: Hebrews 12:22-29
Key Verse: "...that the things which cannot be shaken may remain." Hebrews 12:27

No matter what pinch of human history we pluck from the annals of time, we wonder at the violence, misery and torment that man visits upon man. Our grandfathers recited long lists of wars and famines, of wicked national leaders who led their people into times that shook their faith, their hope, and their survival.

Again political machinery is sputtering and whirring ever faster in this day, making the old world shake from center to circumference until wise men wonder whether the old planet will stay in its orbit any longer. On what can we lean that will not shake us from our footing? For what can we stand with bravery and certainty? There are some things that cannot be shaken. I will only mention those which are fortified and made absolutely sure by revelation of Scripture.

The throne of God cannot be shaken, no matter what may take place in the world material and the world ethereal. We have seen earthly thrones topple and fall in the dust. Autocratic or democratic, they are sure to fall to the brush heap. But while the thrones of the earth totter and fall, the throne of God endures forever. The Scriptures say so.

The world does not need another treaty or economic program to straighten it out. The only salvation for the souls of men is to satisfy their spiritual needs through Christ Jesus. God lives and still holds His scepter and always will.

Another thing remains in the midst of the shaking process, and that is the Word of God. Literature and history may be lost but the Word of God endures. So say the scriptures. It comes from God and is the Divine authority and His revelation to man. No great piece of oratory ever came from any other fountainhead. Patrick Henry had it at Virginia. Abe Lincoln on the battlefield of Gettysburg had it, Daniel

Webster and Wendell Phillips all had it. They had the authority of God's Word and referred to it as unchanging truth.

Beware the ministers today who have lost that authority. They preach on politics or popular themes. They preach anything but the burning message of this old Book, burning with a Holy passion and ready to sweat blood, backed up by the message of divine authority, the Book of God from cover to cover. Not that the word of God is in it, but that it is the Word of God.

Something else remains; it is the Church of God. God's own Son is recorded in the Holy Scriptures as saying that the gates of Hades shall not prevail against it. He built His church not on any philosophy, He built His church on the fact that God in the person of Christ came into this world and died on Calvary to save men. There is no true church in the world that does not rest on this foundation. If there is no word about Christ or humility, no word about repentance or the Holy Spirit or looking to God, if there is only the selling of someone's idea, then that is not the Church of Jesus Christ.

With a deathless conviction that breaks my heart and wets my face with tears I shall continue to remember the throne of God, stand in the shadow of the cross, hold the Book to my heart and preach the glorious gospel of the Son of God, and believe in its everlasting triumph through the coming King. And so, my friend, what of you?

Dearest Almighty God, how comforting to know that in this changing age, some things remain unchanging and unshakable. Lord, if testing is in my future, please help me to stand firm in You, Your Word, and Your Church. In Jesus's precious name, amen.

February 12   The Two Builders

Scripture Reading: Matthew 7:24-28 and I Corinthians 3: 9-15

Key Verse: "Therefore, whoever hears these sayings of Mine, and does them I will liken him to a wise man who built his house on the rock." Matthew 7:24

Have you noticed how Jesus is constantly dividing folks into two groups? There are those who have the wedding garment and those without it. There are those who travel the broad way and those who travel the narrow way. There are those who are spiritually alive and those who are spiritually dead. Whether we relish such divisions or not, He makes them constantly.

Now both builders are constructing something. They are building their own character, their own soul home, the temple in which they are to spend eternity. Will they build a temple or a sty?

We are building all the time. Everything we do, every thought we think, every word we speak, and every ambition we cherish, all these go to make up the material that enters into the structure that we are building for the ages. Some of us are putting shoddy material into our buildings. That oath you swore, the foul story you told, the unclean thing you did, that time you remained silent when you should have spoken, all these were poor stuff to put into your temple. You remember that time you clutched your money in the face of a need, or the time you passed by on the other side in face of a wounded soul? This is very flimsy stuff going into your building.

Then, some are building staunchly and beautifully. That was fine material the widow put into her building when she threw in her two mites for love's sake. That was fine material Daniel put into his own soul palace when he purposed in his heart he would not defile himself.

Now, the next fact our Lord brings out is this, the buildings we are building, the characters we are constructing, are going to be tested. For this reason we are not to build for fair weather only. We must build with a view to a time of storm. All men's works will be tested. Upon some, heavy storms have already broken. Some have seen their lives crash in ruins because their faith was simply a plaything the winds and tempest dashed ruthlessly aside. Some remain victorious, still standing strong after the battering gale. But all will be tested in different ways.

Sometimes the storm breaks over us in the guise of a great temptation, or the agony of great personal loss, the dissolving of the tenderest ties or loss of health or job. Then the storm may be of a different character. Instead of blowing away your wealth, it may be the coming of it in greater abundance. Prosperity tests our building also.

The final fact that Jesus brings out here is that all whose lives are not founded upon Him and His teachings are not going to be able to stand the test. What a bold and daring declaration. Yet He makes it and He makes it without flinching. No apology, no modification, if you do not build on Me your house will not stand. "For no other foundation can anyone lay, than that which is laid which is Jesus Christ."

Those who have built their lives upon the rock, Jesus Christ, who put their trust in His saving grace, will stand the hurling storms of testing. Regarding such a life it will be written in time and eternity, "It fell not!" He is like a tree planted by the river of water; he remains steadfast. For the world passes away, but he that does the will of God abides forever. We're building anyway; let us build rightly on Him.

Lord God, I don't want to waste my life in useless busyness. Let me learn to listen and obey and build my house only on Christ, the solid foundation. Amen

February 13   Reward for Faithfulness

Scripture Reading: I Samuel 30:1-25

Key Verse: "...But as his part is who goes down to the battle, so shall his part be who stays by the supplies; they shall share alike." I Samuel 30:24

While the army defended their country against invaders, the foe came in and carried away the families of the absent soldiers. David's men returned to empty homes, and they were overwhelmed with sorrow. After receiving guidance from God, David pursued the captors. But, at the Brook Besor, a third were just too weary to continue, so David swept on with the remainder, until he caught up with the enemy and decisively won the battle. When David returned to Brook Besor, some selfish men began to protest about sharing the spoils of battle. So, David fashioned this statute for his people, "As his part is that goes down to the battle, so shall his part be who stays by the supplies; they shall share alike."

As not all in David's army were equally strong, even so in Christ's army. Some are endowed with much while others have little. David reminded the 400 men that the victory they enjoyed was all of God's mercy, and all was from God's hand. When will we learn this truth? All of Christ's soldiers, great and small, rich and poor, clever and ordinary, shall share alike in the reward, provided they are equally faithful at their posts of service.

Let me tell you of a missionary, Dr. John Clough, whom I met as a young seminarian. He was so broken in health that he had to be wheeled into the room in a chair. Some of us younger men clung to his every word, and one day he asked, "Would you like me to tell you an early chapter about myself?" Oh, of course we all wanted to know how the great Dr. Clough got his start in working for the Lord. He began:

Well, I was converted in a little country church, but for my daily work I followed the plough. As I followed the plough daily, great impulses stirred my heart to be a preacher. One day I ventured to tell the senior deacon of my impulse to be a preacher, but he promptly suppressed me, or tried to do so. 'Why John,' he said, 'you would never make a preacher. God does not call dullards to be preachers. A man must have some gift of speech to preach. You go on and be a good churchman, and follow the plough.'

John went back to the plough, but the desire burned ever deeper in his heart. Finally, that awkward country boy got up with stammering words and painful embarrassment to tell people in that country church of his impulse to preach. When it was over, the people said, "Let us give John a chance. Let's send him away a year to school." One man gave 100 bushels of corn, another 80, yet another 100 again. Soon, the tuition was raised, and off he went. At the end of the year, John came back to preach his first sermon in the little country church. People from far and near came to hear him. And, when he got up to preach, the Spirit was with him. His tongue was loosed; his words burned like fire in dry grass. Women sobbed, strong men broke into tears. They got around him and cried, "Truly, God knows best. John is God's man." Dr. Clough went to India and did a work among the outcasts that was unprecedented; in one day alone in 1878 he baptized 2,222 new believers. Dr. Clough said to us, "If there is any reward coming to me, God will give the same reward to those humble farmers who prayed for me and sent me to school."

Yes, at home, at church, in business, everywhere, be faithful at the post to which you have been called. For all will share alike.

Dear Lord, let me be faithful to You wherever You place me in life. I know that there is no task too small, if I do it for You. Thank You for Your faithfulness. Amen.

February 14 — Service Calls

Scripture Reading: Ephesians 2:1-10

Key Verse: "We are His workmanship, created in Christ Jesus for good works, which God prepared beforehand that we should walk in them." Ephesians 2:10

God says that all souls are His and He has a distinct purpose for each life. He imbues each life with sufficient resources to achieve His desire for our lives, according to His riches in Christ Jesus. God has already prepared a mission for each of us, and now He is preparing us.

We have confidence then, as we look out on life, of the sure knowledge that if we walk in obedience to His will, God is not only prepared to unfold His program through us, but that all grace will abound toward us. We, having sufficiency in all things through Him, may abound to every good work.

Look at our Lord on the Samaritan route. We are told in John 4:4 that "He needed to go through Samaria." What a glorious example of Christian service. Now the Jews took the circuitous route on the east bank of the Jordan in order to avoid Samaritan territory. There was bad feeling between the peoples of Samaria and the Jews, and they did not voluntarily meet. Yet the Master, with a love that broke all barriers, went through Samaria in obedience to God's will.

You know, in our human life we may be guided by our senses, responding only to our likes and dislikes. Or, we may be guided by our own will and choice. But the best guidance of all is when we submit ourselves to the guiding hand of our Lord, seeking and following His will and purpose. Listen for the call to service God whispers to your heart.

It is a most significant fact in the ways of God that when He gives directions, He also furnishes the needed strength or material to carry them out. When Moses received the directions for the tabernacle and returned to the people to build it, he also found there was exact and adequate provision for it in the gifts of the people to the Lord. Our God will supply.

Jesus needed to pass through Samaria, and because of His one conversation with one forsaken woman a whole town comes to the Lord. That is service grown into fruitfulness. Peter went to the house of Cornelius, though as a strict Jew he had never entered a Gentile house. Philip left a great revival in Samaria and went out to the forks of a lonely desert road for the coming of a chariot. Paul left Ephesus on the left and Galatia on the right and make straight for Philippi. And every believer must allow his steps to be ordered by the Lord. His ways are greater than our ways; we cannot see beyond the sunset to the tomorrow of His plans. Our hours are ordered in the economy of eternity. We must listen for His call on our hearts, and answer it.

What task is it that God has prepared beforehand for you? Satan is making a masterful attack upon Christians, trying to sidetrack us from our task. Beloved, do not be deceived. God has a purpose for your life here on earth. He has gifted you with everything you will need to fulfill His mission for your life. Rely on Him.

The strength of the love of God is the foundation of Christian service, the secret of all great sacrifice, the key that unlocks the hearts of men and women and wins them to Christ. Pray today, won't you, for a flood of God's love to fill your heart that you might fulfill that work that God has prepared beforehand for your life.

Dearest Father, it is so humbling to realize that You have a purpose, a mission for my life. I ask right now that You would strengthen and guide me towards fulfillment of Your trust in me. Give me boldness in my service, and love for those I serve. Let every cup of cold water I offer, be offered in Jesus's name, amen.

February 15   Please Pass the Salt

Scripture Reading: Matthew 5:13-16

Key Verse: "You are the salt of the earth; but if the salt loses its flavor, how shall it be seasoned? It is then good for nothing but to be thrown out and trampled underfoot by men." Matthew 5:13

The Master here is giving us a compliment, and Jesus is not given to slathering His compliments as some do. He is discerning in His remarks. He is saying that we, His people, are to this earth all that salt is to the world.

How insipid is food without salt, notwithstanding the doctors' preaching. It is tasteless and flat. We are meant to add zest and tang into the world even as salt does to food.

Salt is also a life-giver. In Ohio among the steel mills, I saw a container of salt pellets hanging on the walls. Every few minutes a man who was stripped to the waist would walk there, take a glass of water, drop a pellet into it and drink it. Why? Because, salt must be replaced to meet the awful exertion and wasting away of the man before the fires.

The nature of salt is also to preserve. You do not salt a living thing, but you salt dead meat to preserve it. So, here is a grave judgment that God is making of society. He says that society is corrupt and tending to corruption. It is a distasteful likeness.

Christ says we are to go in His name, take His life and influence, and permeate society with the preserving influence of Christianity. The presence of a good man hinders the devil from having elbowroom to do his work. We are to be felt, wanted or not, in society.

Salt is also a great thirst creator. It creates thirst in the body of those who partake of it. Is that your experience? Are people made thirsty for God because you have associated with them and have been in their company? If we are living our faith and partaking of the abundant life God gives us, there will be those who thirst for the One who blesses us.

Now, how may these things be done? Well, salt does its best work when it is brought into close contact with that which must be saved. We must not seek to withdraw ourselves from contact with evil, but seek to cast our influence upon evil and be rubbed into the corrupted thing. Then salt does its work, silently, inconspicuously and gradually.

Let us be the salt Jesus likened us to, touching the world with its pungency, life-giving power, healing and health, and ability to preserve. What a blessing to the world, our families, and our communities we can be.

Lastly there is a note of danger here, a tragic note, the grave possibility of salt losing its savor. We who are Christians can lose our penetrating pungency that stops corruption. We can lose that which distinguished us from the world. Do we "tolerate" wrong until we match it? Remember, you are the salt of the earth, but if you do not salt the earth, the earth will corrupt you. Is your salt being infected by the corruption, or is your salt purifying the corruption? Do we allow the world, the flesh, and the devil to cool our fervor and influence our walk until the world is in us and we become savorless and useless?

Oh beloved, let us return to the Lord. Let us keep so near His life, His love, and His standards, cultivating the habit of communion with Him so that our power, our character, and our influence may be as salt leading a thirsty world to Christ.

Dear Lord, may I enter the influence of God into the world and may I be protected from the influence of the world. Let me be penetrating salt everywhere I go. Amen.

February 16   Life's Seasons

Scripture Reading: Luke 16:19-31

Key Verse: "And being in torment in Hades, he lifted up his eyes..." Luke 16:23

God has appointed seasons to our lives. There is a time to plow, a time to sow the seed, a time to cultivate the crop and a time to reap the harvest. To gain the fruit, man must fit himself into these seasonal opportunities. Nothing turns back the hands of God's timepiece. A season past cannot be regained. So, in our text, the rich man had his day of opportunity, and lost it. It can be too late to mend.

There is a period when we can and must learn. At such a time, habits of study are acquired and the ability to apply oneself patiently and persistently. Let this critical season pass and it is forever too late. History tells us that when Hannibal could have taken Rome, he would not, and when he would have, he could not.

Character development, too, is not something to risk on a second chance. There is a short space of time when a child's hand could stir a mixture of concrete. But later, when it is hardened, it will blunt the edge of sharp steel. Characters are formed in just that way. Opinions harden into convictions slowly but surely. Train up a child now, for in that way he will go.

Also, every individual has what is termed a moral sense, and the capacity for spiritual enjoyment. Cultivate this and encourage the soul, that it may be drawn into the circle of Christ. Neglect it, and it withers and weakens. That is why those who resist the appeal of the Jesus weaken the claim of the gospel on their heart.

And here, in the rich man, we see the tragedy of postponed interest. Suddenly, he finds that all his wealth is useless. His family relationships, though of the finest sort, will not help him. Before the throne each must stand for himself. Salvation and damnation are matters of personal responsibility; in that sense we are the captain of our own soul. Opportunity is limited to our earthly experience. What you decide here, determines the hereafter. As we acquit ourselves in the flesh, so we reap in the spirit.

"Father Abraham have mercy on me," pleads the rich man, yet through all the years of earth's experience he never, so far as we know, ever offered a single prayer for the mercy of God. During those years a prayer for mercy would have been honored, if uttered sincerely. But now it is too late. The season for that decision is past. What an absolute tragedy.

The rich man in this parable is like the father who rushes home one day suddenly full of concern about the neglected family altar. Once home, his wife reminds him that their children are all grown up and scattered. It is forever too late. The season for that task was past.

Luke 16:10 says, "He who is faithful in what is least, is faithful also in much; and he who is unjust in what is least is unjust also in much." Is the still small voice of God prompting you? Don't let the season of opportunity pass you by. Is the Holy Spirit guiding you to some small task? Respond, dear one. Like a faithful steward, be faithful in the little things. The little things are training for the larger ones.

In which season of life are you? What are the tasks of that season? Attend to them now, for the season will soon pass, and with it the opportunity to be faithful in it.

Father I must admit that so often I see the daily tasks of my life as necessities rather than a stewardship. Help me be content in the season of life in which I find myself, wishing neither to return to seasons passed nor to rush this one through so I may begin the next. Rather, let me bring glory to Your name as I faithfully minister for You today. Amen.

February 17   The Worried Face

Scripture Reading: Luke 10:38-42

Key Verse: "Martha, Martha, you are worried and troubled about many things." Luke 10:41

The scene is so homelike and honest that we can easily imagine it. In one of the nicest homes in Bethany, famous no doubt for its hospitality, Jesus has come to his dear friends.

Martha had greeted the Savior and excused herself to the kitchen. Mary doubtless went along, at least for a while, but soon she came back from the kitchen and left Martha to carry on alone. Martha probably looked from the kitchen with flushed face and angry eyes. At last the volcano in her heart makes an eruption and she hurries out of the kitchen to explode upon the company in the parlor. "Lord!" she asks, "Do You not care that my sister has left me to serve alone?" It is quite evident that Martha's patience is worn threadbare. She feels that she is being mistreated. She is sure that her guest is going to rebuke her sister.

But, instead, He rebukes Martha for being worried. Now, Jesus was a foe of worry, for He knew the futility of it. He knew how it spoils life.

And what was worrying Martha? She was entertaining an honored guest, and she wanted everything to be correct. She desired that his visit would be as delightful as possible, isn't that understandable? She was worried that the dinner would be a flop. And, Mary could be very annoying at times, and this was certainly one of those times.

How tragic that Martha is more fretful, more peevish, than she would have been had Jesus not have come. Such a story would be unbelievable if it had not been repeated in so many of our lives. Our religion sometimes annoys us more than it gladdens us. So, here is Martha worrying over her dinner, her sister, and even over Jesus. No wonder her devoted Friend finds it necessary to rebuke her.

Jesus knew that her worry had spoiled the day for Martha. She should have been the happiest woman in Bethany, but instead was the unhappiest. And her worry made her hard to live with, so she not only spoiled the day for herself, but for others. Martha made it hard on Mary, and through her worries grieved and disappointed Jesus. Out of the gathering storms surrounding Him, with a world full of turmoil, hostility, and confusion, Jesus had come to Martha's house for a day of quiet rest. But, instead of bringing joy, His coming proved a source of annoyance. There is tender grief in the heart of Jesus as He rebuked Martha.

When we worry, we hurt ourselves, hurt our fellows and we grieve and disappoint our Lord. But what can we do about it? How can we keep from worrying when so many things burden our minds and break our hearts?

We must realize that the conquest over worry does not depend upon our circumstances. We must take time off and sit at Jesus's feet. And, we must put things in their right place. Martha was worried because she allowed the secondary to shut out the primary. She got so worried about the meal that she largely forgot her Christ. Oh, the tyranny of things! To conquer worry we must put Christ in His right place. Jesus wants you before He wants your service. Anxiety and a true sense of God's presence cannot live in the same heart.

Dear Lord, Right now I want to lay all my worries out for You to tend. I give them over to You, Lord. I recognize that You can use all these things for my benefit, and I don't want to waste another moment in needless and futile anxiety that I could be enjoying Your presence. Please remind me, Lord, to pray and praise You instead of fretting. Amen.

February 18   An Expensive Haircut

Scripture Reading: Judges 16:4-20

Key Verse: "But he did not know that the Lord had departed from him." Judges 16:20

Samson the Nazarite was self-willed and determined. He walked with the wrong company and deliberately strode into temptation. As a young man he married a Philistine girl against the wishes of his parents. That was his first big mistake. Later, he went down to Gaza to have another illicit meeting with a woman. Even after this, God gives Samson the strength to tear up the gates of Gaza. Yet, as he ran up the mountainside with those gates on his shoulders, he carried a greater weight of sin upon his soul.

Samson's sin was slowly getting the better of him, though he did not seem to know it. One sin unrepented always makes way for more. So, next came a third woman to fill up the cup of his shame. This was Delilah. Knowing Samson had an impulsive, ardent temper, she set about to weaken his will using every charm that she possessed. She coyly asked him how he could be bound so that he would be unable to get away. And three times he playfully answers. Each time, Delilah had Philistine men stationed just outside the room, and each time as the Philistines rushed in, Samson broke loose and laughed in their faces. It is not hard to know why he did not discern the evil against him. Samson was blind.

That's right, long before they put out his eyes; his infatuation for this impure woman overruled his sense of duty to his God. So, he told her all, "No razor has ever come upon my head, for I have been a Nazarite to God from my mother's womb. If I am shaven, then my strength will leave me, and I shall become weak, and be like any other man." And when he was shorn, and the Philistines burst in upon them, Samson awoke out of his sleep and said, "'I will go out as before, at other times, and shake myself free!' But he did not know that the Lord had departed from him."

There are several things evident in this Scripture passage. First, it was the Spirit of the Lord resting upon Samson that made him strong. "And the Spirit of the Lord began to move upon him," we read. There was nothing in his seven locks of hair to make him strong; it was the gift of heaven that made him a conqueror. Secondly, it was sin that caused Samson to lose his power. Sin bound and blinded him; sin made him grind at the mill. Oh, the blinding power of sin. It bores out the eyes of the soul until the distinction between right and wrong fades away. Sin always robs us of the power of God. Also notice that it was an unconscious loss. There he was, with his strength gone before he knew he had lost it. Had there been no emergency, he would have gone on unconscious of the awful tragedy that had taken place.

But the beautiful part of this story is that the Spirit of the Lord was given again to Samson. He saw the frightful mistake he had made and out of the depths he cried for help and for the strength of God's presence again. Yes, the best part of Samson's story is that the Lord heard his penitent cry, made him once more a miracle of strength, and saved him even in the moment of his tragic death. Truly we cannot recover the past, but we can reassert ourselves for the future and turn again to God, and His Spirit will come upon us and fill us again for His service. If we will but bring our lives with all their mistakes, sorrows, and sins and place them in the hands of our loving Lord, He will make of us men and women of peace and power again.

Oh, dear Lord, forgive me. You know my weaknesses and my failures. Please strengthen me, and fill me with Your Holy Spirit, that I may accomplish great things for You. Amen.

February 19   The Melting Pot

Scripture Reading: I Corinthians Chapter 13
Key Verse: "By this all will know that you are My disciples, if you have love for one another." John 13:35

Where is such a work to be initiated—that all will know? Where can such a global effort begin? Why, right in our own local congregations. Here we must love one another across social lines and economic barriers and cultural gaps and racial lines. Every church should be a melting pot. Here the heart must be melted, broadened, and sweetened. Here the spirit of good will and sympathy will begin and overflow into wider fields until all men shall know. Salvation of the lost will only come about through love. Unity among believers will only come about through love. But, in many cases, people do not even know one another.

We have multitudes of professed disciples who have no understanding of the New Commandment. If the church is to be a church after the mind of Christ, it must be a brotherhood, a family, in whose life the heart is trained to come close to other hearts. Oh, folks, this is what the church needs. Jesus wants it, you need it, and the world needs to see it and imbibe it.

This is applied Christianity. This world, this nation, and this city are waiting for a society of men and women who will love across all dividing social, political, ecclesiastical, and racial lines. The church must give herself to her supreme task, "Love one another." I make a plea, I sound out a cry: Let us all set ourselves to work to find out what Christian love really is and put it into practice.

Why leave that word vague which is the keystone of the Christian arch? Why ignore "As I have loved you" when such love is the test of discipleship and proof of the divinity of our religion? Why waste time and money and effort in revivals and campaigns and programs to save souls and get people into our churches, if our organizations are devoid of the very fundamental thing by which we are to be known as Christians?

"Love one another as I have loved you." This is the passionate desire of our Lord. It is His dominant longing in the last hour of His flesh, and it is His longing still. Even in His prayer before going into the garden to pour out His soul unto God, He cried, "...that they may be one as We are." He is saying there is only one way by which the world can be persuaded that God sent His Son, that the world can be saved, or that we may be perfected. That is, that you love one another as He has loved us.

The power even of human love is immeasurable. Many years ago in Scotland, it is said, a gigantic eagle carried away a tiny infant lying asleep on the lawn by a hillside cottage. Despite the frantic efforts of villagers, the baby was lodged by the eagle high up on a cliff. A strong young sailor first tried to scale the cliff and rescue the infant, but he failed, as did a robust highlander who also sought to climb the rocky crag. Then a poor peasant woman hitched up her skirts and braved the face, successfully rescuing the baby. Why? Why could she succeed where others, stronger and more able, failed? Because between her and the baby was a bond of love. She was the child's mother.

Where love is miracles happen. So, let there be this tie, this bond, of love between us in our churches today. Take the time, and love.

Dear God, reveal to me the ways in which I can love my brothers and sisters in Your body. Help me show them love, help me take the time to reach out to them and know them. Show me, Father, what it means to love with such an overwhelming love that it is a sign to the entire world. Thank You, Lord. Amen

February 20

Though He Slay Me, Yet Will I Trust Him

Scripture Reading: Job Chapter 1

Key Verses: "...The Lord gave, and the Lord has taken away; Blessed be the name of the Lord." Job 1:21. "Though He slay me, yet will I trust Him..." Job 13:15

The supreme reason we trust God, is God. Our religion is not founded upon our ability to understand God, nor upon our ability to recognize a logical course in His procedures. We trust Him because He is God. In days of great turmoil, sorrow, and troubled hearts it is good to look at this man of faith in Scripture, Job. His compelling experience is a true tale of a truly great man.

Consider Job. Feeling the sting of pain, bracing himself against severe loss, enduring hardships in every form, absorbing the mockery of his friends, and resisting temptation, Job endures. You know it is quite easy to write soliloquies and poems on life and how it should be lived, but the test is to live life! Job is the impressive figure of a man who proposes to stand anyhow, because he is convinced that God is trustworthy. He does not pretend to understand his troubles, but that does not alter his faith. And that is the great fact for us to practice in life.

There are two derivative facts that are essential to the condition of real trust in God. First, we must realize that faith in God will come to places in life where there will be absolutely no discoverable reason for it. There is Job: his body tortured, his friends urging him to curse God, his wife even is given over to despair. He is alone, tired, and stripped, yet he pushes them all back and declares in a triumph of faith, "Though He slay me, yet will I trust Him." Yes! It sounds like a tragedy, but it is a triumph. It is positive. It is trust straight through without concern as to what the end may be. Job has realized that it is God's part to be God, and see to that. Man's part is to trust Him because He is God, and to refuse to surrender faith because of something that happens to him. I trust God not because of *me,* but because of *Him.*

The second fact is the conclusion that though the seeming results of our faith may sometimes bring sad experiences, they nevertheless bring us final triumph. So many of us sit so close to the fire that we cannot see the stars beyond, and therefore we think the night is dark. Or, we keep our eyes on the dirt so near the plow that we do not see the field beyond. Remember that "all things work together for good to those who love God, to those who are the called according to His purpose."

Job worked and lived beyond his horizon. He understood that his life counted beyond what he could see. All of us need to realize this. It might be easy for me to suppose that my solitary little life does not count for much. But in truth I cannot dare to speak in such cheap estimate of life. The facts are that my life is a sacred trust that is inter-related with many others. There is more than one man in any one man's life.

Therefore, you cannot judge your life by yourself. Like Job, we do not need to understand our trouble. No, the heroic thing, the Christian thing for us to do is to be able to stand on our faith in God anyway. Faith is not understanding God, beloved, it is trusting God.

There will be times in our lives when we cannot see the way, when the road seems too rugged and rough. But the truth remains unqualified, He is God and I can trust Him. God's way is the right way. God's way is the best way. God's way will be my way.

Dear Heavenly Father, Job's declaration cuts across the centuries of time like an eternal trumpet set at the lips of experience. I, too, trust You. I know that whatever my circumstances, You are mightier. I am too near the fire to see the stars, dear Lord, but I trust You that they are still there, and that Your light still lights my night, and my way. Amen.

February 21   The Bequest of Peace

Scripture Reading: John 14:25-31

Key Verse: "Peace I leave with you. My peace I give to you; not as the world gives do I give to you. Let not your heart be troubled, neither let it be afraid." John 14:27

Years ago an armistice was signed closing a war and bringing peace to a bleeding world. We thought we were fighting a war to end war, but were we? In less than a quarter of a century the world was steeped in another World War that made the first one look like a skirmish in comparison. Today, the embers are being fanned into a flame and many are sincerely asking, "Are we facing another war? Shall we never have peace?" Our internal peace must be built upon more than a marching army, planes, tanks, and bombs. These alone cannot insure our peace.

"Peace I leave with you." When these words were spoken, the air was thick with rumors. The betrayer had gone out and was already engaged in his treacherous mission. Even Peter's loyalty threatened to surrender to the popular will. Christ's enemies were at the gate. It was in this turbulent, stormy time that our Lord quietly claimed to be in possession of deep and mysterious peace. It was a gracious achievement, a vital, effective, holy minister conveying inconceivable treasures to the hearts of men.

When the Lord Jesus brings His peace into your heart and mine they become inherently sound by becoming fundamentally at one with God. The peace of God means a recovery of healthy fellowship between the soul and the eternal God. Our Lord had this peace independent of the seasons, all through the changing days. He had it at Bethany and at Calvary.

So, we can say this about peace, it can exist in the midst of apparent defeat. One does not have to have success to be assured of it. We can have God's peace and be apparent failures to the world. All that is requisite for us to possess the gift is in the power of the Lord Jesus

Christ. It is not the attainment of painful effort and service. It is not the refined fruit of prolonged culture. It is a legacy. It is a gift. It is Him.

Lastly, there are two ways in which this gift of peace differs from the gifts of the world. When the world seeks to give peace it addresses itself to conditions. The Lord however, addresses Himself to character. The world deals with things. The Lord deals with kinships. The world keeps in the material realm. The Lord moves in the spiritual realm. The world offers to put us into a fine home. The Lord offers to make us a fine tenant. The world will introduce us into fine society. Jesus will make us at home with God.

Secondly, the Lord differs from the world in the manner of His giving. The world always gives its best at the beginning. It offers gaudy garlands, brimming cups, and glittering crowns. It makes an imposing fire but we are soon left with ashes. It blinds us with the garish day, and then come solitary night. Jesus keeps the good wine until the last. He leads us from grace to grace, from faith to faith, from glory to glory. His gifts grow deeper, richer, and fuller right through the eternal years.

Peace is love resting in the believer's heart. Have you the gift of it?

Dearest Lord, You have given me peace and sometimes I forget that I have it. I focus on the circumstances that swirl around my feet. I am like the disciple who when trying to walk to You on the water began to sink because he took his eyes off of You and placed them on the swirling waters. Thank You that through the most terrifying and agonizing situations Your peace is always there as Your gift, and Your legacy of love. Amen

February 22   God's Way

Scripture Reading: I John 1:5-10

Key Verses: "If we say that we have no sin, we deceive ourselves, and the truth is not in us. If we confess our sins, He is faithful and just to forgive us our sins and to cleanse us from all unrighteousness." I John 1:8-9

    One of our great pastors lay dying. A brother in the ministry asked him if he had any word to give to his brethren. He said, "Yes I have. Tell my fellow preachers to make it plain to the people how to be saved." Let us respect his wishes today.

    First, there is no escaping the fact of sin if one is honest with one's own conscience. If you are ever to be saved, you will have to settle the sin question. It is possible in the most vital things of life to be mistaken and when it comes to sin the natural impulse is to deceive ourselves. Some years ago there was a "Dog and Pony Show" in the city where I lived. One act of the program was a jumping contest among the dogs. There were dogs ranging from a Russian Greyhound down to samples of little scraps. The ringmaster put a barrel in the ring. All jumped over it except a couple of little canines. Then he put a washtub on the barrel, and most made it. Then he put another tub on that, but most dropped out until only the Greyhound was left. The ringmaster put yet another tub on the pile. The dog backed to the far end of the tent and came running like a cyclone. With one mighty bound he went over and landed in the sawdust on the other side. After that great achievement, he turned modestly and crept up to the feet of the ringmaster, laid his great head on his paws, and looked up into his master's eyes. So too our greatest achievements bring us to our master's feet. The higher we reach toward God the humbler we become, for no matter how high we go, one more washtub and only the master can carry us over.

    There is another direction this self-delusion may take. There are some who after the claims of Christ have been presented say, "I'm not such a bad fellow. I pay my debts. I don't steal. I don't get drunk and beat my wife." But don't deceive yourself. God looks deep into every heart knowing our purposes and motives. Sin is in every human life. It is grief to the Father's Holy Heart and He cannot but hold us responsible for He is righteous and just. The sin question must be settled.

Is there a way out? Yes. If we confess our sins He is faithful and just to cleanse us from all unrighteousness. What is confession? It is simply taking God's side against your own sin. As long as you justify yourself, you take sin's side. Instead, say, "O Father, I have sinned. Here are my sins. I love them no more. Forgive me. I accept Christ as my Savior and Lord."

You say, "How may I know my sins are forgiven?" Not by feelings. God's way is not feeling, but fact and faith. The assurance is that He said so. His Word in the Holy Scriptures is our sealed contract.

But, we are not only saved, but cleansed. Think of it, not a sin left, not a spot left. The whole of our lives washed white. That is God's business. That is why He sent His son Jesus Christ. <u>He</u> forgives and justifies. But <u>He</u> also cleanses us. It is not a barrel that we can jump over ourselves. Only our master can do this work. If we believe on Him and confess our sins and trust Him, He will not only cleanse us for this world, but He will take us home to Heaven. This, beloved, is God's Way.

Holy Almighty God, please forgive me. I do believe that Jesus died to pay for my sin and I accept His free gift of the salvation of my soul. Thank You for forgiving me and cleansing me and making me pure in Your sight. Amen.

February 23   Light Mindedness

Scripture Reading: Matthew 22:1-14

Key Verse: "But they made light of it and went their ways...."
Matthew 22:5

The Master-Teacher relates the parable of the king who arranged a marriage feast in honor of his son. Everything was ready. The invited guests were called. And then we read, "But they made light of it and went their ways." They were a picture of the light-minded, making light of Christ and His salvation.

Now some dear souls make much of every circumstance. Such people become grumblers and hopeless bores. The Apostle Paul urges us to discriminate in the spending of our time and concern. He says, "For our light affliction, which is but for a moment, is working for us a far more exceeding and eternal weight of glory." The key question is, will it make an eternal difference? It may hurt terribly for the moment, but will it last for eternity? If not, is it worth our concern?

Doesn't that whittle our list of complaints and distresses down to just a few important things? What if affliction strikes our job, our fortune, or our health? Even if it is agony, it is only agony for a little while in comparison to the promise of a tearless eternity. The question is what can we learn from it? We may become bitter and twisted by our affliction on this earth, or we may learn to turn our gaze elsewhere to those things lovely and eternal, and give what the world calls unbearable the slight attention it deserves. After all, what is it that is worthy of our focus in the fleeting years on earth? It is only that which we can take with us into the vast eternity that awaits us. The pain and distress of birth is trivial compared to the wonder and adventure of life. Just so, our slight affliction in life is to be acknowledged, dealt with, and then we move on to occupy ourselves with the weighty things of eternity.

What are these things? Well, people are eternal and we must concern ourselves about them. The effect of earnest prayer is eternal. Yes, this is most definitely worthy of our time. Salvation is eternal. Whose salvation?

First, our own, then we must concern ourselves with the salvation of others. Our devotion to the Word and time in communion with God bears eternal fruit and is not something to take lightly.

On May 31st 1889, the current of life flowed evenly and happily in the thriving city of Johnstown, Pennsylvania. Then came a man riding furiously upon a foam-flecked horse. "Run! Fly for your lives. To the heights!" The respectable citizens were shocked at his mad capers. Who, pray, was he? What was it he said? They made light of it and went their way. Suddenly there was an ominous roar, the ground trembled, and then in one furious onrush the waters of Lake Conemaugh, 100 feet deep, struck that city like a hammer of doom. 2500 lives were lost. As truly as people of that day made light of the warning of the man on horseback, so, today people make light of the words of the Lord Jesus Christ.

What had the good people of Johnstown been concerned with that day? How their business was doing? Whether their living rooms were tidy enough to receive the ladies' society for tea? I do hope they had given priority to the eternal things, for these other matters are of little consequence to them now. They stopped at the grave. And what of us, beloved? Should the unthinkable happen to you or those you love or your neighbor, were the eternal things considered?

Almighty God, my life and eternity are in Your hands. I submit myself to You with the desire to spend the gift of my life doing things that will count for eternity. Amen.

February 24   A Nation's Greatest Asset

Scripture Reading: Psalm 119:1-16
Key Verse: "The entrance of Your words gives light; it gives understanding to the simple." Psalm 119:130

Our greatest national asset today is the Bible. The masterpiece of God, our Bible is a complete code of laws. It is the most authentic history ever published. It has been expounded by the greatest intellects, and stained with the blood of countless martyrs.

This Book addresses itself to the universal conscience, speaking with binding claims and commanding the obedience of mankind. It gives the only source of information on the world's creation, the soul's salvation, human destiny and the realities of eternity. It makes nations and civilizations breathe and grow. It has outlived all other books as a mighty factor in civilization. It is unique and peerless.

What makes the Bible so valuable to civilizations? Well, it is identified with the promotion of liberty, the pioneer of commerce, the foundations of civil government, and the source and support of literacy and education. It is the greatest treasure we have, enduring and impervious to the assaults of doubt.

The Bible is the major factor in maintaining spiritual progress, without which material progress is a failure and a farce. Now, I realize that this declaration brings down upon me the denials of the skeptic. But I humbly declare unto you that the material progress of our nation is insecure and even dangerous without spiritual progress. That is what Woodrow Wilson meant when he said, "The sum of the whole matter is this, that our civilization cannot survive materially, unless it be redeemed spiritually."

What are we profited, if with wood enough to house the world, coal enough to warm the world, and cotton enough to clothe the world, we forget the worth of the Bible in the production of lives of spiritual quality? If our eyes are on gold, and not God, we will become like old Rome, dead. The Bible is our greatest asset because it is the one foundation adequate for a great superstructure. You cannot build a skyscraper on a playhouse foundation, you cannot put ocean liners in brooks, and neither can we build a great nation with less than the Bible for foundation.

Now, the Bible has been built into the moral fiber of our nation. The whole constitutional fabric of America is permeated with the teachings of the Word. Samuel Chadwick said, "The greatest need of England is a return to the Bible to which it owes its soul." We can well apply these words to our own nation.

Finally, the Bible is our greatest asset because it is the enemy of all wickedness, maintaining standards which prevent decay. Do we need a reverence for laws justly administered? The Bible teaches that. Do we need sound principles of commercial ethics? The Bible stands for and urges them. Do we believe in honesty and righteousness? The Bible stands for that. Do we need wisdom for the continuance of our country? The Bible says "The fear of the Lord is the beginning of wisdom."

The Bible is the old-time Book, the new-time Book, the all-time Book. It is the Book, final, supreme and absolute. It is the compass that has guided men in darkness and distress. It is the Rock of Ages, and if we build on it, we are building for eternity.

Dear Holy God, I come in frank shame at the place the Bible holds in my country today. I confess that I am of a people who do not know the Bible, have not read it, and do not esteem it. Yet, Father, I ask for Your mercy. I ask that You would draw us as a country. Revive the place of Your word in national debate, in national issues, and in national esteem. Amen.

February 25   Judas Iscariot's Sermon

Scripture Reading: Matthew 27:1-10

Key Verse: "Then Judas, His betrayer, seeing that He had been condemned, was remorseful and brought back the thirty pieces of silver to the chief priests and elders." Matthew 27:3

Here, in the words of our text, Judas preached one of the most powerful sermons ever delivered on the subject of sin. It was delivered by the art of drama and was all together unintentional. Judas eloquently declares that sin does not pay, as he dashes down the pieces of silver before the priests and then goes out and hangs himself.

The terrible death he died is an eloquent message of warning to us all. See him swing from the limb. See the rope break and watch his body plummet downward over a precipice. A horrible picture, you say? Yes, not very refined. You see sin is not refined. This sermon is lived by Judas in the last hours of his life, and it is an example to us of a wasted opportunity, a wasted influence, and a wasted eternity. Let us learn from it.

Few indeed have had the opportunities Judas had. He was with Jesus and heard Him preach. Judas was at the side of Jesus for three years. He heard Jesus pray as no one had prayed before. Judas heard God the Father speak from heaven saying, "This is my beloved Son."

When Jesus took the loaves and fishes and fed the multitudes, Judas was there. When Jesus healed the sick and opened the eyes of the blind, he was there. When Jesus healed the lepers and unstopped the ears of the deaf, and settled the tempest and raised the dead, Judas was there. Yet, Judas died without Christ as much as the most godless heathen.

But you say, wasn't Judas saved? No, it is clear to me that he was never saved. Jesus, in His High Priestly Prayer said, "None of them is lost except the son of perdition, that the Scripture might be fulfilled." Again, He said, "Did I not choose you, the twelve, and one of you is a devil?" Judas wasted his magnificent opportunity.

Judas could have been another Simon Peter, a great evangelist, telling the story of Christ and winning thousands to the Lord. He could have written one of the books of the New Testament. Yet, the only thing he left behind is this glaring example of wasted influence.

My friend, God has given you a great gift in your influence, and by it you either lift people up or drag them down. Whether large or small, I urge you to offer your influence to God to use for His glory. It is one of the most beautiful opportunities He gives to have eternal effect.

Not only did Judas waste his opportunity and his influence, but he also wasted his eternity. The Scriptures tell us that one day Jesus will be seated upon a throne. Around Him will be the twelve apostles judging the twelve tribes of Israel. And think of it my friend; Judas might have occupied one of those thrones. But instead, he wasted his eternity and his influence.

Inquire of God how you might better develop your gifts. Let us learn from a fallen man, who even at the end would not repent and ask forgiveness for his waste, but took the traitor's willful path even in death. If you are a Christian, I beg of you to live for God. If you are not a Christian, then make a start now. Life, my beloved, is God's gift to us, and how we choose to live it is our gift back to Him. Let us seize it with joy and enthusiasm and use it to His glory.

Father in Heaven, I want my life to count for You. I want to use the gifts You give to me to Your glory and honor. Please help me to be all I can be for You. Amen.

February 26   Beginning With Prayer

Scripture Reading: Acts 3:1-10

Key Verse: "Now Peter and John went up together to the temple at the hour of prayer." Acts 3:1

Here is the story of a prayer meeting in the early days of the church with Peter and John in attendance. Now had they been absent they might have been excused when you think of what a time they'd been going through. They had just witnessed the crucifixion, experienced the resurrection and the ascension, spent ten days in prayer and fasting, and seen the Holy Spirit descend upon the church. They had seen God bring 3,000 souls into the church in one day, yet with all these experiences, they still felt the call of God to prayer.

It is not stylish among some people today to gather for the purpose of corporate prayer. I cannot in my deepest imaginings discern why. Where are the praises? Where is the thanksgiving? Where are the heartfelt petitions for the intervention of God? The joy of communing with God is multiplied when it is practiced together.

Note any fellowship of believers that has even the smallest speck of power or life and you will find believers gathering to pray. It might be a powerful God-centered prayer and worship assembly, or it might be two elderly sisters kneeling by their rockers faithfully lifting up their church family to God, but if there is life there is prayer going on somewhere.

Well, on this day in our text, Peter and John took time to go to pray at God's house. Tell me how often you pray, and I have found your spiritual pulse. It is the secret of power and victory. Is there a barrier in your life? Pray it down. Is there trouble in the home? Pray it out. Is there confusion, defeat, or strife? The victory is found in prayer.

You will notice that the early Christians were praying Christians. As a result, they were unified. You notice that Peter and John went up together. The Scriptures say that they were all filled with the Holy Spirit, and how did He come to them? He came as they prayed with the others in the upper room.

They served. Peter and John went to service a little early and found a man to take to church with them, for prayer puts a burden for others upon our hearts.

They were people of vision. "They fastened their eyes upon him." Oh that you and I might see the lame man, the lost and wounded all around us today. We need only to walk in that vision, pay attention, and respond in love and faith when He places someone in our path.

They were people of love. Peter took the man by the right hand and lifted him up. Think of a beautiful stone needing only the heat and warmth of a hand to bring out its beauty. There are so many who need the touch of God through us.

They were people of power. They lifted the man up. God is in the lifting business and so must we be, not shirkers or fussers or people who knock others down, but uplifters.

They were people who praised. The man leaped up and stood, praising God. Our time in prayer leads to others seeing a difference in their lives and wanting to praise God for it.

They were a growing group of people. Notice that the man entered with them into the temple and surely he too became a worker for God. As lives are healed and changed the circles of ministry grow wider and wider. Good news spreads fast. Pray that as it was with Peter and John it will also be with us.

Tarry in prayer with your Lord.

February 27   The Blind Man's Creed

Scripture Reading: John 9:1-41
Key verse: "One thing I know: that though I was blind, now I see." John 9:25

The healing of this man born blind was the seventh great sign in the book of John, and led to a distinct rupture with the organized religion of the day. This blind man had lived in the dark, but the first person whose face he ever saw was the Lord Jesus.

Remember, the mission of Christ was not to explain the mystery of evil, but to remove the cause of it. So He made clay with spittle and anointed the eyes of the man and told him to go wash. The man obeyed and came back seeing.

His neighbors took him before the religious authorities. Why? Because the miracle had been performed on the Sabbath. Jesus made clay on the Sabbath. The blind man had his eyes opened, but they could not see that. They saw only the violation of the Sabbath.

During the questioning the Pharisees laid the charge, "We know that this Man is a sinner." The healed man said "Whether He is a sinner or not I do not know. One thing I know: that though I was blind, now I see." This blind man who had received his sight was finding that he could not get away from the man who had opened his eyes. Something was happening to his relationship with Jesus.

Then they excommunicated him. He could never again return across the threshold of the synagogue. Organized religion had thrown him out. But he was thrown right into the arms of Jesus. Jesus found him and said "Do you believe in the Son of God?" And the man cried "Who is He, Lord, that I might believe in Him?" Then Jesus gave him a full revelation "It is He who is talking with you." To this statement the man responded with devotion as he fell at Christ's feet, crying. "Lord, I believe." And he worshipped Him.

Now look for a moment at the Blind Man's Creed. "One thing

I know: that though I was blind, now I see." That is his creed, his catechism, his confession of faith.

You may know a great deal about religion, about the Bible, but the one thing you must have is an experience with Christ. Now your experience may not be like mine or this blind man's, but you must have a basic experience of acceptance of Christ, of forgiveness of sin, of salvation. A creed is like a tree. It starts with one stalk ("one thing I know") and that goes on branching and dividing so long as we feed it at the root. You must grow.

Sight does not consist in understanding how we see. Health does not consist in understanding the organs of the body. And, salvation does not consist in knowing how we are saved, but in knowing that we are saved. This man had little knowledge of why Christ saved him. But this one thing he knew (and stuck to it) "that though I was blind, now I see." This short, personal, simple creed led not only to sight, but led to a personal worship of the living Christ.

Oh beloved, have you come to the place where you and Jesus live and work and love together? Do you have a creed, and has your creed led you to Christ? Have you been received into relationship with God in the act of submission and obedience of faith?

Obedience to Christ leads to the worship of Him who owns all things and made all things and was before all things, and in whom is life eternal.

Heavenly Father, I want to wash the clay from my eyes and see You clearly. I want to obey and worship You and call You my Lord. I want the vision You long to give me. I receive You totally and with great joy. Help me to grow in You every day. Amen.

February 28   Defiant Devotion

Suggested Reading: Daniel 6:1-23

Key Verse: "Now when Daniel knew that the writing was signed, he went home. And in his upper room, with his windows open toward Jerusalem, he knelt down on his knees three times that day, and prayed and gave thanks before his God, as was his custom since early days." Daniel 6:10

The defiant devotion of Daniel reveals the sterling stalwartness of a man fully devoted to God. The favor with which the king viewed Daniel had fomented seething jealousies within the courts of the King. They called all their ingenuity to bear in planning Daniel's destruction. They devised a trap for him, which centered in his religious faith. This shows us that those around Daniel knew of his religious customs. So, they inaugurated a royal statute that if anyone should be found praying to any God or man, save unto the King, he should be cast into the lion's den. Daniel's devotion to the Lord, however, was unaffected by the decree. He prayed three times a day, as was his custom.

Daniel would not be swayed by popular opinion. His religious convictions were not for sale. His religion was not a mere convenience, it was a consuming passion. He would not capitulate, even in the face of the lion's den, to a decree that interfered with his soul's right of worshipping God. And so, Daniel took his stand. He refused to be regimented. His devotion was unequivocal and Daniel did not waver even when death roared.

Daniel was a man who believed it was wrong to run when we should stand. He believed it was wrong to be weak when we should be strong. As the Sunday School song teaches, we should all dare to be a Daniel!

How our day needs unalloyed, uncompromising men like Daniel. Daniel would not be coerced to do wrong, even by a king's decree. He was as faithful in his spiritual life after as he was before the decree was signed. No earthly authority could tongue-tie Daniel's loyalty to God. His convictions concerning God were deep as life itself, and dearer.

Bernard Palissy, a poor French potter, was imprisoned on account of his faith. King Charles visited him, and said, "I'm forced to give you up to die unless you forsake your religion." Replied the prisoner, "They that force you, King Charles, cannot force me. You and all your nation cannot compel me to compromise." Devotion like that is sufficient for the supreme and extreme tests of life.

Daniel showed utter obliviousness to consequences. He lived dangerously, but victoriously. He was not careful about his life, but he was careful about his conduct. Neither Daniel, nor Paul, ever asked, "Is this a safe course for me?" Their question was, "Is this right?" Daniel marches down history's thoroughfare with strident step because he would not compromise with the world.

Dauntless devotion to Christ is not only reformatory, it is revolutionary. Would to God you and I had more of it in our lives today. And we can if we are willing to pay the price, the price of full surrender to God. Our hopes can be stronger than our fears; our faith can be stronger than our doubts, if we make God our stay. What are fiery furnaces or dens of lions, if we are God's, and God is ours?

Dear God, Oh, I want to be steadfast and courageous of faith, like Daniel. I want to stand for You, when the world pulls me away. Help me to sink the roots of my faith deep into your unchanging character, God, and allow Your strength to flow through my weak moments. Be strong through me, I pray dear Lord. For Your glory, amen.

February 29　　　　　　　God of the Sparrow

Scripture Reading: Matthew Chapter 10

Key Verses: "Are not two sparrows sold for a copper coin? And not one of them falls to the ground apart from your Father's will. But the very hairs of your head are all numbered. Do not fear therefore; you are of more value than many sparrows." Matthew 10:29-31

The Master here in Matthew is giving good counsel and cheer to His disciples who are faced with persecution and so are now in fear of their persecutors. To these in that day and all of us in this day God gives words of enlightenment, comfort, and strength. He reveals His nature and protecting care and power in most intimate terms. We find here the nature of God, the tenderness and love of God even toward the smallest creatures of His creation.

Here also is revealed the character of God. He will destroy wickedness without mercy, yet He sees, knows and cares about the death of that little sparrow. In the terms of the world, worthless, two sold for only a penny, yet He cares. Yet more, a single hair falling from the head is of trifling consequence to us. But every one of your hairs is numbered by Him.

Most men think of Him as a God controlling great and weighty matters. But here is Jesus saying that God takes care and cognizance of the smallest and most trifling things. Therefore we may be sure He cares for us.

Our God is a personal God who causes the sun to shine and the rain to fall. What maintains those mysterious throbbings of the earth? Who causes the grass to grow and the flowers to bloom? Our God is a God who knows. See the preparation made for man: air, water, minerals, food. Yes, my heavenly Father knows my needs and has made provision for them. And He knows me. He knows the good in me and the bad in me. He knows our ups and downs, our sorrows and disappointments, what medicine we need and when to call us home.

Our God is a God who can. He has spilled the heavens full of stars and His glory. In the lily He revealed the beauty of His sweetness. But God's greatest work is man. Until man came the earth was a house without an occupant, a book without a reader, an instrument without a player. All things waited on man's coming. He is God's masterpiece, fearfully made.

Our God is a God who cares. Some people think God too busy running the universe to notice our own individual affairs. But His heart is touched with our grief. When the long nights are dreary I know my Savior cares. He is the Shepherd who left the ninety and nine to find the one lost sheep. He cares.

Our God does. A drunkard is more interested in deliverance here and now than what God will do with him in the future. No doubt the sick man is glad he will someday be in Heaven, but looks to God to restore him now. The poor, the weak and the oppressed want not a God who did speak but a God who does. The failing and despairing sinner needs not a God of a future paradise as much as a God who cares for him now in this world. He does.

Do you think God would save the souls of man and have nothing for the body which is the temple of the soul? There are two streams of blessing. He says you are loosed from your infirmity, go and sin no more. Here is restoration and regeneration from our God who loves and cares for us so much.

Father God, thank You for loving and caring for me. You made a beautiful creation for me to enjoy and it awes me that you keep track of a whole universe and still know my name and all about me. Thank you. Amen.

March 1 — My Good Samaritan

Scripture Reading: Mark 12:28-34
Key Verse: "...You shall love your neighbor as yourself..."
Mark 12:31

The parable of the Good Samaritan in Luke 10 has as its background an intense conversation about doing the law, and yet doing not just the law but the spirit of it. Jesus showed the lawyer that legalism, doing of just that which is required, is not what true faith is about.

In fact, the parable of the Good Samaritan, while certainly a literal instruction for us in how to treat our fellow man, also paints a greater picture of Christ's earthly mission. For, there was a certain man here on earth, and his name was mankind. He found himself bruised and battered by sin, helpless and without hope. He had gone down from Jerusalem, the city of God representing the state of purity in which man was first created, to Jericho, the city of bondage and wickedness.

But mankind fell among thieves on his journey. Notice the thieves were already there, lying in wait for him. Our adversary Satan was already on the job in the garden. He has held the human race in his bondage ever since. The result is that mankind is left dead in sin, wounded in character. Without the garment of righteousness, he is naked and bruised, utterly unable to help himself. He is dying by the roadside of life.

See who is coming along? It is the priest and the Levite, representing the Law. The Law says, "Do this and you will live." But this mankind could not do anything, he was helpless. So the best the law could do was to gaze upon his condition and pass by. The Law and the ceremonies of religion are all helpless to save a soul.

But in due time God sent forth His Good Samaritan Son, Jesus Christ. He cared not about boundaries of race, color, religion, and nationality. He came to the Jews, yes, but also to the Gentiles. He, too, rode upon a donkey, but He got off and humbled Himself to the death of the cross. His blood was spilled to redeem us, and with the oil of healing and the wine of gladness He brings us back to God and to righteousness in Him. He lands me safe at the Inn, God's appointed place for the saved soul. What more is the church than a spiritual hospital, a place to grow in Him and become strong? Jesus gives us the innkeeper, the Holy Spirit, to minister to our every need. And He leaves with the promise, "When I come again," for He is coming back.

In this allegorical reading of the parable, we must not fail to notice that the wounded man was a willing patient. He did not resist the assistance the Samaritan offered. He recognized his helpless state all too well. His life was spared because he entrusted himself to the hands of the Good Samaritan.

Oh, dear friends, we should never lose sight of the fact that Jesus did what was not required. He did not just pass by in judgment, but stooped to save us. Nothing chilled the love of our Good Samaritan for us. Our bonds of sin did not repulse Him, the ugliness of our wounded lives did not prevent Him, and the enormity of the required sacrifice did not daunt Him.

"Love your neighbor as yourself," He said. And if our benevolence would be of the highest order, we must do all out of gratitude to Him who was the Good Samaritan for us.

Dear Lord, I don't always remember that my condition was hopeless, wounded, and battered, until You lifted me up. Please stir my heart to see those lying along the roadside of life with the compassion of a fellow traveler, and to extend to them Your hands of help. Amen.

March 2   The Tragedy of Prayerlessness

Scripture Reading: Luke 18:1-8
Key Verse: "Then He spoke a parable to them, that men always ought to pray and not lose heart." Luke 18:1

This is our weakness, is it not? It is a mighty privilege to be able to pray when temptations come, when sorrows strikes, and help is needed. We are weak in the very thing that ought to be our strength. Here is where ministers and laymen alike fail. God has placed this mighty gift at our disposal if we will but use it. God can use this gift to make us useful Christians, great ministers of the gospel for Him.

Prayer is a clear and definite command of God. Suppose I should ask how much you pray? How many minutes or hours? What would your answer be? If you find yourself compelled to admit "little" or "none", there is your answer for your lack of spiritual vigor. Prayer, my beloved friend, is necessary. It is obligatory. It is noble, essential, efficacious, and profitable. God answers prayer. Why would you not pray?

Just as we fail to pray, we will fail to grow. Without prayer, one's spiritual life is dwarfed. With it, one cannot fail to grow. Prayer, after all, is communion with God. What a blessed privilege, what a delight, to talk with God. Have you not known friends whose very fellowship was a benediction? In their company, you are blessed, feeling strong and happy. Think then of the power and blessedness of God's fellowship. Think of the bonds of fellowship and friendship that will come between you and God if you only pray. There is no fellowship like the fellowship of prayer. Go to Him. Prayer changes things.

No wonder the disciples cried, "Teach us, Lord how to pray." If we only knew how to use prayer for all times and occasions, we would have a new joy and thrill in our Christian life and service that cannot be found otherwise.

Like the disciples, we Christians need to study to take Jesus' prayer life as our example. It was after a night of prayer that Christ chose the twelve disciples. Organization is needed, but prayer comes first. Of

Christ it is said, "Having risen a long while before daylight, He went out to a solitary place and there He prayed." Now, if Jesus had to start the day with prayer, what about you and me? Before the raising of Lazarus, He prayed. And if we want to see men dead in sin raised to life in Christ, we must pray.

There is a story of Christian Evans, a great Welsh preacher. One day the people of his church missed him from his pulpit. One of the officers of the church went up to the tower-room, and there he heard someone talking. He came back down and said he had found the preacher, but he was talking with somebody. They said, "Well go back and listen, perhaps you can tell who is with Pastor Evans." The man did, and he heard Evans praying. "I know who is with him" he told the congregation. So they waited. For thirty minutes, they waited and at last he came. He climbed into his pulpit with his face all aglow, and tears running down his cheeks. He got only as far as his text when someone cried out, "O, God, what must I do to be saved?"

Oh, it is this power of God that we need, and this power comes only through communion with God in prayer. Why go on anymore without it? Go to Him now.

Dear Lord, thank You for giving me the privilege and the responsibility of access to Your throne of grace. I yearn for more consistency and depth in my communion with You. Prompt me, Lord, to come to You. Wake me up; rouse me from my spiritual drowsiness when I forget. Help me Lord, to make my time with You my priority. Thank You. Amen.

March 3   He Restores My Soul

Scripture Reading: Psalm 40

Key Verses: "I waited patiently for the Lord; and He inclined to me, and heard my cry. He also brought me up out of a horrible pit out of the miry clay, and set my feet upon a rock, and established my steps." Psalm 40:1-2

When my soul grows sorrowful, He revives it. When my soul is sinful, He sanctifies it. When my soul is weak, He strengthens it. Yes, the believer is liable to fall, but not to fall away. When we fall, when we are weak, when we are sorrowful or discouraged, we have a mighty Lord to whom we can cry out knowing He will hear and aid us. When we fall, He waits to bring us up.

The believer is liable to fall. Even the apostle Peter fell, but he fell only as far as the prayer of Jesus allowed it, "Simon, Simon! Indeed, Satan has asked for you that he may sift you as wheat. But I have prayed for you; that your faith should not fail; and when you have returned to Me, strengthen your brethren." Jesus predicted and provided for Peter's restoration before Peter was aware of the need. Jesus knows your needs as well.

Yes, we must have restoration from our Lord. The twenty-third Psalm speaks of green pastures, yet what are they without the accompanying, "He restores my soul"? We must hear His voice saying, "Peace, be still" and feel His hand quieting us before we can lie beside those still waters. What good, after all, are still waters to a turbulent soul? We must "be still" in order to "know that I am God."

And so, this Psalm is precious. We all need God's reviving, restoring work in our lives on a daily basis. We hurry, hurry, hurry in the race of life, often drifting aimlessly rather than pursuing goals purposefully. The urgent things of life drive us, while the still small voice of the Lord goes unheeded. Soon, like David, our "iniquities have overtaken" us. Yes, our enemies (whether flesh or spirit or circumstance) may seem to conspire against us. But, God will not fail. He will not withhold His compassion from us. Time after time, Israel turned away from God. Yet, time after time, as they repented and turned to Him, He would send them a deliverer from their spiritual or physical bondage. Our great God never changes; He is still willing to receive us back, too.

There are certainly times of spiritual declination in every believer's spiritual life. Remember that we are always in the battle between our flesh and our new nature in Christ. The law of the spirit of life in Christ Jesus has made me free from the law of sin and death. Nevertheless, I fall to the temptations of the flesh. Whether it is neglect of the Scriptures, unconfessed sin, or disobedience to the voice of God calling me to some service or calling me to prayer, sin comes quietly and quickly. There really is no excuse, for we ought to live with Christ between us and temptation, with Christ between us and sin. But, God has made provision. "If we confess our sin, He is faithful and just to forgive us our sin and to cleanse us from all unrighteousness," we are told in IJohn.

Isn't it a delight to know that whatever the cause of our falling, whatever reason it is that we find ourselves in the miry clay, He waits to restore and to revive us? Isn't it a joy to have the assurance that He wants to restore to you the old strength of faith, the lost peace in the storm, the sweet song in your heart? Wait patiently on the Lord, for He will answer.

Yes, Lord, I call to You. I call out in thanksgiving and gratitude for You are certainly an ever-present help in trouble. I call out asking that You would set my feet firmly on the rock of Your strength. I am waiting in wonder for Your sweet restoration. Like David, I will not hide my love for you! Thank You, my Father. Amen.

March 4   Under New Management

Scripture Reading: Galatians 2:11-21

Key Verse: "I have been crucified with Christ; it is no longer I who live, but Christ lives in me; and the life which I now live in the flesh I live by faith in the Son of God, who loved me and gave Himself for me." Galatians 2:20

    Let us examine these great, illuminating facts of life a little more closely. First, the old tenant in your life and mine has no place anymore, for Christ on the cross died to redeem us from the power of the evil one who has had us all our lifetime subject to bondage. The old tenant is dead; the old "I" with its mean nature, its unkindness, and sin has in the cross of Christ received its deathblow. Christ died that you may live! But you also need to know that Christ died that you might die. In the economy of God, the old Adam nature is crucified.

    How well I remember, as a boy, catching those June bugs. When you pick that bug up it would play possum, play dead, and lie there without moving. You could then turn it over and push it around but there it would lie to all outward signs as dead as a door nail. Are we playing dead or have we truly released the old ways?

    But there's the coming in of the new tenant. "I have been crucified with Christ, it is no longer I who live, but Christ lives in me." What a blessed tenant has moved into your life and mine. In Glendale, California, there was an apartment above our own. Those folks turned night into day. All night long it seemed they raised "Ned," then slept half the day. Mrs. Meade and I were about exasperated but we did not wish to complain. We did not know how much longer we could endure. Then one day I returned home to see new curtains at the windows, the hallway swept, and the door all clean, and I said, "What's up? What's happened upstairs?" And she said, "The old tenants have moved out and new ones have moved in and they are grand people, nice, and clean and transforming things around here."

    Oh beloved, I tell you, the cross is not only a redeeming power, it is a transforming power. Our lives are no longer a stagnant pool, but a flowing river with the power of Christ streaming constantly in, and then constantly out to the world around us.

Said the pool to the stream, "Why do you work so hard and struggle along, look at me, I'm taking life easy, see how pretty and blue I am? I would not give myself as you do. Soon you'll dry up and you'll be no more. But me, I'll be here in all my contentment and glory." But the stream just said, "I've got work to do," and went on its way making the grass green, giving refreshment, and soon other little streams joined it and it grew. Its banks were lined with flowers, and its streambed deepened until it became a deep and beautiful river running on into the ocean to lose itself in the bosom of the deep. But, soon the hot sun poured down, the pool began to dry up, the bugs infested it and disease polluted it. In a few months it had died without a bit of benefit to mankind, but rather its life had been a hindrance. Which are you making your life, a pool or a river?

Lastly, with this new management in your life may I ask, where are you putting the manager? He wants full charge of every room, every cupboard, now. That is the secret of peace. That is the secret of power; when we, like Paul, see that our life is not our own. It belongs to this new master and we are "under new management."

Lord, I struggle with letting go of control. I am sometimes of the opinion that I know better the circumstances of my life. How like the pool. Lord. I'd rather die to myself and my will and have the river of Your power, love, wisdom and mercy pour through me in a constant stream. Amen.

March 5   History Repeats Itself

Scripture Reading: Amos 5:10-15

Key Verses: "Seek good and not evil, that you may live so the Lord God of hosts will be with you, as you have spoken. Hate evil, love good; establish justice in the gate. It may be that the Lord God of Hosts will be gracious to the remnant of Joseph." Amos 5:14-15

    As the varied instruments of a symphony orchestra, under the skillful direction of a gifted director blend into the harmony of a great motif, so the Old Testament prophets scattered in time, diverse in personality and circumscribed by varying conditions, lift their voices in unison attesting to the immutable sovereignty of God. Among all the prophets, no one deserves to rank higher than Amos. For Amos, religion consisted not in a ritual, but in righteousness.

    But, how could a herdsman from the hills of Judah gain a hearing in the religious center of her northern rival? He was diplomatic in his approach. Instead of arousing animosity at once by attacking the sins of his hearers, Amos denounced the cruelties of surrounding nations, starting with Syria and then one nation after another, until he came to Judah, next door to Israel, "I will send a fire upon Judah, and it shall devour the palaces of Jerusalem." What glee must have filled their hearts as he scorched these neighbors, these rivals, of theirs. Yes, up to this point, Amos was very popular.

    But, wait. He has one more word to say and this to Israel herself. "For three transgressions of Israel, and for four, I will not turn away its punishment." This refrain had sounded like sweet music when it told of the enemies of God's people. But it must have struck terror in the hearts of the Israelites, at last face to face with their own sin.

    What could they plead in self-defense? They were God's chosen people, with greater responsibility because they had the greater blessing. Their privileges were the measure of their responsibility. Then, Amos thrusts the sword of God into the heart of their wickedness. He tells them that not only are they guilty of the destruction of the poor, not only are they so cruel and grasping that they cannot wait for the crops to ripen so that they can begin another season's cheating, but that they profane the very altar of God. Amos utters a call to seek God, to offer contrition and confession.

What of our day? Yes, indeed. Let us, for the moment, not be concerned with the sins of the nations of the world. Oh, our own eyes are too full of beams! We, too, have become a rich and wicked land.

We, too, have built great cities where men and women and little children shiver in shacks. We, too, allow these people to live in squalor, drawing rags about their numbed bodies and tightened belt-buckles. Close by are palaces, light, laughter, food, drink, and here and there a house of God. We have banquet tables and garbage pails with men and women created in the image of God gathering at each to eat. What self-defense can we plead? Have we even offered them the Bread of Life, to satisfy their hunger? Or a crust of earthly bread to fill their stomachs?

Remember, that in the last analysis, the thing that called down Israel's doom was its spiritual decline. Material degradation is always preceded by spiritual destitution. The light of the Son of Righteousness has shone upon us, and the measure of the light is the measure of our responsibility.

Oh God in Heaven, I am so shortsighted. Help me to see beyond the boundaries of my own feeble life. Help me to see beyond my busyness. Help me to see both the physical and spiritual desperation in those around me. And then, help me to help them. Amen.

March 6   Yesterday, Today, and Forever

Scripture Reading: Hebrews 13:1-9
Key Verse: "Jesus Christ is the same yesterday, today, and forever." Hebrews 13:8

I pity the lecturer on current events. By the time he has prepared his speech, his current events are out of date and breathe the fragrance of lavender and old lace. In such a breath-taking age men look here and there for a point of permanence. Some rely upon financial investments, but money has been setting a record for a quick getaway. Others seek to endure through fame, honor, or position, but bricks follow bouquets and the famous are soon forgotten. Some rely upon friends but too many friends are like shadows and follow only in sunny weather. Thousands of others seek to escape life's boredom through "fads" and "isms" of many a shade and hue. Men wander in a wilderness of cults seeking lasting satisfaction.

A man who had been a Baptist, a Methodist, a Disciple, and a Presbyterian told his temporary pastor, "I'm planning to join the Congregationalists." Thoughtfully the old minister replied, "Well, I don't think it does any harm to change labels on empty bottles."

Millions of empty bottles today think to fill themselves by a change of label.

After all, the proof of Jesus Christ is to know Him. For those who do not know Him, no mere argument is enough. For those who do know Him, no argument is necessary.

Let us first acknowledge and reassert afresh the pre-existence of our Lord. He did not just begin at Bethlehem. Strictly speaking, there is no past tense with Jesus Christ. He said, "Before Abraham was I AM." John tells us "In the beginning was the Word," and Jesus is the Word.

Consider this Christ. He was born in another man's stable, buried in another man's tomb, lived in a land about half the size of Illinois, was never more than 100 miles from home, wrote no books, lead no armies, trusted his truths with a few plain and unpromising disciples, and died the death of a criminal outside the city wall. Yet that life stands alone the one perfect chapter in all the annals of time. There is no answer save that of Peter. He said, "You are the Christ, the Son of the living God."

As He did not begin in Bethlehem, He did not end in a sepulcher. It would not be enough to relate the facts of the Christ, if somewhere down the road He should cease to be. A few days after Calvary His disciples were defying the world with a message of victory. They were not the same, and never were again. This Jesus had come from the grave with a new body, had promised them His presence, had returned to the Father, and had sent them the Holy Spirit. No other explanation can account for the early Church.

He is, however, not simply a distant memory. He lives. He is healing broken bodies through prayer and consecrated physicians and nurses, ministering through the slums by the Salvation Army, teaching the word in faithful pulpits, and living in the lives of millions of ordinary Christians. Oh, we must remember that at the very heart of our faith stands a person. He is a living person, eternal and everlasting. The altogether lovely, the real, living, pulsating Christ, waits to make Himself real to you.

But, I have good news. The best is yet to come. He has promised to be with us always, even unto the end of the age, and He has promised to return for those who know Him. What with Him is possible, He is soon to make actual. Praise His Holy Name.

Dearest Father, Thank You for sending Your Son who was with You in eternity past, is with us, and will be with us for eternity future. Amen.

March 7 — He Lingered

Scripture Reading: Genesis Chapter 19

Key Verse: "Then the men said to Lot, 'Have you anyone else here? Son-in-law, your sons, and your daughters and whomever you have in the city- take them out of this place!'" Genesis 19:12

Here we see the old, notorious city of Sodom. The whole city was plunging rapidly towards destruction due to the collapse of morality and righteousness. We are prone to write much and think much on economic collapse, but what can be compared to the moral and spiritual collapse of a people?

Sodom was a center of wickedness and infamy, and yet Lot had carried his family there. Despite warnings and entreaties, the city had gone from bad to worse, until now the city was on the brink of being destroyed; for as men sow, so must they reap.

God even sent two messengers to warn Lot and his family of the impending disaster, and to urge them to flee for their lives, as we read in the verses of our text. God's messengers clearly place the responsibility of authority, of command, and of leadership upon Lot, the father. "Bring them out of this place," he is told.

A city is the nerve center and the storm center of a civilization. But the chief human institution in the city is the home. The first institution God gave to human society was the home and it is the basis for all other society; for as goes the home, so goes the city, and ultimately the world. God was thinking and planning for the saving of this family when He sent messengers to warn Lot to get his family out of Sodom.

So, God's messengers go to Lot's house. They urged and persuaded and incited him to go; they ended up by using holy violence upon him. All of this was to keep that father and his family intact.

Lot had become quite involved in the city life, for he was found in the gate. Oh, when he came to Sodom he was going to clean up that city, but the city took him for a cleaning and when the end came, what a tragedy. Lot had lost all his influence for God. His sons-in-law laughed at his religious talk. Had he ceased to protest against the evil around him? In gaining political and social status, had Lot failed to take a stand for righteousness? We don't know; we can only surmise.

Despite the fact that God sent special messengers to warn him to leave Sodom, and despite the fact that he was not only exhorted by the angels, but was actually pressed into flight, yet we read the horrible words, "He lingered." Lot lingered in Sodom when sin was wrapping around his family like hoops of steel. He lingered until his children lost all faith in their father's religion. He lingered until when tragedy came, his family sneered at his serious pleadings. Lot lingered, until even Mrs. Lot was lost to her love of the world. Lot lingered, until his two daughters became the mothers of the two most wicked tribes in the entire Bible. To linger in sin, when God calls you out of it, is dangerous indeed.

Is Christ the Master in your home? Are you leading the way to God? This old age has about run its course. Have you loved ones that are unsaved? Do you pray for them? Do you talk to them? Do they know by your life and your words that you take a firm stand for Christ? Purpose today in your heart never to become so like the world that your own family would doubt the sincerity of your faith. And when God calls you to lead, don't linger.

Lord, the unsaved members of my family do weigh heavily on my heart. Draw them to Christ, I pray, Lord. And expose in my heart any sin or offense I may harbor which would be a stumbling block to my family, because, Father, I do not wish to linger. Amen.

March 8

Shall We Crown or Crucify Jesus?

Scripture Reading: Matthew 27:11-23

Key Verse: "What then shall I do with Jesus who is called Christ?" Matthew 27:22

We live in a strange world. Scientifically it is round. Spiritually it is flat, and it never has been more flat than it is now. We live in a generation that ridicules all the sanctities of life. It has become the fashion of the times to sneer at all venerable institutions.

But we Bible-believing Christians feel no alarm. We are not losing sleep for fear that some scientist will dig the foundations of our faith from under us. Nor do we expect to make a hit with the times, but then this generation really knows less about the great matters of life than the generation before it.

We lead the world in mass production, but we have failed in man production. We produce, but we don't create. Other generations left art-galleries, we leave signboards. We have printing presses, but no Shakespeare, and fiddles, but no Stradivarius. We send words around the world in a split second, but who is saying anything worth hearing? People, forgetting they are training for a race, live as though they were racing for a train.

But, we Christians are not the ones who honeycomb the land with class-hatred. It is not we who are destroying the sanctity of human life, home, and marriage. And, we insist that the supreme issue before men today is the old, old question: Shall we crown or crucify Jesus? On that historic occasion Pilate faced the greatest question of all time. That question was, "What shall I do then with Jesus who is called Christ?"

In this trial of the ages, Pilate faced three decisions. First, he asked Jesus, "Are You the King of the Jews?" In John we read that Jesus declared His kingdom is a kingdom of truth and that everyone who is of the truth hears His voice.

Pilate shrugged his shoulders as he asked wearily, "What is truth?" He had listened to oriental jugglers, Roman lawyers and Greek philosophers rant about truth until he was in no position to believe that this One who stood before him was not only One who knew the truth, but actually was the truth.

So, standing before the greatest moment of his life, he did what millions have done since. He shrugged his shoulders, crowned the cynic, and crucified Christ. We live in the age of the cynic who sees the price of everything and the value of nothing. It is a strange day when the less one is sure of, the more he is thought to know. If a minister says, "We may well suppose," he is brilliant. If he declares the Scriptures and says, "Thus saith the Lord," he is called a fanatic and a bigot. We call this generation "hard-boiled," but it is really half-baked, like Ephraim who was "a cake not turned."

Nobody need ask today, "What is truth?" For truth has been revealed. The Lord Jesus Christ said, "I am...the truth." No one should criticize the gospel until he has tried it. There are no reasons for being a cynic, only excuses. And remember, an excuse is only a skin of a reason stuffed with a lie. Skepticism is but a smokescreen thrown before a sinful heart.

So, instead of asking, "What is truth?" come to Him just as you are. He will prove Himself to be the "whom" where all your "whats" will find their answer.

Dear Lord, the tug of this world pulls at me from every direction. The many branches of the media make frank statements that don't agree with each other; it is hard to discern truth. Thank You for revealing Yourself so completely in Your Word and in our relationship as we walk together every day. It is true. Once truth is tasted, it is truly recognized. And You are truth. Amen.

March 9 — Shall We Crown or Crucify Jesus? II

Scripture Reading: Matthew 27:22-31

Key Verse: "Then he released Barabbas to them; and when he had scourged Jesus, he delivered Him to be crucified." Matthew 27:26

Today, let us continue with the lessons we can learn from the situation in which Pilate found himself. The first decision Pilate had to make about Jesus was whether to trust his own cynicism and crucify Christ, or to believe that Christ is the truth. He couldn't believe that Jesus IS the truth. The second decision was regarding the criminality or innocence of Christ.

It was customary to release a prisoner at the Passover. Pilate chose to release Barabbas and crucify Jesus. If we do not choose Christ, we choose the criminal. Life is a choice between the best or the beast. When we crucify Jesus, we release Barabbas and he was a murderer and a robber. It is very evident that Barabbas is loose in these tragic days. Jails and penitentiaries are filled with criminals to the bursting point. And I say to you, criminality is the natural consequence of the rejection of the Lord, for Christ is the only cure for crime. Crucify Jesus in the souls of men and women, boys and girls, and Barabbas is set free.

Pilate's third decision was to find if his loyalty lay with Caesar or Christ. That was the finishing blow. Pilate ought to release Jesus, but the mob cried, "If you let this Man go, you are not Caesar's friend. Whoever makes himself a king speaks against Caesar." It was Caesar or Christ and Pilate chose Caesar.

Today that Rome has passed and Caesar has passed, but Christ remains, the same yesterday, today, and forever. Oh how many of us must confess, if we are really honest, that we have no king but Caesar? We have sold out to the god of the age. We are a befuddled generation, sick of old conditions and unable to create better. Our eyes are glued to stocks and bonds, clothes and cars, and all the tinsel trappings of life's mad masquerade. Do we call Him Lord but refuse to do the things He commands us? Do we sing and talk about Him but live in Rome and do as the Romans do?

On an old slab in the Cathedral of Lubeck this inscription was found. "Thus speaketh Our Lord: Ye call me "Master" and obey me not. Ye call me "Light" and see me not. Ye call me "Way" and walk in it not. Ye call me "Life" and desire me not. Ye call me "Wise" and follow me not. Ye call me "Fair" and love me not. Ye call me "Rich" and ask me not. Ye call me "Eternal" and seek me not. Ye call me "Gracious" and trust me not. Ye call me "Noble" and serve me not. Ye call me "Mighty" and honor me not. Ye call me "Just" and fear me not. If I condemn you, blame me not." "Truly, not everyone who says to Me 'Lord, Lord,' shall enter into the Kingdom of Heaven but he who does the will of my Father which is in Heaven."

Today we face the same alternatives that confronted Pontius Pilate. Shall we take the way of the cynic and try to find our way through life by the small, feeble candle of reason? Shall we crown Caesar and crucify Jesus? He is the answer to cynicism, for He is truth. He is the answer to criminality, our guilt, and sin; because when we put on the Lord Jesus Christ we do not fulfill the lust of the flesh. He is the answer to Caesar because when we accept Him we become citizens of Heaven.

Oh that you and I may crown Him now in our hearts so that one day we may have a part in that final coronation when the nations will lay their crowns at His feet and crown Him Lord of all!

Lord Jesus, I want to crown You King in my heart, not shrug my shoulders and deliver You to be crucified out of my life. I love You Lord. Amen.

March 10 Threefold Secret of a Great Life

Scripture Reading: Philippians 3:12-21

Key Verses: "I do not count myself to have apprehended; but one thing I do, forgetting those things which are behind and reaching forward to those things which are ahead, I press toward the goal for the prize of the upward call of God in Christ Jesus." Philippians 3:13-14

Everybody is keenly interested in the lives of those who have succeeded. Today, let us turn our attention to a most remarkable Christian of the centuries, Paul the apostle. One day, writing to the Philippian Church he let out the secret of his marvelous life. We will study that threefold secret now.

The first element in Paul's success in life was his whole-hearted concentration. He says "this one thing I do," not a dozen or two. Many a life has failed not from lack of ability but from lack of concentration. The whole world is a witness to the power of focus. In the spiritual realm, which is the highest, this element holds sway just as much. No man can serve two masters. "His disciples followed Him." Focus, or concentration, is a prime requisite in the victorious life.

The second secret is that he cultivated a wise forgetfulness of the past. We are to remember certain things but we must have that factor of wisely forgetting. Many a man hobbles crippled through life because he cannot forget. Let me give you a few things as teachers and workers we ought to forget.

Forget our blunders. The best of men are but men at their best. We are to learn how to make our blunders bridges to victory by letting them teach us. Forget our losses; think of the big man who lost his property and sobbed, "I have lost all." His little girl said, "No Papa, you have Mamma and me yet." It is our choice whether we cry over our losses or rejoice over our blessings.

Forget life's injuries; we must refuse to harbor them. Think of a hillside where the waters drain endlessly down one path. Soon erosion has robbed the hillside of its strength. God has given us the ability to turn our thoughts. "As he thinks in his heart, so is he."

Forget our successes; there is a danger in success and it is sensible to be aware of it. And let us learn carefully the purpose of success. It is to glorify God, not ourselves.

Forget our sorrows; take them to Jesus, ask Him to overrule to His glory. Consider the oyster, pierced in the side, a grain of sand irritates and injures his insides to the point of distraction. It is through this process that a pearl is formed. "For our light affliction, which is but for a moment, is working for us a far more exceeding and eternal weight of glory." Face the fact that God allows the grains to produce the pearls.

And forget our sins; Christ knows our failures and loves us. It is our job to ask forgiveness and go on. He has already done the rest.

Now Paul's last secret, "I press toward the goal." Have you the right aim in your life? What good is it to reach the top if your staircase is in the wrong building? You have no aim, no goal? Then that's what you will hit.

May we press forward toward the mark, living true and pleasing lives to our precious Lord. He wants to give us life abundant, not an existence of aimless boredom or useless drifting from one diversion to another. He loves us so much more than that.

Dear Father God, I want my life to be glorifying to You. At this moment in time I'm not sure where to go or what to do for that to come to pass. Will You please guide me through Your Word and through the counsel of my brothers and sisters in Christ to Your magnificent plan for my life? I will watch and listen eagerly for Your direction. Amen.

March 11

Out, and In, and the Way Between

Scripture Reading: Deuteronomy 6:20-25

Key Verse: "He brought us out from there that He might bring us in." Deuteronomy 6:23

God's action and His intention in the history of His people, Israel, are here brought together. We read that He brought them out of Egypt, that He might bring them into Canaan. Here we see the purpose of God for Israel. This brief statement of our text is of profound significance, for this experience is traceable in the lives of Christians through all the ages.

God had, by a wondrous demonstration of His power, delivered Israel from Egyptian bondage and guided them to the border of the Promised Land. They came so close, only to rebel and return to the wilderness where they wandered for years. What a tragedy. An entire generation perished. God brought them out, but most of them never went in. This sad story of failure to submit to God runs through both the Old and New Testaments.

All the Epistles are addressed to believers. And in all of them we are face to face with the disparity between what we are and what we should be. Every Christian is come out, but not everyone is gone in. Paul makes it clear that one may cease to be "natural" without ever becoming "spiritual" and that a Christian, throughout life may remain "carnal." Between Egypt and Canaan lies a wilderness in which regenerated souls may wander through life. It is tragically possible to have a saved soul and a lost life.

The unconverted soul is under the power of sin and self. But, the unyielded Christian is freed from the power of sin, but abiding under the power of self. Only he who is fully yielded to God is living in the power of the Holy Spirit. The carnal Christian has a Savior, but has not submitted to the Lord. Only the yielded Christian has both a Savior and a Lord. The carnal Christian is stuck between Passover and Pentecost.

He is on the right side of the cross, but he is on the wrong side of the throne. The Christian who follows his own will rather than God's is wandering, not abiding.

The practical question for us is, "What is my relation to the purpose of God for me?" First, have I confessed my sin, turned to God for forgiveness, and by faith received Christ? Nothing can substitute for saving grace! And, am I living in joyful submission to the Lord? If not, why not? Don't spend your life out, but not in.

Look at Terah, Abraham's father. They left as a family from Ur of Chaldees. Their objective was the land which God promised to show them. But the record says that they came unto Haran and dwelt there and, "Terah died in Haran." Here is an illustration of intention unfulfilled and worthy purpose unaccomplished. Terah came out, but never went in. He made a goal of a stopping place. Being the head of the family, he impeded the progress of them all while he lived. No Christian can stop like that on the journey, without delaying others also.

God's will for all of us is to pass clean over Jordan into the land of our inheritance. For this end were we redeemed. God brought us out that He might bring us in. By faith we came out and by faith we must enter in. Say to our Lord in this quiet hour that you are willing to enter in joyfully and fully; that you are submitted to His will and His work in your life.

Dear Lord, I know that You are Lord in fact, but I don't always joyfully submit to Your will, even when all outward signs would say that I do. Thank You that Your purpose for my life is more than rescue from sin. Thank You that You have a life of purpose set out for me. Please accomplish Your will through me. Amen.

March 12   Can You Recommend Your Religion?

Scripture Reading: Psalm 66

Key Verse: "Come and hear, all you who fear God, and I will declare what He has done for my soul." Psalm 66:16

This is a man who is determined to get a hearing. He has a story that simply will not keep. "Listen to my story," he pleads with joyful earnestness, "I have a message!" What has he to say that he insists on winning our attention?

It is not that he will discuss the topics of the forum or the market place. Nor is he seeking to share with us the latest discoveries of science. Had he done so, that would have been forgotten long ago. No, he is undertaking to bring us a sure word from God. It is not his own deeds in religion; but it is rather the dealings of God with his own soul.

This man has a message that is the most thrilling, the most fascinating that the needy hearts of men can know. He has found that God is a prayer-hearing, prayer-answering God. In God, he discovered a source of comfort. He found God in the glory of His presence and power, and this is the reality for which the world in all its need is longing, and dying for today.

Yes, here is a man who is bubbling over with a testimony, a personal testimony about his God. Here is a man who had an experience with God about which he is not ashamed, but which he would like to recommend to all. We cannot help but see and feel what he believes about it. He has found that in the crisis of his life, God helped him. He is saying, "Taste and see that the Lord is good." Our faith is supposed to help us when we most desperately need aid. Have you experienced this help in your desperate hour? Have you recommended your faith for such hours in the lives of others?

Crises do not offer the only means of recommending our faith in God. In fact, in our everyday experience all of us have ample opportunity to provide testimony of our relationship with our Savior. All of us give some kind of testimony day by day.

Laying his hand on the shoulder of a young monk one day, St Francis of Assisi said, "Brother, let us go down into the town and preach." They walked arm in arm, they talked and conversed as they went through the principal streets and lanes of the town, and then they started on their way back to the monastery. In surprise, the younger priest said, "Father, when shall we begin to preach?" St. Francis looked down kindly upon the younger man and said, "We have been preaching. We have been seen, our behavior has been watched so that we have delivered a morning's sermon. Oh, my son, it is no use that we walk anywhere to preach unless we preach as we walk."

All of us are constantly presenting our religion through our ordinary, everyday relationships with our fellowmen. In our daily associations, we tell what we believe of Christ and His teachings. We commend, or fail to commend, Christ and His teachings to others as we interact with them.

What is Christianity doing in us, and through us each day? This is our real testimony, which others observe whether we speak or not. Yet, it is our privilege to say a word for Jesus. The words of our testimony have an irresistible quality when they are backed up by a consistent life and an unyielding loyalty to Christ.

Dear Lord, I want to be a good representative for You here on earth. Please help me be mindful that my actions and my attitudes may attract others to You, or detract from You. Help me to provide a good testimony with both my words and my deeds. For Christ's sake, amen.

March 13   What Is a Christian?

Scripture Reading: Acts 11:19-26

Key Verse: "...And the disciples were first called Christians in Antioch." Acts 11:26

A little boy asked his father, "What is a Christian?" The father explained to his son just what a Christian should be according to the Scriptures. But he told him so well that when he had finished, the boy answered, "Father, have I ever seen one?"

I have real sympathy for that boy. In this befuddled age when even the faithful are confused by "isms" and "schisms" galore one feels like rising up in the midst of the bedlam to ask, "Just what is a Christian anyway?" The traveler has been lost in the baggage.

One thinks of the housewife who answered the doorbell to be greeted by a stranger who abruptly asked, "Do you know Jesus?" She was so taken aback that she could think of no answer and closed the door in his face.

When she told her husband of it, he suggested, "But why didn't you tell him that you are President of the Missionary Society and teacher of the Ladies Bible Class and active in all church work?" "But he didn't ask me about that," she replied. "He asked me if I know Jesus Christ."

So, in the midst of the things we do and belong to, it is well to ask ourselves once in a while, "What about you? For all your zeal and church work, do you know Jesus Christ?"

A Christian is one who has a relationship with Christ. Who has accepted His gift of salvation and has chosen to love Him and be in union with him. He is saved. Acts 2:47 says "and the Lord added to the church daily those who were being saved." It does not say those who were sincere, earnest, sanctimonious, or talented. They are "saved." There is a realization that they are separated from the Holy God by sin.

This realization leads to repentance, a Godly sorrow for sin, a change of mind about sin, self, and the Savior. There is faith that receives Him into the heart as the Son of God followed by a confession with the mouth that this is so. The love that comes into the union causes the Christian to desire to yield to and serve his beloved Lord. It is miles away from signing a card or joining a church. It is the most profound experience in human life.

Most have heard the story of the servant girl who worked daily in the home of her master. One day, the wife of the master was taken ill and died. The master, in due time began to notice the servant girl and asked her to be his wife. She accepted, love grew, and they developed a loving relationship. Now it was the love they shared, their fellowship, that was important. She loved to do the tasks of a wife and they were easy because she was in love. Her desire was only to please her husband. She listened to his words, looked for ways to help him and things that had been grueling tasks were now gifts of love. You see, sometimes we get the cart before the horse.

The relationship is what is important. With a wife there has been an acceptance of an offer of love and companionship, a forsaking of other relationships and a desire to give herself completely to her husband. Thus, the Christian, the true church, is called the "Bride of Christ." This, beloved, is the definition of a Christian.

Dear Lord, I'm awed by the thought of loving You like a bride loves her husband. Help me to remember that time spent with You is what You desire, not a frantic running around trying to serve You. Let my service grow naturally out of my deep love for You. Amen.

March 14 — The Shepherd of the Cross

Scripture Reading: Psalm 22

Key Verse: "They will come and declare His righteousness to a people who will be born, that He has done this." Psalm 22:31

The three Psalms of David we call the 22nd, 23rd and 24th Psalms should really be considered together, for they are all Shepherd Psalms. These Psalms correlate with the New Testament presentation of our Lord as a Shepherd with three facets. First, in John 10, He is the Good Shepherd giving His life for his sheep. Then, in Hebrew 13:20, He is the Great Shepherd brought again from the dead through the blood of the everlasting covenant. Thirdly and finally, in I Peter 5:4, Jesus is portrayed as the Chief Shepherd who will one day appear to reward His under-shepherds and take immediate charge of His sheep.

Isn't it interesting that these relationships are also set forth, a thousand years before Christ's appearance on earth, in the same order in these three Psalms of David? Psalm 23 is like a bridge leading from the sufferings of Christ described in Psalm 22, to the glories that will follow, as displayed in Psalm 24.

In Psalm 22, we see the Good Shepherd laying down His life for the sheep. It is a picture of our Lord's crucifixion written a thousand years before the event. The Psalm opens with one of the seven words from the cross, "My God, My God, why have You forsaken me?" The holiness of God could not look on even His own Lamb, spotless though He was. That Lamb was there as a sin offering and upon Him had been laid the crushing burden of the world's sin. II Corinthians 5:21 says that the Son of God was made sin for us, though He knew no sin, that we might be made the righteousness of God in Him.

This sacrifice at Calvary does not appeal to the natural man. We see in Psalm 22 the prediction of how Christ would be ridiculed by those observing the scene. And then, in Matthew 27:39-44, the religious leaders join in taunting Jesus as He hangs on the cross. They called out that since He trusted in God, let God deliver Him. Unwittingly, they spoke in direct fulfillment of Psalm 22:8.

The Psalmist goes on to declare the physical sufferings of Christ. Even His agonizing thirst is described, in verses 14-15, "My tongue clings to My jaws; You have brought Me to the dust of death." All the accompanying incidentals of Christ's crucifixion seem laid out for us here in this Psalm, from the piercing of His hands and feet in verse 16 to the soldiers' gambling for Christ's robe at the foot of the cross. What a detailed and true prophecy. There were at least twenty-five accurate fulfillments of Scripture in the 24 hours preceding the death of our Lord Jesus, irrefutable proof that the Scriptures are indeed the Word of God.

In the middle of verse 21, however, there is a startling change. Down to this verse, the psalm is filled with suffering, sorrow, and agony. Suddenly, He cries in triumph, "You have answered Me!" And from here on, there is joyous acclaim and joyous shouting! From this point on, the suffering is over and the rejoicing has begun. Beginning with a cry of agony, "My God, My God...," it now closes with a triumphant shout, "You have answered me." God is near, the psalmist proclaims. God is our deliverer. Praise our glorious Lord!

Oh my dear Heavenly Father, It is impossible to appreciate the crook of the Shepherd without understanding the depth of His love for His sheep. I join my voice today in the shout of praise, "You have answered Me!" For truly, You answer my every call, and You provide my every need. Praise Your Holy Name! Amen.

March 15   The Shepherd of His People

Scripture Reading: Psalm 23

Key Verse: "The Lord is my Shepherd; I shall not want."
Psalm 23:1

There could be no greater blessing come to your life than that you should look up in every trying circumstance and say to God, "Lead me on" in absolute assurance of His presence, His protection, and His care. Well, this wonderful Psalm teaches us of God's divine care and provision for our future. Finding Christ as our very own shepherd brings contentment as we discover the peace reflected in the Psalmist's assertion, "I shall not want." There are nine reassuring principles we can discover in this Psalm, nine things that will comfort an anxious heart and quiet a wondering mind.

First, the Psalmist says, we have the assurance of possession. "The Lord is my Shepherd." He is mine; I need not fear. Next, we have the assurance of position. "He makes me to lie down in green pastures." Our dear Shepherd intends to help us find rest. Thirdly, we have an indication of His power, which is surely reassuring. "He restores my soul." There is no earthly leader who can restore a man's soul, only this eternal Shepherd of ours.

Next, this Psalm teaches us that God is with us. We can see that He guides our footsteps, "He leads me..." and that He leads aright, "in paths of righteousness." His presence affords us the best, most lasting, comfort. Even when distress comes, we learn that we can lean on Him, and depend on Him for our protection. The protection of our mighty Shepherd-King is an assurance like no other, for as a sheep relies on the Shepherd for defense, "You are with me; Your rod and Your staff, they comfort me."

This section of the Psalm assures us of His eternal plan. Do you notice that the sheep are walking? There is no hurry, when you walk with God. That we walk through the Valley of the Shadow of Death also indicates the steady advance of a soul which knows its road's end.

When we walk in this valley, notice too that we walk "through." We walk out into eternity. Death is but a passage to immortality. Praise God for that assurance!

The Valleys in Palestine are very dark. Enemies would often hide in the mountains surrounding the valley passages to attack as one walked through the way. And so it is that many of us do not fear the way to death as much as we fear the vales of life. Yes, life has its vales as well, but as every valley has a water source, so we can stop in every sorrow and drink of the delight of the Good Shepherd's presence with us. It is a precious comfort in trouble to remember His presence, and His staff of protection as we walk through the darkest of valleys.

And, finally we see that our God has great plans for us. We see His provision, "You prepare a table before me in the presence of my enemies." We experience the sign of His pleasure at our company as "You anoint my head with oil." What more could we desire than to be in the presence of our Lord, anointed and provided for by Him? And, yet, there is more to be learned. For God does not provide stingily. No, we are assured of the plenty of His provision as, "My cup runs over." God's loving care for us is abundant and running over. And our future prospect? It is wondrous! "I will dwell in the house of the Lord, forever." Can there be any greater assurance than the knowledge that this Great Shepherd will be my Host forever? With this Shepherd, I shall lack nothing; I can lack nothing. I shall not want.

Dear Shepherd of my soul, Your watch care over me is humbling. You are so gracious and forgiving. This sheep does know Your voice, and dear Lord, I want nothing so much as I want to follow You wherever You lead. Lead me on, Dearest Lord, lead me on. In Jesus's name, and for His glory, amen.

March 16   The Shepherd King

Scripture Reading: Psalm 24

Key Verse: "Who is this King of glory? The LORD strong and mighty, the LORD mighty in battle. Lift up your heads, O you gates! Lift up, you everlasting doors! And the King of glory shall come in. Who is this King of glory? The LORD of hosts, He is the King of glory." Psalm 24:10

The three Psalms we have been considering have been called, "The Psalms of the Cross, the Crook, and the Crown" with good reason. Each of these tender Psalms is a Shepherd Psalm, each representing a different facet of our Lord Jesus and revealing another aspect of His relationship to us, His sheep. In Psalm 22, the dying One is our Savior, in Psalm 23 the living One is our Shepherd, and in Psalm 24 the exalted One is our Sovereign.

"Lift up your heads, O you gates! Lift, you everlasting doors! And the King of glory shall come in. Who is this King of glory?" In the previous Psalm, David used the language of peaceful assurance; in this Psalm the language is exultant. The theme is "Praise for the King, for our Lord who is come from battle." If Psalm 22 is the Psalm of Good Friday, with the agony and sufferings of the Shepherd portrayed in excruciating detail, then Psalm 23 is the Easter Morning Psalm. Because of His victory, because He lives, we shall not want. The sufficiency of the Shepherd to meet our every need is recited point by point. Psalm 23 is a song of unruffled rest; want is cancelled and weariness finds a resting place in green pastures. And, if Psalm 23 is the Easter Morning Psalm, then Psalm 24 is the song of Ascension.

"The earth is the Lord's, and all its fullness, the world and those who dwell therein. For He has founded it upon the seas, and established it upon the waters." The Psalmist bursts forth in praise for the Creator, of whom we know, "All things were made through Him, Jesus Christ, and without Him nothing was made that was made." This returning Shepherd is also the author of all creation.

Then, in verses 3-6, the Psalmist highlights the fact that no one is able to approach the Holy Place of God, unless they are righteous. There is not one of us who are able to come unto God of our own righteousness. We must depend on "He who has clean hands and a pure heart, who has not lifted up his soul to an idol nor sworn deceitfully." It is only because of the righteousness of Jesus that we have access to God. It is only because of Psalm 22 that we have Psalm 23. It is only because the Shepherd was willing to lay down His life for His sheep, that His sheep find rest and freedom from want.

Finally, in verses 7-10, we find the exultant reception of the King of Glory. Here is the Lord, coming from the battle to the holy city. We find David boldly and repeatedly using the covenant word for God's name, which is represented in our Bibles as "LORD." This name, Jehovah, conveys a wonderful revelation of this King, our LORD, and our great Shepherd.

"Who is this King of glory? The LORD strong and mighty, the LORD mighty in battle. Life up your heads, O you gates! Lift up you everlasting doors! And the King of glory shall come in. Who is this King of glory? The LORD of hosts, he is the King of glory." Praise His name, the Chief Shepherd has come to reign. Praise His name, all creation! Praise His Holy name!

Praise the Name of the King of glory! Praise the Name of the Lord of Hosts! My heart sings with the words of this Psalm when I recall that this mortal life is but a fleeting instant. My eternal home is with You! Thank You, tender Shepherd, for Your willingness to face the cross for me, for the continued guidance and protection of your crook, and for the promise that I will see You wear the crown! Amen, and amen.

March 17   The Field Preacher

Scripture: Matthew 6:25-34

Key Verses: "...Consider the lilies of the field, how they grow: they neither toil nor spin; and yet I say unto you that even Solomon in all his glory was not arrayed like one of these." Matthew 6:28-29

Today, with the Master as our interpreter, let us go out into the great temple out of doors. Let's wander to the church whose dome is the sky, and whose carpet is the green earth, whose walls are the far-flung horizons and whose music is the sighing of the wind mingled with the songs of the birds. There we are going to listen reverently and attentively to a winsome field preacher, whose name is Lily.

We find ourselves tingling with a delightful thrill of expectancy, and the Master, who above others has a seeing eye and an understanding heart, is lavish in His praise, "I say to you that even Solomon in all his glory was not arrayed like one of these." And we wonder, what is it exactly that is the glory of the lily? It is not in its richness of adornment, nor in the wealth of what is in its pocket.

Its glory does not consist in its rank. The Master did not call attention to the lily because it bloomed in the temple, or on the steps of the throne. No, its glory is not of position. Nor is its glory in its social setting. Our attention is not directed toward the lily because of its aristocratic neighbors. Is its neighbor the American Beauty Rose? Or does it rub elbows on one side with the "sour dock" and on the other side with "ragweed"? We don't know. Its glory is inherent in itself. It is the glory of naturalness.

Yes, the lily is natural. When you stand in the presence of this lily, you are impressed with its sincerity, its utter freedom from affectation. It is not putting on a lily-face to hide a dog fennel heart. There are no thorns hidden behind its velvet. What a fine virtue is genuine, frank, openhearted sincerity. How repellent is the counterfeit of hypocrisy, and insincerity.

The second glory of the lily is its unspottedness. You could not help but notice its purity. The lily is unspotted. What a virtue that is! Yes, the lily is unspotted, but do not forget that the same God who gives spotlessness to the lily is able to make us whiter than snow. So, you see, we have in this field preacher the very graces that we most need and most desire.

We ask the lovely lily how it became so winsome, and fragrant, beautiful and unspotted. And, if it could, it might answer, "I grew." The Master says, "Consider the lilies, how they grow…" You see, the lily was once only a little homely bulb. There was a time when it was buried in the soil, trampled on by the hooves of cattle and sheep. But, it grew. Not all at once, but little by little did it grow. And, it did not grow independently, Oh no; back of its birth is God. God is the source of the lily's very life; God is the source of the lily's beauty. You see the garment this lily preacher wears? Human fingers never wove one so beautiful. It was woven by His hands. In His soil the lily is rooted, in His sun the lily warms, and in His light the lily stands.

And to think, God has done all this for the lily, who is to live but for a day. If God does all this for the lily, how much more will He do for you? Depend upon it, God who gives much surpassing beauty to the lily that blooms but for a day, will give yet a greater and surer beauty to His human flowers that bloom through all eternity.

Great Creator God, when I do consider the lilies, I am left speechless by your power and majesty. Your creation is so overwhelming, that it makes me tremble to realize it is but a pale reflection of Your glory. Thank You for reassuring me through the lily that I, too, am under Your care and provision, eternally. Amen.

March 18   Even as a Child

Scripture Reading: I Samuel Chapter 3

Key Verse: "But Samuel ministered before the LORD, even as a child, wearing a linen ephod." I Samuel 2:18

    Hannah gave Samuel to the Lord when he was yet a child. She did not think, as so many do today, that it was necessary for him to attain adulthood before he was capable of following God. She believed, on the other hand, that God had a right to every day of his life. There are many today who hardly believe it possible for a child to become a Christian, much less to serve the Lord. They believe that people can only come to Christ through repentance after years spent in sin, many tears, and many regrets.

    Now, there is a certain flower in the tropics that bursts into bloom with a report like the crack of a pistol. As you ride through the forest, you hear it and you know that the flower has bloomed. But, that is not the way the roses bloom in your garden, is it? One night you notice a bud. That night, the dew falls upon it, and in the morning the sunlight warms it. And when you look again, it is in bloom. Nobody heard it, and yet it has bloomed just as fully as did the tropical flower the report of whose blooming rang throughout the forest. Just so, the child raised by loving Christian parents to believe and trust in the Lord Jesus, there will be a day of conscious decision, but it follows years of childlike faith.

    A child can be a Christian. In fact, Jesus said it was to them and to those who succeeded in becoming like children that the kingdom belongs. Children can follow Jesus because the characteristics that go hand in hand with becoming a Christian are naturally childlike. The child has a faith that is beautiful and simple. She is teachable and loyal to those who show love for her. It is our duty to turn little ones towards our Father.

    Children also come to Jesus easier than adults, because they have not yet become slaves to bad habits. While they are still sinners, children generally do not have hard hearts. Also, he will be far more likely to escape the bondage of evil companionships.

People who come to Christ as children also make the foundation for the church of tomorrow. While many dear souls do come to serve the Lord as adults, it is by far the majority of Christians who come to know Him as children. In most churches, you will find the active leadership composed largely of those who came to Christ in childhood.

Not only this, but the sad fact is that unless a person comes to know Jesus as a child, the chances are that they will never come to know Him at all. Statistics are clear on this point.

Yes, Hannah was wise. She dedicated her boy to God in his young and tender years. She made him a special coat, for he was ministering in the temple. Now, that coat was not large enough to fit Eli. No, it fitted the boy. So too, your boy can come to know Jesus but remember that he is still a child. Do not expect him to have the experience of an adult. Do not expect him to act like an adult, or talk like one. Samuel did not recognize the voice of the Lord when He called. It took the experience of Eli, whatever his flaws, to recognize that. Yet the Scripture is still clear that "Samuel ministered before the Lord even as a child."

Dear Lord, please lay on the hearts of the Body of Christ the importance of teaching the littlest ones. Bless those who sacrificially work with the children week after week. Let us welcome children into our midst as Jesus did, and help us to teach them to serve in little ways now, that they might grow to be mighty men and women of God in their later years. In Jesus's name, and for His sake, amen.

March 19   In Life's Storms

Scripture Reading: Matthew 7:24-29

Key Verses: "Therefore whosoever hears these sayings of Mine, and does them, I will liken him to a wise man who built his house upon the rock: and the rain descended, the floods came, and the winds blew and beat on that house; and it did not fall, for it was founded on the rock." Matthew 7:24-25

Jesus would remind us here of certainties that are absolutely predictable and come to every human life. Jesus said, "The rain descended." Yes, the rain will descend upon every life. There are all kinds of rain. There is the rain of discouragement when we serve well and selflessly in some position, and no one seems to appreciate our efforts and critics are plentiful. Or perhaps you give yourself to the happiness of your loved ones, but the monotony of the daily round is not broken by a single word of gratitude. Then, too, there is also the rain of bewilderment. Confusion as to which way to go, or what is the right path to follow, leads to a lack of direction in purpose and plans.

But, Jesus also said, "The floods came." And the floods will come upon every life. The floods of temptation threaten to sweep us off our feet. Never were there so many temptations in such alluring and plausible forms. There is no one who is exempt. Yet, even fiercer than this are the floods of anxiety and worry. What will tomorrow bring in this world of unrest and suspicion? Parents are anxious for their children; all of us worry about our economic, political, and spiritual future. The floods of temptation and anxiety blend into the flood of struggle. It is a struggle to live, and also to pay the expenses of living. Well, Jesus said the floods came and beat upon the house and it did not fall, because it was founded upon the rock.

And Jesus said, "The winds blew." Life's winds are very common. The winds of adversity are bitter, biting winds that sweep in with a howl and leave a trail of remorse. The winds of distress also come, whether distress of body, mind, or spirit. Now, Jesus said the winds blew and beat upon that house and it did not fall because it was founded upon the rock.

Oh, we all know that the walls of philosophy, or science, or self-satisfaction are but thin protection against the winds and rain and floods that come. Sometimes the rain, the floods, and the winds come together and beat upon our lives even as they do on a house, then what? Well, unless your life is firmly planted upon Jesus Christ as your Savior and guide, you too will fall, as have others. Only a life built upon and trusting in Christ can battle successfully against life's storms. All other foundations are as sinking sand.

This illustration of the two builders is but a picture of your life and mine. What is the difference between the wise builder and the foolish one? How he built and upon what he built made the difference. Just building wasn't enough. And, two things are commanded of us: to hear and to do. "He that hears and does these sayings of mine…" Notice, however, that he who simply hears and does not do is doomed to fail. So it is not enough to hear God's word, to read the Bible. We must follow it. What is the foundation of your house, today? Are you safe from life's storms?

Dear Father, Thank you, my Rock, for providing me a solid foundation. I so often allow myself to become discouraged by the storms of life, rather than just turning it all over to You. Please help me to remember that You are my strength, You are my provider, and You are my refuge. Praise Your Holy Name, Lord, for You are truly all-sufficient. And, I am truly grateful for Your mercy and grace towards me. Amen.

March 20   The Tempter

Scripture Reading: John 8:37-47

Key Verse: "You are of your father the devil, and the desires of your father you want to do. He was a murderer from the beginning, and does not stand in the truth, because there is no truth in him. When he speaks a lie, he speaks from his own resources, for he is a liar and the father of it." John 8:44

A murderer and a liar, that ought to settle the question as to the personality of Satan. You could hardly call an influence, an idea, or a figure of speech a murderer and a liar. But that is what Jesus called Satan. And either Christ Himself was a deceiver or Satan is a power in rebellion against God and the great and subtle tempter and adversary of men's souls. We see the answer clearly in the Word.

Jesus gave the parable of the wheat and tares, explaining, "The tares are the sons of the wicked one. The enemy who sowed them is the devil…" If Satan is just an imagination of the mind or a figure of speech, then who is doing this work in the world? Who is mixing the fatal draught that poisons the hearts and brains of man?

"The Tempter came," says Matthew. He is always coming. There are limestone caves in Bermuda where you can hear the flow of an underground stream. Those waters, ceaselessly flowing, have eroded those cavernous depths with their vast resounding chambers and fantastic decorations.

The mind reels as it tries to estimate how long that stream has been flowing. While empires have risen and fallen, while new continents have been discovered, that stream has been flowing on and on. So too temptation flows through the life of man, through every generation flows the river of temptation.

It is as new as birth and as old as death. It touches the life of the fool, the philosopher, the prince and the pauper, the savage and the sage, Judas and Jesus. Wherever man goes, temptation goes. It is man's shadow, haunting him. It is the warfare from which there is no discharge.

Now, since Christ was truly man, He was tempted in all points as we are. The time of His temptation was just after His baptism. Immediately after this, He was led (driven says Mark) into the wilderness to be tempted. Here is a lesson: when you are before others in the name of God, when your testimony is the strongest, when you are at a spiritual pinnacle, this is when the devil can't stand it. He makes his move.

The first temptation in the history of the human race took place in a garden where man was at peace with the whole animal creation. The temptation of Jesus, the second Adam, took place in a wilderness where He was with wild beasts. The contrast between the first temptation and that of Jesus, one in a garden, the other in a desert, shows the ruin wrought by sin.

The record says, "He was with the wild beasts," for He had no human companion. Temptation is a solitary experience. Satan never talks to ten or twenty men. He singles one out from the crowd, draws him apart in the lonely wilderness, and then speaks to his soul.

No matter where you may be, you meet your adversary alone. But as Jesus did, (we will see in following days) temptation may be overcome by absolute reliance on the will of God. Let us learn from Christ how to meet this old tempter. The good news is, He has the answer for us.

Lord Almighty, I have a hard struggle with temptations. Sometimes I fall flat on my face and I am anxious to learn how Jesus handled temptation and to have victory in the face of it as He did. Amen.

March 21   The Temptation of Hunger

Scripture Reading: Matthew 4:1-6

Key Verses: "Now when the tempter came to Him, he said, 'If You are the Son of God, command that these stones become bread...If You are the Son of God, throw Yourself down.'" Matthew 4:3 and 5

    The tempter came to Jesus when He was hungry, after forty days of fasting. Oh, Satan knows when to come. Not at the end of the first day's fast, but at the end of forty days. Satan came to Jesus and said, "If You are the Son of God." Satan knew He was and he would try to turn Him away from His great work of redemption. What Satan was trying to do was to persuade Jesus to act in a way unworthy of His Divine Sonship. In the temptation were two factors. First, was the suggestion that Jesus gratify His hunger. Second, was the taunt that if He truly was the Son of God, He could prove it by turning the stones into bread.

    It was the same temptation made to Him on the cross. Come down, You don't need to suffer; you can relieve yourself of Your sufferings and prove that You are the Son of God by coming down. But in neither instance did Jesus yield to Satan. Why not? There was nothing wrong in turning stones into bread. But to do so at the behest of Satan and to depart from God's plan for Him would have been sin.

    Christ answered the temptation with Scripture from Deuteronomy. "It is written, 'Man shall not live by bread alone, but by every word that proceeds from the mouth of God.'" And what is our lesson here?

    Jesus sets the example for all those who in difficult circumstances are tempted to get out of those circumstances in a wrong way. The world says, "A man must live!" Esau had that philosophy when he sold his birthright for a mess of pottage. "A man must live!" that's what Satan said to the three Hebrew children who were threatened with the fiery furnace if they did not bow down to Nebuchadnezzar's image. But they answered, "If it be so, our God whom we serve is able to deliver us, but if not, be it known to you O king, that we will not serve your gods nor worship the golden image."

A man must live, that's what Satan said to Daniel when he read the proclamation of Darius. A man must live! Satan said to Christ. Yes, said Christ, but not by bread alone. Not merely the animal man, but the other man, the man of the soul and of the heart, he must also live.

It is written, written in the Word of God, written in the stars, written on the moral fabric of the universe, written on the heart and conscience of mankind, that man shall not live by bread alone, but by every word that proceeds out of the mouth of God. Tragic is that hour when the man who lives by the Word of God dies within you, and all that remains is animal and bestial.

Let us learn today. The call of the world is "A man must live!" The call of Christ is "A soul must live!" When faced with temptation, we can look to this, surrender our mortal bodies, or surrender our immortal soul. One is fleeting, the other eternal. One choice has fleeting consequences; the other has eternal consequences.

If it is not the time God has appointed in the plan of our life for homegoing to glory, then beloved, we are indestructible. He will intervene as He did in numerous miraculous occasions in the Scriptures. If it is our time to be released from this mortal body, the time that only the Father can allow, let us go with victory and with glory knowing that God's will has prevailed.

Lord, let me always look to Your example when I'm faced with the temptations of the flesh. You answer in the authority of the Scripture, and You take the eternal view, not the expedient view. Amen.

March 22   The Temptation of Pride

Scripture Reading: Luke 4:1-13

Key Verses:"Then he brought Him to Jerusalem, set Him on the pinnacle of the temple, and said to Him, 'If you are the Son of God, throw Yourself down from here. For it is written: 'He shall give His angels charge over you to keep you...'" Luke 4: 9-11

Now the tempter presents the temptation of pride. Jesus had conquered the temptation of bodily appetites and hunger. This was the temptation of the flesh. The first Adam had failed in this temptation when he was shown the fruit in the Garden of Eden and saw that it was good to eat. The second Adam, Christ, did not fail in this, so Satan pushed on to the temptation of pride.

Satan is not easily discouraged or easily defeated. Christ has overcome Satan by absolute reliance upon the will of God. So Satan is going to tempt Him regarding His reliance upon God.

Satan takes Christ to the pinnacle of the temple, one of the great turrets running 450 feet above the Valley of Jehosephat, built by Herod. The devil can tempt a man in the wilderness, in the city, in the marketplace and in the church. Here he tempts Jesus at the temple. From this very pinnacle history tells us that James the brother of Jesus was thrown to his death some years later, because he refused to repudiate and denounce Christ as an imposter.

Here, at the foot of this temple, are collected all the glories of the throne of David. Here all the rivers of prophesy meet. Satan says, "If you are the Son of God, throw Yourself down, for it is written, 'He shall give His angels charge over you and in their hands they shall bear you up, lest you dash your foot against a stone.'"

See how Satan answers Christ with the words of the beautiful 91st Psalm, making a proposal that Christ throw Himself down from the pinnacle of the temple and then be rescued by the interposition of the angels? That would dazzle the multitudes. Instead of taking the long hard way of teaching and preaching, suffering and persecution, it would prove now at the very beginning of His ministry that He was the Son of God.

Jesus scorned this temptation to pridefully make a show. How the world loves a show, and how human nature is appealed to by it. But Jesus scorned it and answered "You shall not tempt the Lord your God." This wild idea of throwing God's Son to the ground was not God's plan nor could Christ be assured that this presumption and pride would assure any angel's interference. God has great plans for His Son, when he will be honored and borne up, with all who put their trust in Him.

How do men tempt and try God? They tempt God when they leave the appointed course of obedience and faith to go in the path of evil and temptation and then expect that they will be delivered. Would a man jump into Niagara and then expect God to rescue him? Or touch a match to a powder keg and expect God to save?

When Augustine, shortly after his conversion, was accosted on the street by a former mistress of his licentious days, he turned and walked in the opposite direction. Surprised, the woman cried out, "Augustine, it is I!" But Augustine, proceeding on his way, cried back to her, "Yes, but it is not I." There was a new Augustine and this new Augustine would not tempt temptation by walking on the old territory of danger.

Father God, I see that Christ again answers temptation with Your Holy Word. He depends only on Your will and not the easy way. May I remember this example when I am faced with temptations of pride. Amen.

March 23   The Temptation of Ambition

Scripture Reading: Matthew 4:7-11

Key Verse: "And he said to Him, 'all these things I will give You if You will fall down and worship me.'" Matt. 4:9

This is no doubt the most powerful temptation. The devil, having failed in his temptation of Jesus by hunger and by pride, now tempts Him by ambition. "The devil took Him up on an exceedingly high mountain, and showed Him all the kingdoms of the world and their glory. And he said to Him, 'All these things I will give You if You fall down and worship me.'"

In a moment of time, Nineveh, Babylon, Persia, Egypt, Greece, Rome and all the World Empires yet to come, flashed their pomp and splendor before the eyes of Christ. All these Kingdoms would be His if He falls down and worships Satan.

Satan was lying, of course. For although great power was his and he is the prince of this world, yet dominion belongs to God. But there was power and subtlety in the temptation.

Dominion of the world has been promised to Christ. Read the second Psalm, "Ask of Me, and I will give You the nations for Your inheritance." Christ was to secure the Kingdom by the path of loneliness, self-denial, suffering, agony, and death. His only earthly throne was a cross; His only earthly crown, a crown of thorns.

Now the devil tempts Him with an easier way, a short cut to world dominion. Instead of asking it of God, He is to ask it of the devil. Jesus scorns the proposal. Here we have the climax of the audacity and evil of Satan as he throws off all disguise and asks Christ to worship him.

And for the first time Christ denounces him as Satan, saying "Away with you, Satan! For it is written, 'You shall worship the Lord your God, and Him only you shall serve.'" Yet today in human life, Satan is constantly saying to man, "All these things I will give You if You will fall down and worship me."

The temptation to silence one's convictions and bow down to

Satan for the sake of securing a worldly aim, comes at the price of compromise with evil. Some surrender their goal of staying in God's will, stifling their consciences, "For what profit is it to a man if he gains the whole world, and loses his own soul?"

But we need not yield anymore than Christ did. He overcame and we can overcome. The same power whereby Jesus overcame is for you and me today. Christ fought Satan as you and I must fight him.

One secret of Christ's victory was His immediate answer to Satan's proposals. There was no hesitation, but immediate refusal of the temptation. He used the Word of God as His defense and so may you and I. The Psalmist said, "Your word I have hidden in my heart, that I might not sin against you."

Christ won His victory by absolute reliance upon His Father. We too can arm ourselves with this omnipotent power of God, "If God is for us, who can be against us?"

The most beautiful thing in this encounter is the last thing. "Then the devil left Him and behold, angels came and ministered to Him."

And when the angels come, when a clear conscience is held, when self-respect is maintained, when fellowship with the Savior is sweet and we hear His "well done" in the end, then we will know that the victory was worth the struggle of the wilderness.

Holy, Almighty Father, I desire the power to resist when I am tempted to leave the path of Your will. Please help me to rely on You, and Your Word, for protection in times of temptation. Help me to not yield but stay the perfect course You set for me. Amen.

March 24   God Is Love

Scripture Reading: John 21:15-19
Key Verse: "Do you love me?" John 21:16

The Bible is a love story. God reveals His loving character, for God is love, throughout both the Old and New Testaments. But, what of us? He wants to know, do we love Him? To Him the two great commandments are to love God and love our fellowmen.

This knowledge helps us to appreciate the question Jesus asked three times of Peter when almost at the end of His earthly ministry. The master had prepared a breakfast for His disciples on the shore of the Sea of Tiberius. When the meal was over Jesus asked Peter one all-embracing question, the ultimate question of life. "Do you love me?" Peter answered that of course he loved him. The question and the answer were repeated three times and each time Jesus gave a command, "Feed my lambs. Tend my sheep. And feed my sheep."

There were other questions Jesus might have asked. He might have asked, do you believe in me? Do you accept me as the Son of God? Will you serve me? Can I count on you, Peter? Will you sacrifice and die for me? All these were included, however in the one ultimate question, "Do you love me?" Jesus knew that if He had his love, He had everything. Peter's love for Christ led him to give everything for the Gospel.

David Livingstone gave the answer when he knelt on his birthday in the heart of Africa and prayed, "Jesus, my Savior, my God, my King, once again I dedicate my whole life to you." Love leads us in joy to do our Master's will. There was once a youth who complained bitterly about the sin and evil of this world and condemned the God who made it. "Why," he said, "I could make a better world myself." "Good," said his pastor, "Go to it, that is just what God put you in the world to do."

Some years ago, 200 Christian American Indians attended a denominational convention where I had the honor of leading worship. Given a reserved section in the front of the auditorium, they made a colorful picture in their native dress. A Reverend Mr. Tyson spoke, "I was once your enemy, for I was in Custer's campaign in Wyoming and I fought you to the death." He was going on to describe the bloody battle and express his remorse when a large, aged Indian man slowly rose and lifted his hand and was recognized. "Mr. President," said he, "I was in that battle, and we fought you like demons."

A thrill like an electric shock brought that crowd to the edge of their seats. He continued, "I was Mr. Tyson's bitter enemy, but now I am happy to hear him preach the gospel and we are brothers in the Jesus way."

Tense with excitement, the President said, "I want you to come to the platform. Shake hands with your old-time enemy, now your Christian brother."

With great effort the broad-shouldered, brown-faced old man made his way down the aisles and up to the platform. As the two men approached each other, tears were in their eyes. They did not stop to shake hands. They could not speak, but they fell into each other's arms and sobbed joyfully. As they stood in that embrace the great audience rose as one and spontaneously began to sing, "Blest be the tie that binds our hearts in Christian love."

Christ's love for us, our love for Him, our common love for others, such love works miracles. Let us say with Peter, "Yes Lord, I love You," and let us take Jesus's next words into our hearts and feed His sheep. There is the miracle of love.

Dear Lord, I want to be part of the miracle of Your love. Show me how to feed Your lambs, tend Your sheep, feed Your sheep, then fill me with Your power to do it. Amen.

March 25   Sent By God

Scripture Reading: II Kings 17:7-20

Key Verse: "Yet the Lord testified against Israel and against Judah, by all of His prophets, every seer, saying, 'Turn from your evil ways, and keep My commandments and My statutes, according to all the law which I commanded your fathers, and which I sent to you by My servants the prophets.'" *II Kings 17:13*

The most neglected of all the prophets are the Minor Prophets. These twelve great hearts are lesser only in the length of their message. But, perhaps we should remember that steam is no less powerful because it is compressed. The man is yet to be born who will discover any unnecessary words in the Minor Prophets.

What did the Hebrew prophets of old preach? They preached doctrine and duty, insistently declaring that the character of God ought to determine the conduct of His followers. Never since that time has any group of men produced a body of ethical teaching so all-inclusive and so heart-searching. To preach as they did required both wisdom and courage. They were men with a message from God.

They reaffirm in us that which we are apt to forget, that the strength of principles is not measured by the number of those who accept them. All who follow in the train of the Minor Prophets must be willing to see beyond the hedgings of life and build upon the assumption that if God be for us, it does not matter who is against us.

Though they lived more than 2500 years ago, what they had to say is as full of rich meaning now as it was then. In God's view, there are no calendars and we are contemporaries of those people to whom the prophets spoke. Our leaders and the general populace are in need of a great repentance as much as the leaders and people of their time.

The whole period of the prophets is covered by the words of our text. For as the earthly kings of Israel became corrupt, God the true King of Israel instituted the prophetic office to deliver His words to the people. And, the summary of their message is as potent for us today as it was then.

They spoke of sincerity in life. God requires truth in the inward life. Anything less, anything else, He refuses. The prophets also spoke of obedience to God. God's servant will keep back nothing in serving Him, not for idols or for selfishness. And the prophets spoke of constancy. He who serves God only under occasional circumstances cannot be a servant in whom there is no offense. And these Hebrew prophets ever kept before the nation the fact that they were a theocracy, created to live among other nations as a revelation of what it means to have God as an actual King.

The prophets returned time and time again to the same fundamental truths: the proclamation of the Sovereignty of God, the denunciation of infidelity to God as the sin of all sins, and the declaration that such infidelity would bring judgment. In every case, however, these prophets also saw a glory and a victory that was yet to come.

All that the prophets said needs saying today. The vital and abiding principles of life have not changed. Humanity has not changed. While we can't always know His plan, we can know Him, and that makes all the difference. We still need to recognize that He desires that we love Him wholeheartedly. And, we need to remember that we are to live as His people, in part that others might see what it is to have God as our King.

Dear Lord, the message of Your prophets is not distant as I had feared. Help me to do what Israel failed to do, to heed the word of the Lord. In Jesus's name, and for His sake, amen.

March 26 Sowing and Reaping

Scripture Reading: Romans 2:1-16

Key Verse: "...who 'will render to each one according to his deeds'..." Romans 2:6

Today I bring to you a very solemn subject. I make no apology for this for we are living in a time when some folks regard God very lightly. In fact, some have put God out of their thoughts entirely.

Let us stop and think for a few moments about God. He is infinite. He is eternal. He is omnipotent. He is omniscient, and if you resist Him to the end, His power must be against you. He knows what you are thinking; He knows what you are doing. These things are written in His books and one day the books will be opened. He is always about you, observing. Think of His greatness. He holds the winds in the hollow of His hand. He speaks and it is done. Now, come to the text again, what does it mean?

It means that God is not to be ignored. If there is a record of our lives, made by Him who knows our sins, and we are to be judged by what is found written by our name, who can stand a judgment like that?

Here is the remedy God in His wonderful love has provided. It is a message of hope, a way out, a way back. It is the way of the cross that leads home. The law says the soul that sins must die. If that is so, what hope is there for any of us? Ah, yes, but the Lord Jesus Christ who died and fulfilled that law and its demands for us says, come to Me and live. Come my friend, God help you to come, just as you are, in all your need. He will meet every need in your life and you can start with Him in the land of beginning again.

Now dear friend, if you have received Christ's gift, rejoice. Give Him thanks for what He has done for you. You are no longer in danger of reaping what you have sown. You are no longer mocking God because you have come into a right place with Him. You have done what He asked of you.

But, what about your son? Is he in a right place with God or must he reap what he is sowing? Your daughter? Your spouse? Parent? Grandchild? Neighbor? Friend? God doesn't want any of them to reap what they sow. He wants all who will to come into His kingdom. That is why He provided His own Son as payment of our debt.

It is their decision. Yes, this is true. But do they know the story? Do they know the way out? The way home? How can they know unless they are told? And how can they be told unless someone tells them? Have mercy on them. Earnestly share what you have found. It is their eternal soul at stake.

Does it seem that their dear hearts are too hard? Do they scoff at the thought of an eternal God? Pray for them, beloved. Pray as if your heart would break. Pray that their hearts would be softened and the veil of deception would be lifted from their spiritual eyes. Call their names daily before the throne of God and ask that He would help them find the truth. Ask that a faithful Christian worker be put in their path, ask that the Holy Spirit would woo them, and call them. It is so important. It is a solemn task. It is solemn and important because of this; it is eternal. God bless you as you travail in prayer for those you love and those God has put in your path. The decision is up to them. This part is up to you. You can be sure that God will do His part.

Dearest Lord, I know You love _____ even more than I do. I ask You now to move heaven and earth to soften their hearts toward You. I don't want them to have to reap what they have sown. Please open their eyes to Your love and save their soul. Amen.

March 27   The Christian Soldier

Scripture Reading: Ephesians 6:1-13

Key Verse: "Put on the whole armor of God that you might be able to stand against the wiles of the devil." Ephesians 6:11

It is natural for Paul to use the figure of a soldier. Being in bonds so much of the time, he had ample time to study the characteristics of the soldier to whom he was chained. Everything that is worthwhile has to be done at the cost of opposition and antagonism, and no noble service is possible without brave, continuous conflict and sacrifice.

Let us consider some of the things incumbent upon a good soldier of Jesus Christ. A child born in these United States instantly becomes an American citizen. But natural birth does not make one eligible for the Kingdom of God, even though the parents are Christian. The child must be born again.

Enlistment as a soldier of Christ is voluntary. God does not draft His soldiers. There is no force or compulsion. There are no conscripts in Christ's army.

Enlistment immediately separates us. When one joins the army he ceases being his own master. His time is fully arranged for him. He is separated from his former associates, his clubs, and all former social attachments. From now on he belongs to his country and his old-time freedom is a memory.

And so we read, "But you are a chosen generation, a royal priesthood, a holy nation, His own special people." Paul reminds Timothy, "No one engaged in warfare entangles himself with the affairs of this life, that he may please him who enlisted him as a soldier." Everything that may hinder the service of God must be forsaken. Seek first the kingdom.

So, every true soldier of Jesus Christ is separated unto God. Paul is proud to tell his Roman friends that he is separated unto the Gospel of God.

To the Corinthians he writes, "Do not be unequally yoked together with unbelievers. For what fellowship has righteousness with lawlessness? And what communion has light with darkness?"

Let us now consider the equipment of a soldier. There is first, the uniform. Obviously the uniform doesn't make the man a soldier. He wears the uniform because he is a soldier. Paul lists the elements of the uniform by first admonishing us to put on the whole armor of God.

There is the girdle of truth. The girdle gathers the loose, flowing garments, making it possible for the man to walk, run, and labor. It also held the various pieces of armor securely in place. Without the girdle the soldier would feel that he was going to pieces. Truth is basic to all other considerations. We cannot build a sound faith on false beliefs. This means more than sincere beliefs, they must be unmistakably true. To have one's loins girded with truth is to have one's whole nature held together by integrity.

So here we stand, ready as a soldier of Christ. We enlisted voluntarily. We left behind our private lives and desires in order to dedicate ourselves more fully to the task ahead of following our Captain. Why? Because we believe in the truth. It strengthens us and inspires us to action because we know it is right. It is a worthy calling to be enlisted in the army of God.

Almighty God, I am Yours. I don't like conflict and war, but in the spiritual realm it is a necessary path and one that I readily accept. I will fight for the salvation of my children. I will wage spiritual warfare for the truth, that the deception, thievery, and murder by the enemy of our souls will not succeed, but through the power of Jesus Christ we will have victory. Amen.

March 28 Uniform of the Christian Soldier

Scripture Reading: Ephesians 6:10-18

Key verse: "Therefore take up the whole armor of God, that you may be able to withstand in the evil day, and having done all, to stand." Ephesians 6:13

After Paul instructs us to gird our loins with truth, we stand ready to accept the rest of the uniform of the Soldier of Christ. That is the armor, our protection from the attacks of the adversary. This armor is necessary because he looks for the way he can hurt us the most. If we are in obedience to God, we are protected. How can we be overcome if there is no opening? Let us examine ourselves to see if we are completely covered.

The breastplate of righteousness protects the front of the fighter, covering the heart, the seat of affection. The breastplate of righteousness keeps us from losing heart in the battle. There are the shoes of peace. God's peace guarantees a march free from crippling feelings of hate, or worry. We are peacemakers in a world crying to be reconciled.

Then, let us consider the shield of faith, affording protection for the whole body. It gives us the protecting calm of His continuing presence. Real faith in God and His Son, Jesus Christ, is an absolute defense against all foes. This shield is large enough to cover us completely. Have you ever noticed that the Lord Himself is called a shield? He was Abraham and David's shield. The Psalmist said, "The Lord God is a sun and shield." Now if Satan cannot wound us, he would seek to destroy our faith. He would hurl doubts at us. To Eve, he said, "Has God indeed said...?" Curiosity supplanted faith, the shield fell and they were instantly wounded to death.

The shield of faith then is the great essential to the Christian believer. Lay not your shield down. Keep your trust continually in the Lord.

Paul urges us, also, to put on the helmet of salvation. This is our protection for the head. Now, the head is the seat of thought, while the heart is the seat of love. How important that they both be guarded. We must keep our head in these unsteady days. How many sun-struck Christians are running after this foolish teaching or that quack philosophy? Put on the helmet of the truth of our salvation and keep it on.

Did you note that these last five parts of our armor are defensive in nature? Let us now examine and take up our weapons of offense. There are two.

First, see the sword of the Spirit, which is the Word of God. With this word Jesus met and defeated the devil and so will you. Philosophy will fail, logic will fail, experience, emotions, and traditions will fail. But the Word of God endures forever and it will never fail. "Forever, O Lord, Your word is settled in heaven." His word is "living and powerful, and sharper than any two-edged sword." It is not our duty to vindicate the word of God, but to proclaim it. Let us be like David who said, "Your word have I hidden in my heart, that I might not sin against You."

And, we have the Christian's spear, "Praying always," adds the apostle. "Praying always with all prayer and supplication in the Spirit." No weapon is as mighty as prayer. No wonder we are encouraged to pray without ceasing. A praying soldier is not defeated. A praying church is a victorious church. Those enlisted in the enemy's army are rendered helpless before it.

A most significant fact remains that we all must see. In all of the Christian armor there was given no protection for the back. And that, dear soldier, is because there is no place in God's army for retreat.

Father God, let me never turn aside and be unprotected; let me keep advancing for Your Glory and for Your kingdom. Amen.

March 29   Be Sure

Scripture Reading: Numbers Chapter 32
Key Verse: "...be sure your sin will find you out." Num. 32:23

This text has been long misunderstood. It does not say that a man's fellows will find him out, but that his sin will find him out. It does not necessarily teach that your sin will be found out, but that you will be found out, which is a far more solemn thought. A man may live a long life of crime and never be detected. He may die as a solid citizen, never suspected of being other than he appears. And yet, this text is true. Your sin will find you out even though no one on earth ever detects the crime.

It is not an evil thing for a sinner to have his sin found out. In fact, it might bring repentance. But, it is a far more blessed thing when a man finds out his own sin. The judging of sin within your own breast is a blessed work. But, our text has nothing to do with that, either. It is not about finding one's own sin, nor others finding one's sin for him, but sin finding him out.

Every sin brings punishment. The wages of sin is death, the Scripture tells us, and though that isn't a popular idea today, it is none the less true. As surely as the sun rises in the morning and sets in the evening, so sure is it that punishment follows on the heels of sin. The harvest reaped by the sower of the seed of sin is punishment. It may not come during the sinner's lifetime here on earth, but come it will. And, how does sin find out the sinner? Sometimes sin finds the sinner in the realm of conscience, as with Judas Iscariot. The thirty pieces of silver for which he sold out Jesus began to burn a hole in his soul until he couldn't stand it. Sin found out that sinner.

Sometimes sin finds the sinner at his deathbed. When finally facing eternity the sinner realizes in horror what awaits him. Many in our age fear death not because it is the vast unknown, but because deep in their hearts they do know what it holds for them.

A coal mine in England has a limestone formation continually being built up. The water is fully charged with lime as it trickles onto the rock and dries, leaving a layer of limestone. Then the men working in the mine cause a layer of coal dust to rise and settle, leaving a thin layer of black on the white limestone. This goes on daily, except for Sunday. On Sunday, a thick layer of white falls, and the miners call that rock "Sunday Rock" because you can just look and tell whether they worked on Sunday or not. So it is with sin. We write our own history to be read at the judgment, and every sin will be laid plain to sight.

Praise God that Jesus came to provide a way out. Praise God that Christ died to wash away those sins. He has already taken our punishment. Praise God that when you look around and see the despairing one, the guilt-ridden one, the fearful one, you have something to share. Yes, sin will find you out; they must know that. But, there is One who has taken all the punishment, all the shame of that sin. They must also know Him. Then, their despair will blossom in hope, their guilt will melt away under the clothing of Christ's righteousness, and fear will be cast out by perfect peace. Praise God that Christ came not to condemn us but to save us.

Dear Gracious Heavenly Father, sometimes it is hard to even remember what it was like to feel the burden of sin, guilt, and shame. Thank you for that innocence in my soul that you have given me through forgiveness. Please help me to look upon the world around me with your eyes. Help me to see the broken hearts, the searching, despairing ones. And, help me to share the hope that is within me. Thank You, dear Lord, Amen.

March 30   Come See A Man

Scripture Reading: John 4:11-29

Key Verse: "Come see a man who told me all things that I ever did. Could this be the Christ?" John 4:29

In the wonderful story of the woman at the well, we see Christ as we seldom see Him revealed in all Scripture. It starts when a tired and thirsty Jesus requests a drink of water from a local woman. She is astonished that he would speak to her as He is Jewish and she a Samaritan, and she asks Him why. He tells her that if she knew who He was, she would ask Him for living water so that she would never be thirsty again.

Although she is not yet ready to receive this water, the idea selfishly appeals to her, so she responds that she will take it so she won't have to draw water every day. It is necessary for the Lord to penetrate to the very heart of her need. A cancer cannot be treated as a skin disease, from the surface.

There are two kinds of sinners. Those who know it and those who do not know it, and there was no possibility of her partaking of the living water, the salvation He offered, until she was willing to admit her lost condition. So Jesus proceeds to reveal to her the urgency of her need, which she has not yet fully realized. "Go, call your husband, and come here," says Jesus. What will be her answer? He is revealing His deity and showing her that He knows the thoughts of her heart and the actions of her life. "I have no husband," she answers, and the Lord shows her the extent of His knowledge. "You have well said, 'I have no husband,' for you have had five husbands, and the one whom you now have is not your husband; in that you spoke truly." He pronounced a revelation, a condemnation, and a commendation in just those few words. What a record she had, and He knew all about it.

The woman is confused. She can see that He is no ordinary man. So she does the best she can to change the subject. She seeks His opinion of an age-old argument and controversy between Jews and Samaritans.

We do the same today. We try to run from the penetrating light of God's holiness and hide behind argumentative questions. In the end, how astounded she must have been at the breath-taking answer of the Lord. In words that could not be misunderstood, He announced simply that He was the Messiah.

In amazement at the revelation of the Person of Jesus Christ the Messiah, she left her water pot and started up the hill in haste to the village. She came to a group of idle men. In the midst of that group she came with these wonderful words, "Come see a Man who told me all things that I ever did. Could this be the Christ?"

The well is flowing, the stream widens. The one who had told her all things is the one to whom she can freely invite others. "Many Samaritans of that city believed in Him because of the word of the woman who testified, "He told me all that I ever did."

Like the Woman at the Well, when we are born again He plants within us new life. Go to a hospital when a new baby is born and you will see that all the attention of doctors and nurses is concentrated upon that baby until they can hear him cry. It is the cry from his lips that announces his birth. If you are a believer in the Lord Jesus Christ, go to those with whom you come in contact and cry, "Come and see a Man." You will find a new joy that you have never known before as the flow of the living spring from within you brings life to thirsty souls.

Dear Lord, I want to cry out like the newborn who has just received life so that all I know may also receive life. Please fill me with Your Holy Spirit and let me overflow with You. Amen.

March 31   There is a Lad Here

Scripture Reading: John 6:1-14

Key Verse: "There is a lad here who has five barley loaves and two small fish, but what are they among so many?" John 6:9

In the Bible there is a message for each of us. It deals with humanity on a world scale, but it also speaks of a boy, a boy moving with a multitude. With spaciousness that knows no east or west it records the birth of a babe, the fall of a sparrow and the amount of food a boy carried in his basket on a holiday jaunt.

This Bible speaks of a little boy who brightens the lives of others and makes a throng happy. Yes, the same Bible that speaks of boundless oceans chanting their hymns of praise to God from shore to shore speaks also of a boy who yields the contents of his picnic basket to a stranger who asks him for it.

He was a lad with a little. Not a sack of flour, but a little. Not a net of fish, but two small ones. Not a bin of bread, but a bit of bread, a little that he had brought for himself as he went with the multitudes that followed Jesus.

He was a lad with a listening ear. Between verses nine and ten of John's chapter six, somebody went to the lad and asked for his five barley loaves and two fishes. There we see him listening to what they had to say. Maybe the disciples, wondering at the large crowd and the small food supply went to him and asked for it. Maybe Jesus himself asked the boy for his food. But the boy listened to those who spoke for God. He listened and heard what God wanted.

He was a lad letting go. There is a time to hold on. There is another for letting go. Samuel Morse endured the laughs and jeers of congress on behalf of his telegraph for nine years, but he held on and manifested glory by so doing.

But this lad has the glory of letting go. He let go of his five barley loaves. He let go of his two small fish. He relinquished his all. And there he stands today in the Lord's hall of fame, along with the little widow who let go her two mites in church.

The lad let go the thing that meant his comfort. He was ready to suffer hunger. Nobody knew that Jesus was going to feed that crowd and make a mountain of meat out of two small fish, and make baskets-full of bread from five barley loaves. The lad let go, nevertheless. He gave it to Jesus and you know the results. The boy learned one thing that we need to learn today. God does not want us always to do the easy things in life. He sometimes calls us to do the hard things.

The lad reached out beyond the day in which he lived, even to the day in which we live, in influence and power for God. He gave the little and it was multiplied by the Master. You say, only a pen, but a pen in the hand of a poet, only a violin, but a violin in the hand of a Paganini. Only five loaves and two fish, but five loaves and two fish in the hand of the Son of God. He was a lad with a little, but Jesus lengthened it out to feed the multitude.

Have you been asking, "What can I do?" Ask the tiny raindrop, sunbeam, or sparkling rivulet. They are nearly nothing, yet they are capable of forming magnificent prisms that color the world. Just so, when our little is placed in the hands of Jesus, miracles occur. "There is a lad here." Are you that lad, my son, my daughter? Then give what you have to Jesus.

Almighty Father, there is something that I know in my heart You have asked me to relinquish. I surrender it to You that You might make a miracle that might benefit many. Amen.

Palm Sunday   An Ending, a Beginning

Scripture Reading: Matthew 21:1-11

Key Verse: "And a very great multitude spread their clothes on the road; others cut down branches from the trees and spread them on the road." Matthew 21:8

It was the Sunday before Resurrection Day. It was also the Passover Feast commemorating the deliverance of the Children of Israel from the bondage of Egypt. It was considered the birthday of the nation, and it was the closing period of Christ's earthly ministry.

He was entering the very stronghold of His enemies. On Friday night and Saturday He stayed at Bethany, the home of Mary and Martha. On Saturday night a feast was given in His honor by Mary, and there she anointed Him. On Sunday morning Jesus sent two of His disciples to a village to bring Him a donkey colt tied there. The disciples placed their garments on it and seated Jesus thereon.

Soon the multitude gathered. They knew He was announcing Himself as King. Soon they were chanting Psalm 118, and shouting Hosanna. "Hosanna to the Son of David! Blessed is He who comes in the name of the Lord! Hosanna in the highest!" (Matt. 21:9).

They came out of their shops and houses. Some joined the crowds calling to Jesus and praising His name, but others simply went back into their shops again, business as usual. Who is this? The answer they received has meant more to the ages than it did to either the speakers or hearers of that day. This is Jesus, from Nazareth in Galilee.

And yet, because of the wickedness of the human heart and the frailty of the human soul, this same Jesus, in less than a week, was killed with no one to own His cause or protect His name. Before they killed Him, they called Him a blasphemer, a glutton, and a wine-bibber. They said He was crazy, had an evil spirit, and was a deceiver, a law-breaker and a tax-dodger.

They found fault because He ate with the lowly. They misquoted Him and made false reports about Him. These led to death-plotting, aggravated by every kindness He did, every good deed He performed, every soul He relieved of suffering. At last, the suffering and the sin of the World was laid on Him and in the fullness of time the King humbled Himself to the death of the cross.

How strange for a nation to kill its King instead of acclaiming Him. For never did a truer King live in all the ages. This king had done nothing worthy of death. Even Pilate protested repeatedly, "I find no crime in this man."

When Our Lord rode to Jerusalem, He knew the hour of His destiny had arrived. There would be no more throngs eager to hear the words of His teaching. No more tenderly anointed feet lovingly dried with the long hair of a grateful sinner. No more feeding 5,000 with the lunch of one small boy. No more walking on the water. That part of His life was ended.

Today we celebrate Palm Sunday. We remember the crowds, and the acclamation. Remember also that Jesus is about to lay aside His servant-king robes and accept the role of the Lamb. He rode that colt of a donkey into Jerusalem and began the week-long journey through the horror and degradation of the Cross, to the final victory, the triumphant Resurrection. And, beloved, He did it all for us.

Almighty God, Who sent His only Son to be our example, our teacher, and our Savior, give me the faithfulness not to follow the whim of the crowds around me. May my praise be genuine and unwavering, not dependent upon the opinions of those around me. Help me to realize the magnitude of the sacrifice Jesus made for me and live my life accordingly. Amen.

Monday   This is the King

Scripture Reading: Luke Chapter 22
Key Verse: "This is the King...." Luke 23:38

Our Lord Jesus Christ, as He hung upon the cruel Roman Cross, was declared King in all three of the great languages of the ancient world: the great language of religious thought, Hebrew; the language of culture, Greek; and the language of law and government, Latin, all declared Him to be King.

How descriptive, how fitting this is. Is it not true that in the religious world He is king? He is king of salvation, holiness, and love. He is the only way to truth and life. In the realm of culture is He not king? Vast treasures of art, music, literature, and philosophy belong to Him.

Is He not King in the political sphere? Empires have been born or dispersed; nations have been founded or confounded upon the name of the King, Jesus. Christ's name is traveling in ever widening circles over the earth until that hour when every knee shall bow and every tongue confess that Jesus Christ is Lord.

Now around the cross are several groups. To each group, Jesus is a King whether they think of Him as such or not. But how vastly different are their thoughts concerning Jesus. One group at the cross had already proclaimed Him and loudly so, as King. But their voices had rung with mockery.

This group, after Jesus had been scourged, took Him into the soldier's quarters so all could enjoy the spectacle. There, Roman mercenaries crowded around, to gloat over His sufferings and to turn His agony and shame into brutal mockery. They cried, "So He claims to be a king, does He? Well, we'll make Him a king." And oh the mockery that followed. An old cast off officer's coat became the robe of royal purple. They cried "A king needs a crown! A crown He shall have!" And so, some thorny briars obtained in the courtyard were formed into a crudely shaped crown and pressed down upon His head.

"No king without a scepter!" So a heavy reed was thrust into His hand.

"No king without homage!" So they bent low with mockery and cried, "Hail! Hail! King of the Jews!" And taking the reed from His hand they smote Him over the head.

Then their travesty reaches its lowest depths as they covered His blessed face with their filthy spittle. Thus the Roman soldiers and their kind mocked heaven's appointed King. With cruel smiting and spitting they insulted the manhood of the Son of Man. With mocking worship they blasphemed the deity of the Son of God.

Oh beloved, can you see the scene in your heart? Can you feel the humiliation? Have you been hurt? Have you been humiliated? Jesus knows. Jesus understands. Jesus felt the sting of cruelty. Jesus has been a captive. He has known degradation and pain from the hands of others. He has been innocent, yet accused and punished. Have you been there? He understands.

Tomorrow let us further examine the King as He suffered and went to the cross, remembering that it does not end there. No, dear one, that is not the end of the story of our King. This week of remembrance ends in victory, and He has assured us that our life will also end in victory, because of Him.

Lord God, thank You for being the One I can come to, knowing that You understand the pain I've suffered. Thank You for Your comfort, Your love and Your care for me that takes me through the times of the cross but does not let me stay there. Thank You Lord, for the end of the story, the victory of the Resurrection. May it be so in the trials of my life as well. Amen.

Tuesday

This is the King II

Scripture Reading: Luke Chapter 23:1-38
Key Verse: "This is the King...." Luke 23:38

As we move forward through this Passion Week, let us consider the reactions of those around Jesus to His claims to kingship. To the religious leaders of the day, Jesus became a despised and rejected king. They had decided they did not want the kind of king Jesus had come to be.

Jesus preached repentance. What an insult! He preached a spiritual Kingdom. But no, they wanted only a visible and literal kingdom or none at all. He preached the necessity for humility and this came into violent conflict with their religious pride and self-righteousness. And their growing bitterness and hatred finally caused them to determine to kill Him.

Observe them as they reject their King and before Pilate choose Caesar instead. This was a fateful renunciation. By choosing Caesar they closed their hearts against the messianic hope of Israel. They sold out their national honor to a pagan nation and bowed to a pagan king. The people themselves chose the ones who within just a few decades would lay waste to Jerusalem.

As Jesus hung upon the cross they gloated over the sufferings of their victim. All sense of decency was gone. Unwilling to let Him die in peace, they poured out upon Him their contemptuous jeers.

They pelted Him in every tone of mockery. They cried "He saved others, Himself He cannot save. He is the King of Israel, let Him come down and we will believe Him. He trusts in God, let God deliver Him now." Thus despised, they esteemed Him not. His own people did not receive Him.

The Apostles had forsaken their Lord and had fled, leaving Him to meet His fate alone. How keenly must our Lord have felt their desertion. Peter had followed afar off, and then denied Him. The others, in fear of their own lives, had scattered. Only John was at the cross and saw His

Master die. How we are apt to shake our heads and bluster, "Not me, I would have stayed by His side, I would have fought for Him."

These were human beings just as we are. They were afraid, even after spending years at the side of the Master. They saw Him heal the sick. They watched as He stilled storms and walked on water. Yet, they were faithless in the end. With all their love for the Savior, they did not yet have the strength and power they needed. That would come later with the sending of the Holy Spirit. No, friends, let us not judge these frightened friends of Jesus. If we were there that day, we would have been as hapless and as helpless as they.

Have you failed the Master? He understands. Have you stood back when you should have stood firm? He knows. Have you fled in the face of trial when the test got difficult or frightening? Jesus understands it all. He's seen it all before.

Return to Him as Peter did. He will honor you, accept you, and trust you with His concerns. He knows our weaknesses, but does not let us stay there. He sent the Holy Spirit to give us strength, power, and victory. We are no longer victims, but overcomers through Christ and what He endured. He did it all for us.

Jesus, I know I've let you down. Like Peter, it seems as though I fail so many tests. Thank You for helping me up, forgiving me and sending me on my way with the Holy Spirit to guide me and give me the power to stand firm or go forward. I am so sorry for the rejection You endured, and so thankful for what You did for me at the cross. You paid my eternal fine with Your very life. Thank You. Amen.

Wednesday   This is the King III

Scripture Reading: Luke 23:39-55
Key Verse: "This is the King...." Luke 23:38

We have been studying Christ as King during the Passion Week. We have seen Him as an innocent King, a mocked King, a despised and rejected King, and a forsaken King. How tragic this week has been so far. It isn't until we near the Day of Resurrection that the victory begins to emerge. What appears to piteous human thought as defeat is transformed in the spiritual world into a momentous triumph.

There was a soul at the cross who even in the face of Christ's apparent defeat believed on Him as King and received Him. This story of the trusting, forgiven thief is one of the greatest examples of faith in the entire Bible. He had doubtless learned of Christ's assertions and watched His deportment as He hung beside him on the cross. He had become impressed with Christ's demeanor and the prayer made for His enemies. In that hour he felt the fear of God. We see repentance in his reproof of his comrade, "Do you not fear God?" And as always is the case when God is near, he saw his own sinfulness. He confessed that sin and in faith he acknowledged Christ as King. The crucified confessing the Crucified. He saw that Christ was King and with full assurance and faith he leaned upon the sovereign power of Christ and cried, "Lord, remember."

What it must have meant to Jesus in that hour! Forsaken by His disciples, yet suddenly recognized by this poor sinner who saw His redeeming Kingship and in faith threw himself upon Christ for mercy. What a joy it gave our Lord to assure the dying thief of salvation and take him into Paradise.

To those who saw Jesus die it was perfectly obvious. This was a picture of absolute defeat. But as we gaze from our present position across the ages to the Cross, we rejoice and thrill to hear the vibrant ring in Christ's shout of victory and triumph. "It is finished!"

Thus He expressed His gratification that He had perfectly fulfilled the covenant of redemption which He made with the Father. Having drunk the large black and bitter draught, He flung the cup away and cried, "It is finished. Into Thy hands I commit my spirit." That is the way God died. Here death became His glory and resurrection climaxed His triumph!

To believers everywhere, Christ is not only a received King, a triumphant King, but a reigning King. The seat of His Kingship is the heart of every true child of God. Each day He is bringing His Kingdom to a culmination in this world.

That day is fast dawning when He will come in full actuality as the reigning King. John saw Him coming, riding upon a white horse. Men who have rejected Him now will recognize in some way the Kingship of Christ, for to Him every knee shall bow. That mighty host of believers from every age will join their voices with those of the angels and burst forth in a mighty hymn as Heaven's King is being crowned, "Worthy is the Lamb who was slain to receive power and riches and wisdom, and strength and honor and glory and blessing!"

And how can believers do otherwise but say "Amen. Even so, come, Lord Jesus," Come quickly, for truly "This is the King."

Father God, what a treasure Easter holds, what promise and triumph! I am reminded that we Christians are to walk by faith, not sight. What seemed a defeat at Calvary was the greatest victory of the ages. Jesus had to walk through the hate and humiliation of others to save them, and me. I am so blessed to have Christ as my Lord and Savior. May I honor Him with my whole life. Amen.

Maundy Thursday   The Crucifixion of Christ

Scripture Reading: John Chapter 19
Key Verse: "Where they crucified Him." John 19:18

At the last supper, the disciples gathered around Christ as He tried to prepare them for the events of the following day. They could not understand the crisis, the miracle, that was about to occur. The scope of what happened confounds us even today.

One of the peculiarities of the Bible is its power to condense great truth into small compass. What other realms of literature take volumes to express, Scripture expresses in one terse sentence. Our text is a case in point, where John reduces the greatest fact in history to four plain little words, "Where they crucified Him." This statement tells us simply and definitely what hundreds of books have tried to declare. Each word in this sentence glitters like a pearl upon the necklace of truth.

Where it took place was in the most spiritually privileged place in the world, Jerusalem the Holy City. Actually, Christ was crucified just outside the city wall, as He was not considered worthy to die within. Jerusalem was the temple site. This was the city that localized the presence of God. It was here that our Lord was crucified. What a contradiction! The Holiest Person dying the most unholy death in earth's most holy place.

They -both Jew and Gentile had a hand in the dark crime of the cross, and the whole world stands guilty before God. Pilate, a Gentile ruler, gave the verdict and committed Jesus to the tree and Gentile soldiers carried out the sentence. Yet here is a great mystery, that the devoutly religious leaders of a professedly holy nation were the ones who rejected Jesus, and insisted upon His death.

Crucified between two thieves: this was the most shameful punishment existing, the extreme limit of the Roman law. Do we realize the horror and shame associated with this despicable word in the Bible? The cross meant the lowest form of death. To be crucified was to be dragged out, beaten, nailed to a gibbet naked and bleeding, hung up between heaven and earth to die a bitter, lingering, painful death. No wonder the sun hid its face! No wonder the world went dark at noon-day! It was too awful a sight for creation to see the Creator dying in nakedness, shame, and anguish, and thus nature provided a robe of darkness.

Him, who is the most exalted Person ever. Jesus the Son of God, your savior, your friend, your Maker, your God was crucified guiltless and suffered in your place for your sin. He paid your penalty, and met its price, there at Calvary. All of us can understand the death of the two thieves, for on their own word they received the just reward for their deeds. But, why should Jesus, the holiest and loveliest and most divine One who ever lived among men, die such a death? And yet, in cold blood, they crucified Him. See His majesty in His prayer, "Father forgive them, they do not know what they do." And after His resurrection, He commissioned His disciples to preach. He said, "Go into all the world," but He told them to begin at Jerusalem. What love! Where these Holy people of a Holy City had crucified Him, begin there!

And, beloved, His grace is still unchanged. These four small words, "Where they crucified Him" tell the biggest story in the world.

Dear God, when I think of the part my sin shared in nailing Jesus to the cross, I feel ashamed, and unbearably sad. Yet, when I think of Christ's mercy to Jerusalem, I can see clearly that the four little words in John are the door into relationship with You. My shame and my sin are gone just as surely as Christ is no longer on that cross, or in that tomb. Praise Your Holy Name! Amen.

Good Friday   Reigning From the Tree

Scripture Reading: Psalm 96
Key Verse: "The Lord reigns." Psalm 96:10

Beloved, Jesus came as King and one of the thrones from which he ruled was not a gilded one, but the cross of Calvary. As Jesus died, His lips were opened in seven utterances, in which we have a striking witness of His sovereignty. The order of the seven cries is Christ-like. He began with His enemies and ended with Himself. All through His life it was others first and self last. Thus, Jesus died even as He lived.

First, there is sovereign grace. The first thing Jesus did when He got to the cross was to seek forgiveness for those who had placed Him on it. He interceded for pardon for His enemies in virtue of His blood now freely flowing from that tree. How kingly and kind.

Do we reign with Christ in the matter of forgiveness? What is our attitude when others wrong us? Our participation in the forgiveness of the cross demands that we forgive as He forgives.

Then, there is His sovereign power. "Today you shall be with me in Paradise." Such a part of the Crucifixion story is like a flower of rare beauty planted among dreary crags of agony and blood. Christ poured an overflowing reward upon the dying thief who recognized His sovereignty.

Guilt, grace, and glory were the three stages of the spiritual biography of the thief on the cross. He became the first subject of the new kingdom of grace. He was the first sinner to enter paradise washed in the blood of the Lamb. Christ died as a King indeed, seeing that He had power to open the door of eternal bliss for a believing soul to enter with Himself. And we, likewise, reign in life when we allow the Cross to fill our vision and deliver us from all self-centeredness, endeavoring to make others the sharers of His bliss.

Then there is His sovereign love. "Woman, behold your son. Behold your mother." He had already made precious gifts. To His murderers He bequeathed forgiveness. To His companion in crucifixion He gave the pleasure of paradise. Now to His mother and beloved disciple, John, He bequeaths one to another. Whatever cross we have, let us determine to manifest the kingly grace of kindness.

Christ displays a sovereign sacrifice upon the tree. None will ever be able to plumb the depth of these awful words, "My God, My God, why have You forsaken me?" Around, there was dense darkness, for the Light of the World was being extinguished. In such a dark moment He felt the terribleness of the load of human sin. But, blessed be His name, He stayed on that cross. He endured that God-forsaken experience that we might be forever saved.

Then, there was the sovereign humiliation. For twenty hours this Royal Sufferer had tasted nothing. For six hours His lovely battered form had hung upon the cross. Vinegar was offered Him but He would not touch it. He could easily have refreshed Himself and numbed the pain with the opiates of man, but He who made all the wells and rivers was smitten by a bitter raging thirst. "I thirst!" Truly He was never as kingly as when in His cry for water He revealed His humanity and humbled himself.

For us there is a two-fold thirst, a thirst for God and a thirst for souls. And all who thirst in these directions shall, unlike our suffering King, be filled.

Tomorrow, let us continue our meditation on the sovereignty of Christ on the cross.

Lord God, may I learn from Christ at His most anguished moments how to deport myself in love and reign with Him through His sacrifice. Amen.

Saturday   Reigning From the Tree II

Scripture Reading: Psalm 97
Key verse: "The Lord Reigns. . ." Psalms 97:1

Today we reach the apex of victory. Let us look at the Sovereign Provision. "It is finished." What a triumph! This is the cry of a victor in realization of His triumph. "The Son of God was manifested that He might destroy the works of the devil." The cross then was the Savior's ruddy throne upon which He stripped all hellish forces of their authority. Calvary was Satan's waterloo.

No wonder the Early Fathers spoke of the Cross as the "Finished work of Christ." It was here that Jesus voiced His victory over sin, death, hell, and the grave. It was here, that He brought to a culmination all the prophecies and sacrifices of the Old Testament. Jesus' work of expiation was a finished work. Therefore, no tears, no works, no deeds of righteousness that we may do can add to His finished salvation. Jesus paid it all.

Then, there is the Sovereign Trust. "Father, into your hands I commend my spirit." A voluntary committal and dismissal is implied by these words. Willingly He had stayed upon the cross until He had drained the dregs of the bitter cup of suffering. "Trust in God" is the whole of all things. Thus, Jesus died as He lived, committing Himself to God.

Would you like to reign in life and in death? Then commit your way to the Lord. Our cross can become a throne as we trust ourselves to God's fatherly care. Are you falling beneath your cross? Or are you a conqueror in spite of your Calvary?

The world stands in dire need of a King, one who can and will govern. That King, who 2,000 years ago reigned upon a tree, is coming to reign upon a throne. But the throne upon which He wishes to reign today is the throne of your heart and mine.

There is a day soon-coming when the nations will have one place of universal administration. (Micah 4:1) "Now it shall come to pass in the latter days that the mountain of the Lord's house shall be established on the top of the mountains and shall be exalted above the hills and peoples shall flow to it."

There will be one plan of universal immigration: (Micah 4:2) "... many nations shall come and say, 'come let us go up to the mountain of the Lord, to the House of the God of Jacob; He will teach us His ways and we shall walk in His paths. For out of Zion the Law shall go forth, and the Word of the Lord from Jerusalem."

Also, God will have one plan of universal arbitration and disarmament: (Micah 4:3) "And He shall judge between many peoples and rebuke strong nations afar off; they shall beat their swords into plowshares, and their spears into pruning hooks. Nation shall not lift up sword against nation; neither shall they learn war anymore."

And then there will be one plan for universal cultivation: (Micah 4:4) "But everyone shall sit under his vine and under his fig tree and no one shall make them afraid."

Finally, we will have a time of universal adoration: (Micah 4: 5, 7) "...But we will walk in the name of the Lord our God forever and ever... So the Lord will reign over them in Mount Zion...forever."

Yes, Beloved, He reigned from the tree, that He might reign from the throne. How great and Holy and magnificent is Our King.

Dearest Lord, I live in such a thrilling time. The curtains of the future are beginning to open and soon we will see these prophecies fulfilled, as were all the prophecies fulfilled regarding your crucifixion. Thank You for the sacrifice You made for me. You are the King of my life. Amen.

Easter Sunday — He is Not Here

Scripture Reading: Mark Chapter 16
Key Verse: "Do not be alarmed. You seek Jesus of Nazareth, who was crucified. He is risen! He is not here." Mark 16:6

These are words that thrill with the deathless joy of Easter! They speak home to our deepest longings, and to our highest and holiest hopes. And what kind of victory is this we celebrate today?

There are some victories so temporary and so trifling that to win them is of little consequence. They are temporary. They do not last. They fail to satisfy beyond a brief season. After the First World War, the Allies shouted of their victory after the signing of the Armistice. But what an unsatisfactory victory it proved to be. From the vantage point of a few years, we can see that it had in it far more of sorrow than of joy, more of war than of peace, and more of death than of life. This is the case with so many earthly victories.

And there are some victories that mean something to a very few, but to the many mean nothing at all. A young man in Birmingham recently won a prize of $10,000 by writing 50 words on a product. The victory was his, and of course it brought him great gladness. His friends, naturally, rejoiced with him. But to the multitude, his victory meant nothing at all.

But, the victory we celebrate today is for all of us, and it abides for all time and eternity. It is an all-inclusive victory. It includes the conquest of every foe that we are called upon to face, victory over sin, victory over fear, victory over death, and victory over the grave.

Yes, we have victory over sin. We are dead to sin in the death, burial, and resurrection of Jesus. "As many of us as were baptized into Christ Jesus were baptized into His death...just as Christ was raised from the dead by the glory of the Father, even so we also should walk in newness of life." Even now as we abide in Him and through Him and He lives in us, in Jesus Christ we have victory over every sin.

We also have victory over every fear. The fact is clear that with all classes of people, fear is an awful reality. People have fears for themselves and for others. They have fear of the future, and fears from the past. People fear sickness, death, poverty, and the unknown. Well, today we shout the victory over fear! For Jesus, in His resurrected power says to every one of us, "Do not be afraid!" Be not afraid of life, He says, for I am the way, the truth and the life. Trust me. Be not afraid of death, for "I was dead but behold I am alive forevermore." The enemy death is destroyed. "O death, where is thy sting? O Grave, where is thy victory? But thanks be to God, who gives us the victory through our Lord Jesus Christ."

Not only does Jesus bid us not to be afraid of life or of death but He also bids us to be unafraid of eternity. In the Christ-emptied tomb, the soul finds its needs supplied, its longings met, and its questions answered. The empty tomb is the gateway to the glory of the Christian's eternity, to the glory of undimmed vision and understanding, to the glory of heavenly fellowship. When we understand the victory Christ has won at Calvary and revealed in the emptied tomb, it will put a song of gratitude in our heart that nothing can hush. When we grasp this marvelous truth, we will face the future with confidence and calm expectancy. Praise God, the victory is won through Christ Jesus!

Oh precious Jesus, I lift my face to the heavens and lift my heart to You. Praise Your Name for taking my place on Calvary, and for leading the way through death to eternity. The thought of Your great love is overwhelming. "Thank You" seems so small, when what I feel is so big. Amen.

Classic Christianity
A Year of Timeless Devotions

SPRING
Daily Devotions for April, May, and June

Based on the Writings of
The Reverend L.A. Meade

Revised and Edited by
Patricia Ediger and Cara Shelton

The Reverend L.A. Meade stands at the pulpit.

Sunday Afternoon Meeting at Dallas, Oregon, 1930.

At fifteen, Lawrence Meade left his home in Brockville, Ontario to head to the big city of Toronto. As the youngest son in a family of Baptist ministers, Lawrence knew the sacrifices of ministry, but he also knew that the call of God on his heart was not to be denied.

At McMaster University in Toronto, Lawrence met the great missionary Dr. John Clough and other noted missionaries and evangelists, including Dr. Biederwolf of Scotland. These men inspired the young seminarian to consider missions work. But L.A. felt a call to a different field. He looked across the vastness of the United States and found his pastorate.

After graduating from McMaster, L.A. did evangelistic work for three years, working with the great evangelists of his day. Then, he accepted his very first pastorate, in a fine farming section of Michigan known as Grand Ledge. In the four and a half years he was pastor there, he was known for his ability in conducting praise services, and in teaching, and for his emphasis on missions. But, evangelism was still his forte. His soul ached to see other souls saved.

During his pastorate, Rev. Meade conducted evangelistic campaigns in and around Michigan. Clearly, his gifting was evangelism, and it soon became apparent that God had plans outside of Grand Ledge for Lawrence.

For the next twenty years he traveled from state to state, spending two to four weeks in each location. The Meade Brothers Evangelists became known for L.A.'s preaching, for Harold's piano, for the children's services they held and their unflagging dedication to God's Word. From Michigan to Florida, from North Carolina to California, they toted their tent, twenty-two hundred folding chairs, and a piano. Motivated by the goal of seeing the lost saved, and the saved fulfilling God's plan for their lives, L.A. preached wherever God opened a door in a community. He was our "Papa," and we gladly share these words in the hope that Papa's words may yet be used to glorify God, and continue to fulfill the mission he was given so many years ago.

April 1   Needed: Warmed Hearts

Scripture Reading: Jeremiah Chapter 20

Key Verses: "...But His word was in my heart like a burning fire shut up in my bones; I was weary of holding it back, and I could not." Jeremiah 20:9

"Did not our heart burn within us while He talked with us on the road, and while He opened the Scriptures to us?" Luke 24:32

If you study American History, you will read about the "Great Awakening" and the "Second Great Awakening" in the previous centuries. Our forefathers knew what we have forgotten: that Christianity is more than reason and intellect. It is fundamentally a great love for our Savior. Yes, the heart of true religion is holy affection. How is your heart? Is it cold, or warmed? This old world is in a sad way, and lately it has plenty of hotheads. But the solution to our world's problems lies not with hotheads, but with hot-hearts.

In the first key verse, Jeremiah is ready to quit preaching. He even tried to quit, but just couldn't. Instead, he developed a bone-fire from the Word of God. Jeremiah had a holy fever; he was a man of God with a burning heart. The other text brings us to the Emmaus disciples after the days of the crucifixion in Jerusalem. They were trudging along a country road, suffering a terrible letdown both in body and spirit when the Lord caught up with them. Now, they were right in their facts. As they said, "This is the third day." But, they were wrong in their conclusions, for since it was the third day, they should have been expecting to see the risen Lord around any bend of the road. Even when the Lord did appear, they did not see. But when He expounded the Scriptures, they developed a burning in their hearts that turned them into radiant witnesses.

How do we obtain a burning heart? Well, first we need to realize that God has provided each of us with a holy fire—the Holy Spirit. This is the fire that Paul urged Timothy to stir up within himself. Every believer has the Holy Spirit, and we must wait on God in the Word, and through prayer for a stirring up of our spirit by His. Jeremiah confirms it was God's Word that warmed his heart, and it was Jesus expounding the Scriptures to the disciples that warmed their hearts as well.

Oh, there are things that can nearly smother the fire. Willful sin will do it. Neglect, too, will dampen the fire. Fear will choke the fire. But these are not of God. God does not give us a spirit of fear, but of power and of love and of a sound mind.

God hasten the day when we look into the blessed face of our Savior, as the Holy Spirit reveals Him through the Word, and when the Holy Spirit vitalizes our prayer life. True prayer is never independent of the Holy Spirit because whenever we pray to God, the Trinity is present. The Father hears, the Son advocates His cause at the Father's right hand, and the Holy Spirit intercedes for us. Prayer brings us into dynamic cooperation with God and His omnipotence.

When we immerse ourselves in His Word and pray earnestly, reverently, and systematically, our hearts will cease to be cold, lifeless, and powerless. Prayer deepens our love, expands our sympathies, and directs our desires God-ward. And His Word opens the shutters of our lives and lets in the light of God.

Dear Father God, I wait before you in expectancy. Please stoke the fire of Your Spirit within me. Draw me nearer to You as I read Your Word. And Lord, let the fire within me rage into flames that catch in the hearts of those around me. Let Your love and Your light permeate and characterize me, I pray in Christ's name, amen.

April 2   God of Those Who Fall

Scripture Reading: Psalm 145
Key Verse: "The Lord upholds all who fall, and raises up all who are bowed down." Psalm 145:14

The God of the Bible is an available God. The Bible is a book of love and sympathy; it is like a mother's bosom to lay one's head upon in time of distress or pain. Its pages teem with cheer for those who are discouraged. It set its lamps of hope to shine in darkened chambers. Its hands reach out to help the fainting and the fallen. It is full of comfort for those in sorrow, and full of special promises for those in need.

Yes, God, as revealed in the Bible, has a partiality of kindness for those who are weak and needy. As a mother pays special attention to the sickly child, so with God. How little the world cares about the broken hearted. The world is selfish and callous. Men break hearts by their cruelty, injustice, and coldness. But God cares. The Lord is near. The Great Physician heals the broken hearted and binds up their wounds. And who is there among us to whom this precious truth brings no comfort? Haven't we all failed? Haven't we all been weak, or in sorrow, discouraged or frightened? This Psalm brings to us a God who loves, who cares, and who saves.

A noted writer has said that so long as there are tears and sorrow in the world the Bible will be considered authoritative for the simple reason that the words of the Bible bring balm to the hearts of humanity when every other remedy fails. Take heart, my friend. Look to Him.

Perhaps you have aspired to something, and the hope has been taken from you. It is oftimes at the cost of worldly success that we can reach spiritual beauty. Michelangelo once said of the fragments of marble flying thick on the floor beneath the blows of the mallet, that while the marble wastes the image grows. So, too, we can often say as God cuts away the externals of our life. While the outward wastes, the spiritual shines out in greater and greater beauty. In your failure and losses remember, they do not drive God from you, but draw Him nearer and nearer to you. "The Lord upholds all who fall and raises up all who are bowed down." That is God's part.

Your part? Oh, that is found in Psalm 121:1-2, "I will lift up my eyes to the hills - from whence comes my help? My help comes from the Lord, Who made heaven and earth." Israel used this song of ascent as they marched up unto Mt. Zion to meet and worship God. And, it is good advice, isn't it? Look up! Don't look around, not down or back, but look up. Oh, if you want to be distracted look around. If you want to be miserable look within, but if you want to be helped? Look up! The hills of Scripture seem to always speak of God in His dealings with man. Mt. Sinai reminds us of God who spoke by law. Mt. Zion shows us God who deals with us through love. Mt. Hermon speaks of God's glory and Mt. Ararat of refuge. Mt. Calvary, of course, is a monument to God's forgiveness. So look up unto the hills. The hills speak of the reality and glory of God. How we ought to appreciate the hills as they stand above the fog and mists and swamps. So God would be for you - above the mists of this world. Mountains represent strength and peace. God is your strength and peace.

So, today, you do your part in looking to God for help in your need. We can assuredly trust our dear, caring Father to do the rest.

Thank You, my God, Oh, Thank You. It is such a blessed peace to know that You care about the needs and problems of my life. I leave my worries with You, today, Lord, and I look to You for help for I know You care. I trust You, Lord, and submit my heart and soul to the Great Physician's care. Amen.

April 3 — Blood Marked

Scripture Reading: Exodus Chapter 12
Key Verse: "...And when I see the blood, I will pass over you..."
Exodus 12:13

George Henry Stuart, President of the Christian Commission during World War I, was passing through a camp; he could not give the password when challenged. The sentry said, "It is my duty to shoot you dead, Mr. Stuart, but I know who you are. Go to the General's quarters and get the right password." Soon, Stuart returned with the right word, and was allowed to pass. "Now," he said to the soldier, "You were anxious that I should know the password. Have you the right password for eternity?" "Yes, sir," the soldier replied, "the blood of Jesus Christ His Son cleanses us from sin." You see, he knew what the bloodmark was.

We think of that most memorable night in all of Israel's history, that night in Egypt when every Israelite home was to be blood-marked. The spotless lamb was to be killed, the blood caught in a basin and then, with a branch of hyssop, the blood sprinkled on both door posts and the lintel. Because the door was blood-marked, the death angel did not bring death to that home, he passed over, and all were safe. Terrible must have been that hour when the death angel passed through Egypt.

The blood of Christ both shelters and separates. The precious blood of Christ forms the base of that platform on which a just God and a justified sinner meet in sweet communion.

That long-ago night in Egypt, the blood was not left in the basin, but was applied to the doorposts. So must Christ's blood be, by your faith, applied to your soul. The law demanded obedience, or death. Jesus gave both obedience for Himself and death for you and me. He kept and fulfilled the law and died for the lawbreaker. He gave Himself for us, life for life.

In spiritual redemption, your soul is brought into a position of freedom from the penal consequences of sin. The purchasing power of this redemption is the blood of Christ. "Without shedding of blood there is no remission," Hebrews 9:22 tells us.

Near midnight on July 31, 1838, the evangelist William Knibb gathered together 10,000 slaves on the Island of Jamaica for a praise meeting and for the news of the Emancipation Act which was then to take effect. An immense coffin was built and filled with whips, branding irons, handcuffs, fetters, slave garments, and other memorials belonging to that horrid system. At the first stroke of the midnight bell, Knibb shouted, "The monster is dying." At the twelfth stroke, he cried, "The monster is dead. Let's bury him!" Then, they screwed down the coffin lid, lowered it into a deep grave, and covered it up, thus burying out of sight, in this ceremonious way, the very things which so long had made human lives a hard, painful bondage. That night, the ten thousand liberated slaves shouted themselves hoarse with the joy of freedom.

Oh, dear one, do you see that your great Emancipator, the Lord Jesus Christ, by the price of His blood, has obtained your freedom and buried your enslaving sins in His own grave? By believing in Him, you apply his blood to the sin-stained doorposts of your life. You faith has set you free in Him. He has snapped the bonds of sin slavery and you are free!

Praise Your Holy Name, Lord Jesus! Praise You for Your holiness, and Your willingness to die for unholy man. Praise You for being my Emancipator, and for taking the stripes for my enslaving sin. Praise You for setting me free from the power and the punishment of sin. Thank You, Lord. Amen.

April 4   Simon the Cross-Bearer

Scripture Reading: Mark 15:16-41

Key Verse: "Then they compelled a certain man, Simon a Cyrenian, the father of Alexander and Rufus, as he was coming out of the country and passing by, to bear His cross." Mark 15:21

If the city of Cyrene is immortal, it is because this Simon, a Jew by descent, a black man by color, was compelled by the stern authorities and ironhanded power of the Roman soldiers to turn aside from his duties, his plans and his routine, and get under the load of another. He was rudely and roughly compelled to assume his humiliating task and carry out this service.

We can well imagine the heat of his indignation and resentment when these rough soldiers manhandled him and this accursed instrument of a barbarous and shameful death was thrust upon his shoulders. No doubt he had come to Jerusalem for the Passover. He wanted only to be left to his worship and private life. Yet, he was gradually touched into some kind of sympathy as he carried the cross and watched this man die. At last yielding to the soul-conquering power of Christ, the hated compulsion blossomed into a joy forever and a glorious privilege. By the time Mark wrote this story, Simon and his two sons were members of the Church and Paul states also in Romans that Rufus and Mrs. Simon were "chosen in the Lord."

I think that in one way or another we all find ourselves, sooner or later, in the grip of some irking compulsion against which we are disposed to rebel. Life itself drafts us for a disagreeable service or brings us face to face with some grim necessity or inescapable burden. We are going our way, attending to our own affairs, when an arresting hand is laid upon us and we find ourselves thrown out of our course, our plans broken and altered.

We might also apply this thought to life's sufferings and sorrows. I am not concerned with that suffering which is avoidable and unnecessary which we bring on ourselves, but rather with that suffering and sorrow that comes to us as one of life's compulsions. We are not responsible for it. It is not the harvest of any seed we have sown. It was flung upon us by providence or somebody else's mistake, stupidity, or sin.

That cross Simon was compelled to bear was not his own, was not intended for him, and was not chosen by him. Neither was it Christ's. It didn't belong to Him. He didn't deserve it. But Christ accepted it, took it upon Himself, used it in His redeeming purpose, and so gave it value His enemies had never dreamed of.

Even so it may be with your cross today. You were going your way, carefree and joyous until invisible hands arrested you and laid some irresistible burden of pain or some suffering cross upon you. It is all so meaningless, so unjust, so unexplainable, and you have been going your way bearing this burden, struggling under the load of disappointment and loss.

But this is the thing that supremely matters. What is your attitude? It is easy to parade down the street when the crowd is crying, "Hosanna!" But it is a harder thing to do when the mob is crying, "Crucify, crucify!" Take your end of the cross and carry it - with purpose and with love.

Almighty Father, I see that Simon was touched by the presence of Christ. That presence turned a wretched burden into a blessing. I surrender my unwanted burdens and sorrows, disappointments and sufferings to You. Please transform them into blessings. Amen.

April 5   Four Ups in the Life of Christ

Scripture Reading: Luke 2:22-40
Key Verse: "He took Him up in his arms and blessed God..." Luke 2:28

Many times a blessed Bible study is hidden in just one word. To illustrate, let us consider the two-lettered word "up" as it relates to the life of Christ. I want to call your attention to four different passages of scripture in the New Testament in which this word is found. In each case it brings forth some outstanding truth about our wonderful savior.

First, a rewarded saint took Him up. When the aged Simeon took the Christ-child into his arms the action concluded three facts. First, a realization of His incarnation, for Simeon had been promised by God that he would not see death until he had seen the Christ. Secondly, knowledge of salvation, for Simeon said, "For my eyes have seen Your salvation." Therefore in Christ alone is there salvation. That salvation is a person, not a creed, or a church. Finally, an assurance of destination, when the words "now You are letting Your servant depart in peace," spoken by Simeon show how mankind is benefited by salvation. Having taken the Christ-child into his embrace, he was ready to depart in peace. He was assured that all was well for eternity.

Secondly, a rebellious people lifted Him up. "And as Moses lifted up the serpent in the wilderness, even so must the Son of Man be lifted up." This refers to the lifting up of the body of Christ upon the cross in sacrificial atonement for sin. It was necessary for Him to be lifted up for our reconciliation to God, for our forgiveness, and for our eternal redemption.

Thirdly, a righteous God raised Him up. Acts 2:24 tells us "Whom God raised up, having loosed the pains of death." Why did God raise Him up? He raised Him up as a vindication of His sonship. Jesus claimed again and again to be the Son of God. It infuriated His enemies and because of it He was crucified. Now God raised Him to vindicate

His claims, also, as the acceptance of His sacrificial death and a pledge for a future life.

Lastly, a rejoicing Father carried Him up. Luke 24:51 says, "...while He blessed them He was parted from them and carried up into heaven." This happened while He was giving His farewell benediction. It was a redemptive blessing and a blessing in which we share today as part of that church of which they were the nucleus. And we read, "They worshiped Him and returned to Jerusalem with great joy, and were continually in the temple praising and blessing God." That is what the blessing of God does for men.

So, we see four great "ups." A rewarded saint took Him up, implying His incarnation. A rebellious people lifted Him up, giving us a glimpse of the crucifixion. A righteous God raised Him up, relating the story of His resurrection. And a rejoicing Father carried Him up. This speaks of His Ascension.

We, as God's people, are urged to "look up," and "be lifted up." We are raised up together and someday soon we expect to be caught up to meet the Lord in the air. See how much this tiny word has taught us today?

Father in Heaven, even the psalmist tells us to lift up our eyes to the hills from whence comes our strength. Thank You for this small word that has shown us the full story of Your life. Now help us to manifest these truths through our lives that many may know You as the Savior and Lord. Today in my work, my play, and my relationships help me to look only to You, that I might disappear and only You remain. In the precious, holy name of Jesus Christ, amen.

April 6   What to do With Life's Burdens

Scripture Reading: Galatians 6:1-5

Key Verses: "For each one shall bear his own load."
Galatians 6:5

"Bear one another's burdens, and so fulfill the law of Christ." Galatians 6:2

"Cast your burden on the Lord, and He shall sustain you." Psalm 55:22

Many burdens may be seen, but the deepest and heaviest cannot be. If we knew what fierce battles are being fought in the hearts and lives around us, the burdens people carry, it would teach us lessons of restraint and charity and contentment beyond any we have ever known.

The Bible has three points to make about burdens. Read our key verses. First, notice that our burdens are non-transferable. "For each one shall bear his own load." Every life is separate and different from every other life. To a remarkable degree every life is lived alone. Born into this world alone, we leave it alone. No man can perform your life and duty for you. Nobody can repent of sin for you, nobody can believe in Christ for you, and nobody can answer at judgment for you. We must each one give an account of Himself to God. God sees you as an individual. Whether or not others do right or not, you must. Whether others stay true or not, you must.

Yet the grace of God offers help with our heavy burdens through the ministry of the saints. "Bear one another's burdens and so fulfill the law of Christ." This means, our burdens are community property in the family of God. We are to share our burdens and others are to share their burdens with us.

The third word is the best, "Cast your burden on the Lord; and He shall sustain you." Who of us have not at some point felt like fleeing, giving up when our burdens are too heavy to bear? But that would not help, for you have your burdens yet.

How will He sustain us when we give our burdens to Him? One of two ways, He will either take it away, or come with divine reinforcement to help us bear that burden and be the victor. Paul prayed three times for the "thorn" to be removed. It was not removed, but God told him that He was sufficient for him. God helped Paul to bear the burden and proceed.

There was a father in yonder city, with a flaxen-haired daughter of five summers. His wife died suddenly of a short illness. The little girl was nearly inconsolable, crying for her mother. He petted and soothed, but finally out of exhaustion and sorrow for him she grew silent. In darkness, the man looked through the darkness to God. "I trust you Lord, but, oh, it's dark as midnight." The girl started to sob again. Papa said, "I thought you were asleep." "Papa, did you know it could be so dark? I can't even see you. But Papa, you love me even if it is so dark, don't you? You love me even if I can't see you, don't you?" He pulled her against his heart and rocked her until the little thing went to sleep. Then he took the child's unbearable cry to himself and passed it up to God. "Father, it is as dark as midnight. I cannot see at all. But you love me if it is dark, don't you? I will trust you even in the darkest hour." God always comes to those who trust Him.

Turn your burden over to the One who cares for you. Trust in Him. Believe in Him. Rest in Him.

Lord God, Thank You for Your invitation to cast my cares upon You. They are too heavy for me and I don't see the answer right now, but I know that You are strong enough to carry my burdens or carry me through them. I do rest in You. Amen.

April 7   Even so Come Lord Jesus

Scripture Reading: Titus Chapter 2

Key Verses: "For the grace of God that brings salvation has appeared to all men, teaching us that denying ungodliness and worldly lusts, we should live soberly, righteously, and godly in the present age, looking for the blessed hope and glorious appearing of our great God and Savior Jesus Christ." Titus 2:11-13

    This glorious hope and important doctrine was the mainstay and inspiration of the early church. Their zeal for Christ, their utter fearlessness, their passion for the lost, and their desire for holiness were all inspired by the hope of the soon return of Christ.

    It is only in the last seventy-five years that there has been a revival of the preaching, teaching, and vision of the Lord's return in the hearts of God's people. For 1500 years the teaching has been dark, forgotten, eclipsed. Today we see and feel the pulse of this blessed hope increasing and awakening God's people to a new sense of devotion and preparation for His coming.

    It is the one event most often recorded in Holy Scripture. The Holy Spirit sets it forth in type, in symbol, in plain declaration and in prophecies. In the Garden of Eden the assurance is given to the woman that her seed should bruise the serpent's head. That act takes place at the second coming of Our Lord Jesus Christ as recorded in Rev. 20, where it states He shall descend from heaven and bind Satan under His feet and with His saints reign for one thousand years.

    Enoch was caught up without dying. Why? It was a figure of the generation that will be alive at the Second Coming of the Lord and who will be caught up to meet Him. Noah and his experience is a prophecy of His Second Coming. The Lord compares the days of His coming to the days of Noah where Noah was kept safely from the flood in the ark, or in the story of Lot in Sodom where the Lord snatched him out of the doomed city just before its destruction.

    Abraham sends his trusted servant, Eliezar to get a bride for his son, Isaac. The servant finds her, shows her gifts sent from the father in the name of the son, and leads her forth to meet him. Suddenly the son comes and leads her to the place he has prepared for her. The Holy Spirit is the servant, the bride is the church and the admonition to the church is that the bridegroom cometh, go out to meet him.

Moses crosses the Red Sea, dry shod, and sings of the second coming of the Lord as a man of war. David strikes his harp and pours forth his testimony to the wonder and glory of the second coming. Isaiah sees the Lord coming with chariots of glory, Jeremiah announces that the Lord will come and make Jerusalem His throne and gather all Israel unto Him. Daniel has visions of His coming in the clouds of Heaven. Zachariah says when the Lord comes the second time His feet shall stand upon the Mount of Olives. And this is only a sampling of the Old Testament's references to the second coming.

Christ's coming for His bride is the most imminent event on the horizon of time. Between us and His appearing to set up His Kingdom there are many foretold events. But between us and the secret, sudden coming of the Lord in the air to take away His bride there is not a single predicted event. That coming may take place at any moment. "Even so, come, Lord Jesus."

Dearest Father in Heaven, I see all around me the culmination of history as the prophecies of the last days are fulfilled. It gives me a sense of expectancy, an urgency to bring my friends and family to the faith, and a desire to reject ungodliness and embrace a righteous and godly life. Amen.

April 8   The Insight and Choice of Faith

Scripture Reading: Hebrews 11:4-27

Key Verses: "By faith Moses, when he was born, was hidden three months by his parents, because they saw he was a beautiful child; and they were not afraid of the king's command. By faith Moses, when he became of age, refused to be called the son of Pharaoh's daughter, choosing rather to suffer affliction with the people of God than to enjoy the passing pleasures of sin, esteeming the reproach of Christ greater riches than the treasures in Egypt; for he looked to the reward. By faith he forsook Egypt, not fearing the wrath of the king; for he endured as seeing Him who is invisible." Hebrews 11:23-27

    The outstanding character trait of Jochebed, Moses's mother, was faith. It was the force that drove her in the face of danger. The thing that accounts for all her daring deeds was faith. Faith gave her insight and that insight took God at His word to see a waving harvest field before the grain is planted, to see the man in the child.

    Jochebed's courage first showed itself in hiding the baby. Faith disobeys as well as obeys. Faith has insight, is courageous and ingenious. She built a boat, and what a boat. Few boats have made such history as did this tiny craft, launched with no pompous ceremony, probably in the dead of night.

    Faith not only enabled her to do a heroic daring deed but that faith gave her energy to carry on for years. Through long nights and days she watched and prayed. She shaped Moses's character and gave him a sense of values that later gave him power to make the choices which shaped history.

    Yes, our choices are determined by our faith and Moses had before him two ways. In choosing one, he gave up the other. He gave up the honor of being the son of Pharaoh's daughter. This meant he gave up the throne. Moses also gave up the treasures of Egypt. One only has to recall the treasures unearthed in King Tut's tomb to glimpse the wealth Moses chose to forsake. Furthermore, he gave up the good will of the king. His faith caused him to have no fear of the wrath of the monarch.

The other path, which Moses chose, identified him with a race of slaves. He did not choose affliction instead of pleasure. He chose right instead of wrong.

And then his faith caused him to endure. He endured himself and his tempestuous nature. He endured murmuring, ungrateful people and life with its reverses. To endure is very hard. Faith makes it possible.

Moses's choice was a voluntary one. He was forty years old when he made it. It was a permanent choice. We can endure for a brief season when we know the pain will soon end. We can bear to have a tooth extracted when we think of the comfort that will be ours later on. But Moses made his choice for all time. He could in no sense ever return to the privilege and luxuries of Egypt. His choice was the choice of a person. He saw One who was invisible and this invisible One became the source of all the springs of his activities and aspirations.

Oh that you and I would fix our eyes of faith upon Jesus this day and by doing so would have insight and courage and endurance to choose right from wrong as Moses did and follow God forever.

Father God, all that Moses went through really does come down to faith. He did not choose the easy, he chose the right. Thank You for the gift of faith that enables me to choose wisely too. Please help me to put it to eternal use. Amen.

April 9   I Saw the Lord

Scripture Reading: Psalm 46

Key Verses: "In the year that King Uzziah died, I saw the Lord sitting on a throne, high and lifted up, and the train of His robe filled the temple. Above it stood seraphim; each one had six wings; with two he covered his face, with two he covered his feet, and with two he flew." Isa. 6:1-2

In the sixth chapter of Isaiah, we read the prophet Isaiah's encounter with God in which seraphim appear, "each one having six wings." We are told, also, that "with two he covered his face" as the majestic angel reacted to the appearance of the Lord. This position of the seraphim is a picture of reverence. And this picture of the seraphim in the sixth chapter of Isaiah is the only glimpse we get of these creatures in all of Scripture.

Yet, though they are only mentioned briefly, we get an impression of strength and honor when we read of the seraphim. Reverence is a sign of strength, just as irreverence is a sure sign of weakness. No man can sneer at sacred things and retain nobility of character. The token of man's highest nature lies not in his ability to comprehend everything, but in his ability to feel there are many things he cannot comprehend, and to bow in reverence to the presence of true wisdom. In Psalm 46:10, we read, "Be still, and know that I am God." Reverence, you see, leads to revelation.

Next we find that "With two he covered his feet." The idea is that the seraphim hid behind the wings that carry him forward. This is the very picture of humility. "I believe," said Ruskin, "the first test of a truly great man is humility." We see that being near to the Lord did not puff up these beings, but rather they were humble in the glory of His presence.

The story has been told that in the old castle of Edinburgh, the way to the crown jewels leads through a very low door, and the visitor who wishes to see these treasures is compelled to stoop in order to pass through the doorway into the passage to the jewel room. Just so, the one who wishes to find his or her way to the place where God keeps His jewels must first pass through a low doorway called humility. In James we read, "Humble yourselves in the sight of the Lord, and He will lift you up." And it was Augustine who declared, "It was pride that changed angels into devils; it is humility that makes men as angels."

So, with the first pair of wings the seraphim covered his face, suggesting reverence. And with the second pair, he covered his feet suggesting humility. Now, we see that with the third pair of wings, "he flew."

In that statement, we find the idea of active service. We are, after all, to be about the business of God. And so, in those who spend their time closest to the physical presence of God, we find reverence, humility and service represented. Isn't that life's message to us every morning when we awake? Each day we should come before God to serve Him with reverence and humility.

As we have seen the reaction of the seraphim to the presence of the Lord, tomorrow let us examine the reaction of Isaiah to this vision of majesty and greatness. For what effect such a revelation must cause in the heart of man! "Be still, and know that I am God." Amen.

Dear Holy God, I come before You in humility of spirit, realizing that all I am and all I do is only from You. I need a truer picture of Your holiness, Your power, Your mighty love for us. Help me to appreciate Your nature, so that I may understand what it is to reverence You in my daily life. Thank You, dear Father. Amen.

April 10　　　　　　　　　　　　　　　　　　　Vision

Scripture Reading: Isaiah Chapter 6:1-9

Key Verse: "So I said: 'Woe is me, for I am undone! Because I am a man of unclean lips, and I dwell in the midst of a people of unclean lips; for my eyes have seen the King, the Lord of hosts.'" Isaiah 6:5

As we look again today at the marvelous vision of Isaiah, we must remember that sorrow is a great sanctifier. To the teachable man, suffering and sorrow, distress and disaster, the loss of all things temporal become, through the grace of God, the dawning of the real and the eternal. In Moses's life, it was in an hour of great sorrow and trial he had his eyes opened to the glory of God. This was true also in the lives of John, Job, Paul, and others. History proves this to hold true also in the lives of nations. Think of Israel's history. Only at a time of great crisis, despair, or want did she realize her need of God and seek His divine guidance and fellowship.

It is evident as we study the life of Isaiah, that up to this hour he had been but a nominal prophet, with little success, in the midst of a wicked and sinful people. It is also probable that the worldly life of his friend King Uzziah caused a sense of apathy to settle upon Isaiah. But suddenly the divine hand of judgment is manifest as Uzziah is smitten with leprosy and dies. It is an hour of self-examination and a time of meditation before the Lord.

God, in a great vision, reveals Himself to Isaiah in new and unending glory. This vision was pregnant with power, and so suggestive of might that the very posts of the "temple doors" moved at the voice that cried. It was so majestic that the beautiful temple could scarcely contain the robes of God's glory. Israel's throne may be empty upon Uzziah's death, but heaven's throne is not. God is there. It is a revelation of the God of Israel as an everliving and everlasting God. In the midst of chaos and despair, our God remains. The throne speaks of rulership and kingship, and its position shows that God is above all competition or contradiction of man.

Seraphim and cherubim were in the act of worship and praise, and yet He who is worshipped by all the heavenly host and by all creation condescended to reveal Himself as the God of Isaiah. This God, maker of heaven and earth, by whom all things were made and through whom all things continue, revealed Himself by a vision to His prophet. What a revelation!

And it is this vision of His holiness, His majesty, and His splendor that we need today. The wisest man of all time, Solomon of old, said, "Where there is no vision, the people perish." Why is it that our society today seems to trust in our scientific achievements and, filled with pride, we attempt to supplant the majesty of heaven with the dignity of earth? Why is it that our tendency is to minimize God and to exalt man?

Now, note that when Isaiah saw the Lord, he finally saw himself. He is immediately smitten with a sense of his own sin and humbled by an understanding of his own feebleness and folly. The loss of the sense of sin, you see, is preceded by the loss of the vision of God. Thus, the world's lack of communion with God actually explains our society's callousness to sin. As Isaiah found, it is only through confession, brought about by communion with God, that cleansing is received.

We need nothing as much today as we need to catch a vision of our great and holy God, ruling in sovereign power and majesty upon the throne of the universe.

Holy God, I come before You hungry for Your presence. I am anxious to sharpen and focus my vision of You. I long for a clearer understanding of Your holiness, Your sovereignty, and Your majesty. I wait, now, Lord, on You. Amen.

April 11 — Lift Up

Scripture Reading: John Chapter 4

Key Verse: "Do you not say 'There are still four months and then comes the harvest?' Behold, I say to you, lift up your eyes and look at the fields, for they are already white for harvest! And he who reaps receives wages..." John 4:35

This encounter is a study in soul-winning philosophy, but it is also a dramatic personal challenge to each one of us who claim Christ. One cannot read this chapter prayerfully and continue in lethargy and laziness. There are three great and imperative commands within this story, that apply to you and me in our day of history as much or more as any other time in the past.

First, "Lift up your eyes and look." The Christian church has been afflicted at times, it seems, with spiritual blindness. We need to have God remove those cataracts and straighten up our posture so that we can stand erect before the world and see. We are God's ambassadors to a needy world, and an ambassador is one who represents his government in a foreign country. He is a man with a mission. We need to realize the sacredness of our calling, and lift our sights upon this needy world of ours. We need to ask God to open our spiritual eyes; for without a vision we will never see the need.

The second command within this passage seems to be calling us to lift up our hearts and pray. We need to lift up our hearts and pray because without prayer our hearts will be self-satisfied and content to go along in the even tenure of our way, serving the Lord in our own strength. We need to pray because Satan is doing all that he can to disappoint and defeat us. And we need to pray because of the awful spirit of egotism that Satan sends. We can be so proud and high-minded, and conceited. But, above all, we need to pray for a passion for souls.

Our lack of concern is a thing to be mortally ashamed of. Remember that the disciples walked right by the woman of Samaria, more concerned over their stomachs than her soul. Jesus saw her, and saw her not just as a woman of the streets, but He saw a redeemed soul.

Finally, this passage urges us to lift up our feet and go. Someone has said, "You can tell a man by the way he walks." That was a beautiful walk that Enoch had, about which the Scriptures say, "And Enoch walked with God." It was a helpful walk that Peter and John had, when we read in Acts that they walked by the temple Beautiful and stopped to heal a lame man. Yes, we must tarry for power in prayer, but we must put feet to our prayers for the harvest is ripe. And we must tarry in prayer until, as we go out to the harvest fields, the people will say of us as they said of the disciples of old, "These men have been with Jesus." Lift up your feet and go, because the time is short, so short. We need to be going—now! Are we making the effort we should to tell other about Christ?

Oh, that God would help us today to get our eyes upon Jesus and stand in the shadow of the cross! And with heaven as our destination, and the world and its pleasure behind our back, lift up our eyes and look, lift up our hearts and pray, and then lift up our feet and go!

Dear Heavenly Father, please touch my spiritual eyes that I might see others as You see them! Help me to see not only the multitude, but help me see the individual souls dying for lack of Jesus. Show me the fields around my home as white unto harvest. Let me show the love of Jesus to those who so desperately need Him today. Amen.

April 12   For Such a Time

Scripture Reading: Esther Chapter 4

Key Verse: "...Who knows whether you have come to the Kingdom for such a time as this?" Esther 4:14

The book of Esther is more fascinating than fiction, yet no divine name appears in it. God's name is hidden because of Israel's sin, yet His overriding providence is evident.

In this desperate and challenging situation, Mordecai confronts his niece Esther with the question of our text, "Who knows whether you have come to the Kingdom for such a time as this?" For every crisis, God has His man or woman on the scene. What a time of anguish confronted the Jews in Esther's day! The decree had gone forth to destroy all the Jews throughout the world. Cruel Haman was willing to do almost anything to be rid of them, with King Ahasuarus unknowingly going along. Mordecai cried with a loud and bitter cry, while Esther and her maiden fasted. And think of what lay in the balance, emancipation, or extermination of the entire race.

Yes, if Haman had succeeded in his diabolical scheme, all the blessing and covenants to Israel would have failed, and the race which was to produce the savior would have been destroyed. The eternal destiny of unborn millions waited upon the success or defeat of Haman's plot. God intervened. It was no accident that Esther had come to the Kingdom for such a time. Was she equal to the occasion?

What emotions must have stirred the heart of Esther as she received the appeal of Mordecai. To learn that she was the nation's hope of escape from complete extermination must have roused her to the depths of her noble being. But, Mordecai's words, "If you remain completely silent at this time..." surely lingered in her mind and heart. So often when a great cause is in danger, one strong voice turns the tide. If that voice is silent, or utters words of unworthy compromise, the cause is lost. Esther might have acted as some of us today in a crisis. She might have maintained a cowardly silence. God pity us if we are afraid to speak in His name.

Expediency might have been another reason for silence. Esther might have argued that to imperil her own position was useless. But she knew, as we do, that expediency is man's wisdom. Followers of the Lamb cannot find it expedient to hold their peace at a time which demands a bold and uncompromising witness.

We also see Mordecai warn Esther, "Relief and deliverance will arise for the Jews from another place." Mordecai knew that Israel was a privileged nation. He also knew that if Esther failed her Lord and her people, God would send deliverance from another source.

How thrilling is the marvelous reply of this woman of faith, "I will go to the King…, and if I perish, I perish." You know the outcome. God was leading; Esther faced the challenge and by the overruling providence of God obtained favor in the King's sight.

May God raise up in our midst a body of men and women like Esther and Mordecai. Mordecais who will refuse to bow to the Hamans of our day. Mordecais who will sit at the King's gate and hold out for God. Esthers who will boldly speak in defense of God's people in spite of personal peril. The King knew Mordecai's record, and God knows our record. Put on the whole armor of God, and enter the fray.

Dear Lord, It is hard to think of the battles of my life as spiritual warfare. I want to stand for you. I understand that I may be in the place I am for such a time as this. Help me to face it wisely. Amen.

April 13   Touched

Scripture Reading: Luke Chapter 8:40-56
Key Verse: "And Jesus said, 'Who touched me?'" Luke 8:45

Here is a miracle within a miracle! Jesus was really enroute to the home of Jairus the ruler of the synagogue, whose little daughter was at the point of death. Word spread quickly that Jesus was going to the ruler's house, and soon crowds gathered and excitement ran high as a procession of people marched towards Jairus's home.

Among those who heard the news was an unfortunate woman. Since Jesus called her "daughter," she must have been a young woman, yet undoubtedly the twelve years she had suffered with this hemorrhage had taken its toll. Not only did this disease weaken her body, but it made her a social outcast in the process. If she was a married woman, she was compelled to leave her husband. She could not go up to the Temple, and the place of sacrifices. If she touched any object, or person, they were defiled. If any person touched her, that person was thereby made unclean.

Such was the sad and terrible plight of this woman. She had spent all her money in search of a cure, but none had been found. Just think of all the things you have done in the past twelve years, the places you have gone and the sights you have seen. The only experience of this poor woman during the past twelve years of her life was to see her strength wane, her health weaken, and her fortune consumed in vain efforts to be healed.

But, this day, she was on the street in the midst of the crowd, for she had heard that Jesus was on His way to heal the daughter of Jairus. Can't you imagine her, crouched against the wall, trying to make herself inconspicuous? Perhaps a neighbor had been testifying to His power. Or, perhaps she knew of Peter's mother-in-law, or the nobleman's son. A flicker of hope lights up her soul, and there she is, hoping that He might pass her way.

How many, dear friend, are there in the world today that are just like this woman? Just waiting, just hoping, they are inconspicuous and hurting. We ought to move carefully, speak gently, and act kindly, for someone there where you are passing is just waiting and hoping for a little light and life.

Summoning all her courage, she resolves to try to touch Him. She steps out through the crowd and works her way, fearful yet determined, until at length she gets close behind Jesus and in a grasping effort, she clutches the hem of His garment. Instantly, the feeling of weakness and sickness that had hounded her day and night for twelve years left. She had been healed.

Jesus told her, "Daughter, be of good cheer; your faith has made you well. Go in peace." It was not the hem of the garment that healed her, but her faith in Jesus that made her whole.

And we should note the interest Jesus took in this one individual. Despite the shortness of His ministry, and the vast truths He had to declare, He always found time for individuals. He saw Zacchaeus in the branches of the sycamore tree. He heard the shout of blind Bartimaeus outside the gate. He spent an hour with an outcast woman of Sychar, and revealed Himself to her. And, to them all, He showed that there was One deeply interested in them. Christ is still here. He passes by.

Dear Lord, I am so thankful to have You in my life. I cannot imagine the pain, the loneliness, the absolute emptiness of being without You in this world. Please help me to notice those around me who need Your touch in their lives, that I might speak a little more gently, move a bit more carefully, and act ever so kindly as I point out that You are still passing by. Amen.

April 14   Truth from the Rocks

Scripture Reading: Deuteronomy Chapter 32
Key Verse: "Of the Rock who begot you, you are unmindful, and have forgotten the God who fathered you." Deut. 32:18

Throughout the Bible, Jehovah is likened again and again to a rock, a strong solid presence with many purposes and benefits. First, rocks are used as foundations. At the close of Christ's great Sermon on the Mount, He instructed men to build their lives on the rock of His teachings as foundational, "whoever hears these sayings of Mine, and does them, I will liken him to a wise man who built his house on the rock: and the rain descended, the floods came, and the winds blew and beat on that house; and it did not fall, for it was founded on the rock."

Rocks are also sometimes used as resting places for the weary traveler, beneath which they may find a place of shade from the sun's rays. Isaiah had that picture in mind when he said, "A man will be...as the shadow of a great rock in a weary land." Of course, in Christ we do find rest for our souls, strength to undertake the journey, and protection from the enemy. How gracious that invitation, "Come to me all you who labor and are heavy laden, and I will give you rest."

How often has a weary traveler come to the rock, there to discover a spring coming forth from the rock in the side of the mountain? God said to Moses, "strike the rock, and water will come out of it, that the people may drink." In Deuteronomy, we also find that "He made him draw honey from the rock." What lesson can we draw from this picture? God does not lead His children into the wilderness except He provides for their need while there. "My God shall supply all your need according to His riches in glory by Christ Jesus." Also, the rock is seen as a sign of judgment. Christ said, "Whoever falls on this stone will be broken; but on whomever it falls, it will grind him to powder." So it is that whoever rejects Christ as their Rock of Refuge will soon discover that to them He becomes a stone of judgment. Today, Christ as a stone of judgment is passive. Those who stumble over Him and His teachings only hurt themselves. But one of these days, this stone of judgment will become active in the great and notable day of the Lord. Then that stone will fall on the rejecters of Christ and ruin them beyond repair.

Rocks also are a symbol of protection. The Psalmist writes, "Be my rock of refuge, a fortress of defense to save me." Again he sings, "Lead me to the rock that is higher than I." Jesus spoke the warning to flee to the rocks and the mountains in the days of great tribulation. Yes, dear ones, that rock behind which we can find refuge is called the Rock of Ages.

A man was sent out on a rocky promontory in Scotland where his signals might help a ship that was working its way through a difficult channel in the midst of a storm. Great waves sent their spray up over that rock and the man signaling was drenched. But he stood his ground, and the ship arrived safely. Afterwards, someone asked him if he did not tremble as he stood on that rock. His answer was, "My legs trembled, but the rock didn't tremble." Friends, today storms and winds are beating. Many are trembling in their places. But rest assured, the foundation of our lives, Jesus Christ, the church's one foundation, does not tremble. He and His will stand through the fiercest gale.

Dear Father God, I bless Your holy name today for the constant source of strength and protection You are in my life. I am fully aware of my weakness, and fully aware of Your solid presence as the only sure foundation for my life. Thank You for Your provision, for Your constancy, and for the rest I find in You alone. Amen.

April 15   The Poor Widow Who Was Rich

Scripture Reading: Mark 12:41-44

Key Verse: "Then one poor widow came and threw in two mites..." Mark 12:42

It is near the sunset of Christ's life. The time is Paschal week, the last week of Christ upon earth. During Passover Week great multitudes came to Jerusalem, possibly as many as three million people gathered there during the seven days of the feast.

A particular treasury was in the court of the women, a large enclosure of the temple holding fifteen thousand women when filled. Here there were thirteen boxes or chests conveniently placed for the worshippers. Nine of them were for temple dues and four for free-will offerings.

Well, Jesus sat down over against the treasury and observed. That's a good place from which to observe. See how people give and you will see far into their hearts and lives. How and for what we spend our money is a good test of character.

It isn't difficult to see the crowd passing before the Savior's eyes. Human nature was the same then as now. The Master notes those with flashing, jeweled fingers, haughty, clothed in purple, as they ostentatiously drop their big coins. And then comes the widow. Her garb denotes that; its quality shows she is poor. She clutches in her hand two mites, the smallest coins in circulation. The Master beckons to His disciples. "See, that little woman there, the one in black?"

"She just dropped in one twenty-fifth of a cent. She ought to be rebuked!" blusters Peter.

"Pretty close-fisted," mutters Judas.

"No, no," the Master tenderly corrects. "She has given more than all the rest. The others have given of their plenty, she has given her all." You see, God's scales are so fine that they weigh not only what we give, but also what is left. Two mites? How small! No, it was all.

But hear me. The Lord sits over against the treasury of our lives. It is a staggering moment when we awaken to the near presence of God.

Nothing can be done in a corner. Life takes on a majestic dignity if we realize that our least endeavors are witnessed by Him who sits upon the throne.

No life becomes real until it becomes sacrificial. We begin to operate with vital forces when we cross the border into the land of sacrifice.

Washington's ragged troops left blood marks where they trod in the snow that awful winter at Valley Forge. Abraham left blood marks in his tracks up Mount Moriah. He was going to offer his only son Isaac as a sacrifice to Jehovah. That was an experience that shattered self.

And here we stand, you and I, before the treasury of God. What will we give? We do give something, for each of us as individuals casts into the world's treasury our little gift. The inventor brings his tools, the author his books, the musician his score, the physician his skill and knowledge, and the minister his sermon and his service. And while the world may fail to note your gift, Heaven never does. What shall we give the Lord? We give ourselves and what we have.

"Moses, what have you?" "A rod, Lord." "Gideon?" "A pitcher." "Joshua?" "A ram's horn." "David?" "A shepherd's sling." Oh, give what you have to God. Yes, you say, but it is small. Never mind that. The widow gave two mites and she achieved the approval of the Master, and immortality.

Dear God, I squeeze my possessions, gifts and talents so tightly sometimes. Help open my eyes to ways I can give freely, joyfully, extravagantly, as You give to me. Amen.

April 16   Are You Making A Living Or A Life?

Scripture Reading: Romans 12:9-21

Key Verse: "not lagging in diligence, fervent in spirit, serving the Lord." Romans 12:11

The New King James Version of the Scripture says "fervent in spirit." Moffett says "Maintain the spiritual glow." What did Paul mean by this songful word?

He meant that to be a Christian is to live zestfully. He meant that to follow Jesus, to call Him Lord and Master, is to be possessed of a glowing heart. Paul had learned this from his Master. He had learned it from his fellow saints, but best of all, it was his own experience. We may find Paul suffering and under much hardship, whipped time and time again, left for dead after being stoned, imprisoned endlessly, but we never find him without a glowing heart.

Jesus lived zestfully. He had a joy that nothing could overshadow. He said so often, "Be of good cheer." That is what He meant when, upon the mountain-side, He said "You are the salt of the earth." It is so simple that any child can understand, yet so profound that the wisest cannot fully fathom it.

What did Jesus mean? He meant that to be Christian is to be different. He consistently expected His followers to be finer than those who did not follow Him. You cannot but detect the tone of disappointment as He asked His friends this question, "What do you do more than others?" When He found them no more giving, no more loving, no more unselfish than those who did not know Him, it broke His heart.

But the richest meaning that Jesus put into this great word is that to be Christian is to find the secret of zest. It is to find the tang in the feast of life and to be able to give that tang to others. Without the salt, life becomes vain and full of nothingness.

Look at the Pentecost Christians. They were so absurdly joyful that their critics could not explain it. But with the fullness of this zest they went out to build a new world. What they had then is the matchless possession of millions since then and can be yours as well.

Paul, in his statement, intimates the sad possibility of losing our glow. That is what Jesus meant when he followed His tremendous declaration "You are the salt of the earth" with the admonition "But if the salt loses its flavor, how shall it be seasoned?"

How shall we maintain this spiritual glow? First, keep busy. That's why old folks have a tendency to think of the Church of yesterday far better than the one of today. They were busy in it then and serving blesses. Secondly, keep our faces toward the future. We cannot go forward by looking back.

Remember the heartbroken disciples on the way to Emmaus? Their Master had been crucified. All their future was past. Then Jesus drew near. They did not recognize Him at first, but when they sat down to supper together and He asked the blessing in his winsome fashion their eyes were opened. They said to one another "Did not our hearts burn within us while He talked with us on the road?" You and I must talk to Him on our way. A kerosene lamp goes out when the oil is exhausted. Electric lights go out when unplugged from the power source. Even so, the radiance will go out of your life if you lose touch with Him who is the light of the world.

Almighty Father, I don't want to be like salt without flavor or a life unlit by You. I want to glow like Moses did when he came down from the mountain. People saw that he had been with You. I want the great joy that comes from being with You and living for You. Amen.

April 17 — Purpose

Scripture Reading: Daniel Chapter 12

Key Verse: "Those who are wise shall shine like the brightness of the firmament, and those who turn many to righteousness like the stars forever and ever." Daniel 12:3

The Bible has many striking things to say concerning fools. The Psalmist remarks, "The fool has said in his heart, 'there is no God.'" Paul says, "Someone will say, "How are the dead raised up? And with what body do they come? Foolish ones, what you sow is not made alive unless it dies." And the Savior added, in telling of the man with a bumper crop who could think only of eating, drinking, and being merry, "Fool! This night your soul will be required of you."

But, the wise are not overlooked in Scripture. The men who bowed before the infant Christ were called wise men. The man who built his house upon the rock is numbered with the wise. And, the virgins who were prepared to rejoice with the bridegroom's party are named "wise" virgins. And also, we find in Proverbs 11:30, "He who wins souls is wise."

Years ago, an old feeble woman might be seen sitting on a small box on a downtown corner of Los Angeles. From six in the morning until eleven at night, she sat there in all kinds of weather, selling papers and receiving alms. Her food was stale bread that she got from a nearby bakery, and discarded fruit salvaged from garbage cans. She presented a pitiful picture of wretchedness that evoked considerable practical sympathy. One rainy day, a passing stranger commented on her condition to a friendly policeman, "It is a civic shame that such a poor old shivering bit of womanhood should have to sit there like that." "Poor indeed she is," replied the officer, "She is dying in misery and loneliness while at the same time, she is unbelievably rich. The very five-story building she is huddling against is hers." Four other downtown properties were hers, to say nothing of many thousands of dollars in the banks. Obsessed by greed and fear, her inheritance had never become a reality to her.

This true story reflects too many Christian lives. Paul informs us that the riches of His grace are all ours. We are joint heirs with Christ. The Holy Spirit has been given us for power and witnessing, and the Lord is our Advocate and King. We are made ambassadors in Christ's stead, and told to go out in the highways and byways and compel them to come in. And yet, despite all the preparation for this work in our lives, we spend our time in spiritual poverty if we don't take advantage of what the Lord has provided.

God has a plan for your life and mine. What a challenge to surrender fully to Him! Through my body, my life, my testimony, my love, I am to serve this community by the will of God. What about you? Have you found your place in God's will? Do you have a testimony about Christ, about salvation yes, but also about what Jesus means to you every day and every hour?

My friends, this world is in crisis, and that is a clarion call to the heart of every Christian. God has a purpose for you in the time and place in which you find yourself. Wisely use the gifts God has provided you. Wisely submit to the leadership of the Holy Spirit in your life. Through our lives, His Spirit will touch others. Through our warm hearts, He will touch the coldhearted. And, "those who are wise shall shine like the brightness of the firmament, and they that turn many to righteousness like the stars forever and ever."

Dear Lord, I am aware that wisdom comes only from the relationship I have with You. Help me to shine with the truth of Your way, today and every day. For Christ's sake, amen.

April 18   The Tragedy Of Neglect

Scripture Reading: Hebrews 2:1-9

Key Verse: "How shall we escape if we neglect so great a salvation...?" Hebrews 2:3

In this land of ours do you suppose men and women are finally lost because they intend deliberately to be? No! No one deliberately intends to miss heaven. Why then do they miss it? One little word in the text denotes the answer. It is neglect, simply neglect.

You see, people do not have to blaspheme God to be finally lost; they do not have to lift up their tiny fists in the face of God Almighty to be lost. People have only to go on down the tide, floating, drifting, neglecting.

Christ came to fit you to live here and now, to fit you for your task. Are you a laborer, a businessman, an executive? Christ comes and offers you His own grace, forgiveness, mercy, and divine reinforcement. He would not only save your soul, but your life, body, brains, influence, and personality. He would leave nothing about you out, even your past. He saves us from our regrets, sorrows, sins, and poor choices. He'll blot it all out.

But that's not all; Christ saves us in our stressful, eventful, important present. Saves us and fights for us our battles, tasks, responsibilities, discouragements, and more. Christ is our supreme need. More than we need bread, we need Christ.

Nor is that all, Christ comes to those who will honestly be a friend to him and tells us to not be afraid of the future. For you see, He is also there in death and in the judgment. We do not need to be afraid to face Jesus at the judgment bar if we have not neglected our salvation.

What arguments shall I marshal to help you, to persuade you, to encourage you? Let me say first, you should give up the neglect of your own salvation because it is unreasonable. "'Come now, and let us reason together,' says the Lord. "Shall a human being, made in the image of

God turn his back on his own Creator? Human beings are made to live when the stars and sun are blotted out forever. We shall all live in the world to come, eternal in its duration, so can it be reasonable to ignore our destiny and fail to provide for that future?

Cease your neglect of yourself and your soul's welfare because it's not right. No bodily suicide is right, neither is spiritual suicide right and God will not be at fault if you miss the way He holds forth to you in love.

Lastly, your neglect is not safe because this life is not all. There are a thousand gates to death, I ask you, are you ready? What I am summing up to you is a choice between two masters; one is a friend, the other a foe. A choice between two lives, one of unceasing usefulness, the other of want and purposelessness. A choice between two worlds of the future, one of peace, bliss, and life forever, the other world of waste, loss, defeat forever.

If on the outskirts of this city a little woman you don't even know, with a wagonload of vegetables, tipped over in a deep ravine and was unable to extricate either her team or herself, and I said, "Are there those who would go tonight to save her?" nearly everyone would rise. Yet, right now, I am talking about your very soul that will soon be in an eternal world. Your own soul! Make the right choice, before it is forever too late.

Dear Jesus, I come to You. I want the salvation that You promise and I realize this is the moment You have given me to make the choice. To neglect to choose You is to still make a choice, a choice that leads to a sad eternity. I choose You, Lord. Amen.

April 19   The Other Prodigal

Scripture Reading: Luke 15:11-32
Key Verses: "Now his older son was in the field...But he was angry and would not go in." Luke 15:25,28

Perhaps this story would be better named, "The Parable of the Two Sons." Usually, all interest centers in the prodigal and when we see him clasped in the welcoming arms of his father, we turn aside satisfied. Seldom do we attempt to cultivate acquaintance with the elder brother.

To begin with, the story of the prodigal was provoked by the fact of the Pharisee's criticism: "This man receives sinners and eats with them." Several parables follow, forming Jesus's answer to their accusation. First, Jesus is the shepherd who goes out after the lost sheep. Then, He is the woman who searches for the lost piece of silver. Jesus is saying to the critical Pharisees that He receives sinners because they are lost, and that His mission is to save them. Next, Jesus presented to them a life-sized picture of themselves in the immortal story of the elder son.

We notice that self-righteousness blinded the elder son. He had many excellent qualities. He remained with his father. He was industrious, making his living by honest toil. His reputation was secure. But, oh how much he missed in life despite his good qualities.

Would it not have been wonderful if Jesus could have told the story another way? What if the elder brother, seeing his father's distress, had gone out in search of the prodigal? Jesus would have loved to tell the story that way, for it would have been a true picture of Himself and His ministry. He, our elder brother, left the highest heaven to come to earth in search of a race of prodigals, to bring them back to the Heavenly Father.

But no, the elder son said, "Lo, these many years I have been serving you." That is just where he should not have been. He ought to have been out on the mountains, seeking his lost brother in the land of sin and want.

The elder brother reminds us of the Pharisee who prayed, "God, I thank You that I am not like other men." His self-righteousness completely blinded him to the state of his brother. He emphasized his brother's sin to his father, casting him in the worst possible light. The self-righteous always have a low estimate of others.

Then, this elder son turned on his own father, desiring him to act as a judge, and not a friend. He saw only parental authority, and ignored parental affection. He wanted to see condemnation and not compassion. But, we read that the father ran to meet and greet his erring, penitent son as God the Almighty runs to welcome every grief-stricken returning sinner.

And so, we see that Jesus was showing the Pharisees the contrast between Himself and His Father, and them. Jesus seeks and searches for and brings the lost home to a welcoming Father. The Pharisees sit in self-righteous judgment of the prodigal, feeling assured that they should have the prominent position in God's favor.

God forbid that any of us would be linked in any sense with the elder son of our story. Instead, let us make our churches a place of refuge for the tired and buffeted, a place of welcome for the suffering. Open your arms wide to the seeking sinner, as Jesus does.

Dear Father, Oh You know how I do struggle with those very feelings that surged in the heart of the elder son. Too often I feel no compassion for those trapped in sin, judging them when You would be reaching out to them. Forgive me, Father, for the sin of self-righteousness. Help me to see each lost one through the eyes of Your love. Amen.

April 20   The Fear of Faith

Scripture Reading: Genesis 6:9 to 8:1

Key Verses: "Thus Noah did; according to all that God commanded him. . ." Genesis 6:22

"By faith Noah, being divinely warned of things not yet seen, moved with godly fear, prepared an ark for the saving of his household, by which he condemned the world and became heir of the righteousness which is according to faith." Hebrews 11:7

Faith is not as cold as steel. No, in fact, functioning faith produces emotions and crystallizes into deeds. Noah is one of the best known of all characters in Old Testament history, for even though others lived in his day, the Bible says, "As was in the days of Noah." Noah's life was so significant that his name was given to the time in which he lived. His life was a dividing point in history because of his faith.

Faith produced an emotion in the heart of Noah, and it produced four distinct results as well. First of all, what was the emotion produced by Noah's faith? It was fear. Now, it was not fear for himself, nor was it servile fear or fright. No, it is a godly fear, a reverential awe. So, what did this fear produced by faith do in Noah's life?

The fear of faith gave Noah the power of appraisal. Noah had the power to see the difference between what was good and what was bad. It gave him the power to see the truth in its proper light. If a man cannot distinguish between good and evil, he cannot have a noble character. Just as a musician must be able to make the distinction between harmonious tones and discord, and just as an artist must be able to distinguish colors that blend and complement, so Noah had this distinction in regard to life. This godly fear made him able to discern right from wrong. After all, we know that "The fear of the Lord is the beginning of wisdom."

This fear also gave Noah the power of protest. He did not resign himself to evil. He did not merely acquiesce to evil tendencies. Noah's life stood out as a protest against sin. Every Christian should stand out as a living protest against evil. Paul said, "... do not be conformed to this world, but be transformed by the renewing of your mind, that you may prove what is that good and acceptable and perfect will of God." Noah, we are told, "walked with God."

Noah's faith also enabled him to overcome great difficulties, obeying God when it seemed ridiculous to do so. In the midst of a wicked world, a world marked by unbelief and sin, Noah persevered. Perseverance is impossible if one lives only for the present. Noah's faith enabled him to live for the future. He firmly believed that God would eventually make His enemies His footstool. Functioning faith expects final victory.

Finally, Noah's faith, and the reverential awe it produced in him, created a sense of individual responsibility in Noah. Believers have a collective responsibility, like that of a fighting army on a battlefield. Unless each soldier does his part, the army will fail. I am only one, but I <u>am</u> one. And if I fail to carry my obligations, no one else can or will fill my place. The responsibilities that God entrusts to me are mine to carry out with His guidance, aid, and wisdom. He does not ask us to do that which He will not assist us in doing. But, we must do it.

Dear Father God, my faith in You is growing, and maturing, yet it seems so small when compared with the faith of Noah. I, too, desire the kind of faith that changes the world, that leaves a mark for Your Kingdom upon people's hearts. Please use me as a vessel through which Your love can be shared, and Your compassion delivered to this hurting world. In Jesus's name, and for His sake, amen.

April 21   He Blessed Them

Scripture Reading: Mark 10:13-16
Key Verse: "And He took them up in His arms, laid His hands on them, and blessed them." Mark 10:16

We are not told who brought the young children to Jesus, but most likely it was the mothers. Blessed are those who have so believed in Jesus as to bring their children to Him.

In Belgium, boys are taught to run up to religious leaders and ask them to bless them with the sign of the cross. Are we anxious that the sign of the Cross should be impressed upon the lives of our offspring? If so, let us bring them to Jesus.

A mother casts the longest shadow over the lives of her children. The prayers of patient Monica turned her gifted son, Augustine, from a profligate into a saint. George Washington confessed that he owed his character to the influence of his mother.

The disciples were disturbed about the children milling around. They had no time to listen to their prattle, but not so with Jesus. Here is a revelation of Christ's love for children, and this scene teaches us that even little children should and must come to Jesus. The scene also tells us that children are welcome to the arms of Jesus. Allow them, let them, and encourage them to come. Parents, this is your primary responsibility. Lead them by your precepts, by your example, and by your counsel. The rest of us can find ways to help as well.

God help you if you are a hinderer. Jesus says, "Do not forbid them," by omission or commission. You know the ways. Never hinder a precious child in its earnestness of heart from coming to Jesus.

Now this story says they brought "little children" to Him. When should a child make its decision to follow Jesus? When that child knows right from wrong, is old enough to realize that sin is bad and doing right is good. That age is dependent in part upon the environment the child is brought up in and the training that child has received. Some of the greatest Christian leaders were saved when very young, even at the age of four, five, six, or seven. A child does not need to know the philosophy of salvation to become a Christian. He has but to open his heart in faith to the Savior.

The disciples, like some folk today, rebuked those that brought the little children to Jesus. Those who stand in the way of children are at heart out of sympathy with Him in His great saving grace. Let us not let children be hindered by long sour faces and bombastic phrases about theology.

Children are fit subjects for the kingdom of God. Not that they are innocent, as any schoolteacher will tell you. It is that the characteristics of the child are those which all must have to enter the kingdom

They have pure faith, dependence, and simplicity. They lack intellectual pride and worldliness, are free of anxious care, and have a faculty for living in the present with great imagination and joy. They are examples to others in how they receive the kingdom of God without doubt or questioning, but with an honest, simple heart. What they are naturally, we strive to become, not childish, but childlike.

The end of all training and care is that they should by voluntary act draw near to Him. Let us not hinder their coming but rather give every effort, remove every hindrance, help them come now, to Him who is the friend of little children.

Lord, I bring to You in prayer those children who are within my influence and care. May I consistently point toward You in counsel and example and may I never, never be a stumbling block or hindrance to their knowing and loving You. Amen.

April 22   Jesus, a Man of Prayer

Scripture Reading: Luke 11:1-4
Key Verse: "...He was praying in a certain place..." Luke 11:1

There are those today for whom prayer as a working force is unknown. Many drift into the habit of prayerlessness, allowing the prayer-hour to be crowded out by duties that seem more pressing. Because of this, it is wise for us to consider what Jesus teaches about prayer.

Jesus demonstrated prayer's worth by making constant use of it. At the beginning of His ministry as He came up from the waters of baptism, it was as He was praying that the heavens opened and the Spirit of God came upon Him. In fact, you will note that prayer marks the entire course of His ministry. His whole life was one of constant communion with God the Father. When He was at the end of the way, His last breath was a prayer, "Father, into Your hands I commit My spirit."

The question comes to mind, then, "How did Jesus pray?" First, Jesus addressed God as Father. Only in His hour of darkness on the cross does He vary from this fixed custom. The single word, "Father," was rich and dear enough without any qualifying adjectives such as "Dear" or "Loving." So, we see that sincerity is necessary, flowery speeches are not. Next, we see that Jesus prayed everywhere. He prayed with His disciples, rather like a family prayer that a father would lead at home. He also prayed with them in lesser groups, and also Jesus prayed alone.

And, when did Jesus pray? We must answer that He prayed without ceasing. He prayed not only as He faced a coming conflict, but He prayed with equal diligence after the battle was won. When deliverance has come, how often we cease to pray! Jesus never blundered after this fashion. We find him going out to pray time after time, after days of miraculous ministry. We also find Jesus in prayer concerning all needs and interests of life. He prayed for Himself and for His disciples as a group. He prayed for the Church, and He prayed for individuals.

Finally, Jesus knew that prayer was not the mere preparation for battle; He considered it the battle itself. All else was merely the going forth of a conqueror to receive the spoils of battle. In our local paper recently, we saw the picture of a brave young man who was receiving the Distinguished Flying Cross. How easy and grand to receive such a medal, right? But the medal was not won that day. It had been won through days and nights of toil, daring bravery, and courage in the face of unrelenting hostility. Just so did Jesus win his fight in the place of prayer, and then go out to conquer with seeming ease.

This concept is illustrated throughout Christ's ministry, but nowhere with such force as in the Garden of Gethsemane. Gethsemane was the arena of victory, you see. Gethsemane was the place of blood, and of tears. Then, when he hung upon that cross, even a highwayman could discern His kingliness and His victory.

Now, if prayer was central in the life of our Lord Jesus, shouldn't it be so in our lives today? If Jesus won His battles in the secret place, where ought we expect to win ours? Prayer is a privilege we cannot afford to neglect.

Father, today as I go out to meet the day, let me see the people around me through Your eyes. Help me to stand firm on Your word in the face of opposition, but help me to love with Your love when faced with the unlovely. Clothe me in your armor, and fill me with Your spirit that every word I speak and every deed I do might be a testimony to You. Amen.

April 23   One Cubit

Scripture Reading: Matthew 6:25-34

Key Verse: "Which of you by worrying can add one cubit to his stature?" Matthew 6:27

Perhaps there never was another day in history when there were so many worried people as there are at this moment. Nor can we explain this wide-spread worry merely in terms of circumstances, for worry is not a child of circumstance. Whether you worry or not depends not upon your situation, but upon you. If you are robbed of your joy by worry, it is always an inside job.

Worry is so useless. Isn't this the very heart of what Jesus implies in the words of our text? Now, we have all done plenty of useless things, but nobody ever did anything more useless than to waste their precious days and nights with worry.

Did you ever wake up on a cold night, about half frozen and remember that there was a blanket not eight feet away? But, instead of getting up and getting the blanket, you simply lie there half asleep and freeze the rest of the night? Such conduct does not get you warm, it just makes you miserable. Such behavior is akin to worry.

Finally, we need this warning from Jesus because worry is so harmful. Not only is it harmful to the one who worries, but it makes that one hard to live with. Those who worry are a burden to themselves, a burden to others, and a sorrow to the Lord. How often when Jesus was upon earth did He remark to His friends with pained amazement about how little they trusted him, how small their faith. This is also true of you and me, when we worry.

Now since worry is such an ugly foe, we must get rid of it. How? In our own strength, we will fail. We must redirect our thinking. As the apostle Paul says, "Whatever things are true, whatever things are noble, whatever things are just, whatever things are pure, whatever things are lovely, whatever things are of good report, if there is any virtue, and if there is anything praiseworthy - meditate on these things." Paul is not urging us to blind optimism; he is rather urging upon us the sanity of seeking in our world, in our situation, in our church, in our friends, and in our loved ones the things that are lovely.

But the supreme cure for worry is faith. Jesus reminds us that the same fatherly God who looks after the needs of the birds can be trusted to supply our needs. We are to rest in the Lord and wait patiently for Him; we cast our care upon Him in the realization that He cares for us. Above all else, we are to make a habit of prayer, "In everything by prayer and supplication, with thanksgiving, let your requests be made known to God; and the peace of God, which surpasses all understanding, will guard your hearts and minds through Christ Jesus."

Many years ago, an aviator was making a flight around the world. About two hours after leaving an airfield in Egypt, he heard a noise in his plane which he recognized as the gnawing of a rat. It had gotten in while his plane was grounded. The pilot was desperate, for at any moment it might cause disaster and death. Then he remembered that a rat was only a rodent. It is not made for the heights. So, the pilot began to climb. He went up, up, up until he was 20,000 feet in the air. Then the gnawing ceased. When he came down a few hours later, there was a dead rodent in the engine pit of the plane.

Worry, too, is a rodent. It cannot live in the secret place of the Most High. It cannot breathe in an atmosphere made vital by prayer.

Dear Lord and Father of mankind, forgive our feverish ways. Reclothe our minds in the joy and peace that only You can give. Amen.

April 24   Living As He Lived

Scripture Reading: I John 2:1-17

Key Verse: "He who says he abides in Him ought himself also to walk just as He walked." I John 2:6

When Jesus concluded His Sermon on the Mount, He said, "Why do you call me 'Lord, Lord,' and not do the things which I say?" His purpose was not to champion a creed, but to inspire a deed. He wanted us to live as He lived. A man can have a religion about Jesus; he can preach a great creed, and yet be full of racial prejudice. He can have a religion about Jesus and yet pay his employees a starvation wage, lie about his neighbors, and be a devil in his home. But, he cannot have Jesus and do these things. If we have truly surrendered to Him it will change our thoughts, it will change our ideals, and it will change our practices.

To men and women in this world fraught with care, chaos, and misunderstanding, in a world filled with anger, violence, and hurt, there is only one thing that cannot be laughed off, only one thing that will haunt men and women and prick their conscience. It is the person who walks as Jesus walked. "By who's preaching were you converted?" they asked a sophisticated young man. "Not by anyone's preaching," he answered, "but by my mother's practicing."

Though I speak with the eloquence of an orator and have not the Spirit of Christ, I am none of His. Though I be a prophet and foretell the future, though I be a philosopher and understand the marvels of thought, though I be a scientist and discern the mysteries of space, earth and heaven, and though I be a psychologist and understand the mysteries of life, and have not allowed love to master my prejudices and suspicions, I may make a lot of noise, but be of little service to the Kingdom of God.

Ours is not the task of convincing skeptical minds that the walk of Jesus is reasonable. When God is lifted up by the imitation of Christ in our lives, He will draw all men. Ours is the task to stay close to Jesus, let him fill us with the Holy Spirit so that our life overflows with God's love and joy, and to forbid the world to crowd out our love for Him.

The philosophically minded will say, "Think it through." But that is not enough. The spiritually minded will say, "Pray it through." And that is imperative, but it is not enough. If we are to become Christ-minded, we must begin to live it through.

Jesus went too far in neighborliness, and He said we should go and do the same. He went too far in forgiveness, for He said "forgive seventy times seven." He went too far in the matter of loving our enemies, for He tells us that it is absolutely essential that we do love those that despitefully use us. He went too far in surrender, for He went to Calvary and died for all.

There was no limit to His love and service, and if we are to live as He lived, it will mean giving until we feel it. It will mean vigorous co-operation in the struggle of daily life. It will mean travail for the souls of men. It will mean concern for your friends and neighbors. It will mean a refusal to hate or become embittered in a world torn with strife. It will mean sincere striving to bring justice where there is injustice, and to bring peace where there is pain.

"He who says he abides in Him ought himself also to walk just as He walked."

Dear Father, It is not possible for me to be good and perfect and always loving, but it is possible for me to surrender to You and let You live through me. Lord, fill me up with Your love so that I may spread it all over the earth. Forgive me when I fail and help me as I walk in Your footsteps through this life. Amen.

April 25   Three Little Words

Scripture Reading: Luke 19:1-10

Key Verse: "The Son of Man has come to seek and to save that which was lost." Luke 19:10

The three greatest words of our Christian faith are "lost," "sought," and "saved." Originally, the Lord Jesus Christ spoke those words after he went to the home of Zacchaeus and people found fault with Him for it. In answer to them, Jesus spoke the words of our text, "The Son of Man has come to seek and to save that which was lost." That is why He came into the world. That is why He died on the cross. That is why He was raised from the dead. That is why He is interceding in glory, and that is why He is coming again to make the kingdoms of the world the Kingdom of our Lord and Christ.

And for 2000 years, He has kept this promise. He has never turned any away. If people have had faith as a grain of mustard seed, they have been rescued from the jaws of hell. Yes, these 2000 years have proved that Jesus Christ is able and eager, anxious and willing to save every woman, every man, and child, every sinner.

But you know, nobody will come to Christ who does not realize that he or she is lost. We are not going to send for a doctor until we know we are sick. We will not take any medicine until we need it. We have many things we may lose. It is a trial to lose one's money, or property. It is a tragedy to lose one's health. But frankly, beloved, death will heal the loss of fortune. Death will heal the loss of mind, or character, or health. But, there is no healing outside of Jesus's blood for a lost soul.

One may lose his wealth, health, money, and friends, and yet go to heaven. But on the other hand, if a man should accumulate all the money there is in the world, what good will it do him if he dies lost? We know that we will die, and if we die without Christ, we die lost, not for time, but for eternity.

Oh, thank God that I don't need to stop there! There is a way out. There is a plan of escape for every one of us. The Bible teaches that not only has God given His Son for us, but He invites every soul, no matter what condition, to come - to come and accept His gift of grace.

Some years ago I saw a card. On one side it said, "What must I do to be saved?" Just below that was written the verse, "Believe on the Lord Jesus Christ and be saved." On the other side of the card, however, was written, "What must I do to be lost?" And in a square with black mourning draped about it, was just one word, "Nothing."

God is ready. He is willing. He is eager, anxious, and waiting for the opportunity of washing away the sins of every soul in the precious blood of His Son. But, His grace and forgiveness are restrained by man. If any person wants to be saved, God will accept that one today, immediately. But, if they do not, God will not force their hand.

What is our place in this picture? Well, first of all we need to be sure we are right with Him. Have you believed what God has said? Next, what about those around you? Do they understand what the Bible says about the state of man? It is not a difficult thing to share what you believe, not in a threatening way, but in a gentle manner. Ask God for the privilege.

Dear God, truly You are a merciful and loving Lord, to provide a sacrifice to cover our sin. I am so thankful. Please provide me the opportunity of sharing this good news with one who needs to hear it. And, please help me to meet every opportunity to share the truth with the beautiful simplicity of Scripture. For Christ's sake, amen.

April 26   Back to Bethel

Scripture Reading: Genesis 35:1-15
Key Verse: "...Arise, go up to Bethel and dwell there; and make an altar there to God..." Genesis 35:1

Have you ever wondered if God has allowed us to look a little more closely at the lives of some in the Old Testament because He knew there would be so many more like them in the world today? Let's take a look at Jacob's experience, and go with him back to Bethel.

With a bundle of belongings in one hand, Jacob first came to this barren waste which would be called Bethel. While the stars shone down upon him, he made his pillow of stone and lay down to sleep. As he slept, he dreamed of a great ladder to heaven with angels going up and down, and Jacob heard the voice of God. In the morning, that vision and voice so impressed him that before he left the spot, Jacob made a vow to God that henceforth he would do the will of God and be all that God would have him to be. Oh, all looked good for Jacob at Bethel!

This is the first instance in the Bible of a man making a vow to God, and oh, the pity of it is that it was so soon forgotten. Jacob traveled north to Paddan Aram to meet his Uncle Laban, in whose household he would work for 20 years, marrying both of Laban's daughters. By the time he has a household, children, and livestock of his own, he also has the household idols of his father-in-law. The time came, however, when he returned home, and the angel of the Lord met him on his way, and wrestled with him. By dawn's break, Jacob cried out to the angel to bless him. The angel replied, "What is your name?" "Jacob." And the angel replied, "Your name shall no longer be called Jacob, but Israel." Now he was Israel, a prince of God, for Jacob had met God face to face.

Yet in the very next scene of Jacob's life, he met Esau, who told him to come on home. But Jacob deceived his brother, and hurried away in another direction, toward Shechem, and became a freeholder among that wicked city. It wasn't until after a terrible tragedy that Jacob was willing to hear God's command to, "Go up to Bethel." Jacob turned to his family and said, "Put away the foreign gods that are among you, purify yourselves, and change your garments. Then let us arise and go up to Bethel."

Yes, we must put away anything that has separated us from God. We must make a housecleaning in our lives. God will bless a clean, contrite soul. He wants a surrendered, pure people. And Jacob did it. He went up to Bethel, and God met him there.

First, God spoke to Jacob there at Bethel, reminding him of the old promises. Next, Jacob set up another stone pillar, after 30 years. Oh, can you imagine the joy that must have filled his heart as he worshipped there? Have you been wondering, "Where is the joy that once I knew when first I saw the Lord?" Well, it is just where you left it. Arise, go back to Bethel!

Listen, dear one. It is no different for you or for me than it was for Jacob. If you have strayed, why not go back today? Put away those foreign gods. Be clean, clean in heart, habit, and soul. Change your garments, say goodbye to Shechem, and bury the past beneath the oak. Finally, rebuild the altar in your life, the altar of prayer, love, and service. Joy, peace, and God's presence will be yours back in Bethel.

Dearest Father God, thank You that You do not move. I know that if I feel the absence of Your presence, it is not You who have changed position, but me. Oh, Lord, hold me firmly in the center of Your will and Your way, for Your glory. Amen.

April 27   The Call of Calamity

Scripture Reading: Joshua Chapter 1

Key Verse: "Moses My servant is dead. Now therefore, arise, go over this Jordan, you and all this people, to the land which I am giving to them—the children of Israel." Joshua 1:2

Moses was Israel's Napoleon. He was worth any thousand men. They could have spared anyone better than he. Moses was the leader of God's people. He seemed the one man of all the vast multitude that could not possibly be spared, and yet we read, "Moses My servant is dead."

Why, he was the man who began the great enterprise of Emancipation. He it was, who had seen the burning bush, heard God's call to deliver His people, fought with the hard-hearted Pharaoh, and won. When they faced the Red Sea, it was he who smote the waters and God parted them. It was Moses who struck the rock when they were parched with thirst. And when they fought the Amalakites, it was Moses's uplifted hands that brought them victory. He had carried them upon his broad shoulders, nursed them, and interceded for them for almost half a century.

But, however reluctant we are to admit it, facts are to be faced. Moses is dead. What will be the attitude of Joshua, and of all Israel, at this hour?

They might have assumed an attitude of hopelessness and despair. That would have been natural, for there was no one like Moses. Isn't this the attitude we often assume in the presence of the dead Moseses of our lives? We meet one great defeat, are wounded by one great sorrow, go through a period of real testing, disappointment, and loss. We come to a crisis; we sit down by the coffin of Moses and say, "What's the use?" We nurse our sorrow, and we magnify our calamities and cry, "Moses is dead."

But God's counsel and command is not the call to surrender or to give up. "Now therefore, arise, go over this Jordan." That was God's plan then, and it is God's plan now. "Therefore, arise, go." Go, because God needs men to lead. But, while God works through mankind, we need to remember that no one person is essential to the success of His enterprise. God can take His workmen home to heaven and still carry on His work. It is a good thing to face that fact again and again. The work of the Lord does not necessarily depend upon this or that individual, or Moses. We need to get our eyes off the Moses in our lives, and get our eyes on God. God uses men to complete His plan. But, no one man is essential. God alone is essential and God abides.

Centuries ago there came One to this world who gave Himself unreservedly to the cause of building up the Kingdom of God. He drew about Him a few choice men and women into whom he infused a spirit like His own. But, while that company was a mere handful and the enterprise seemingly in its infancy, He Himself was killed. He was dragged before Pilate and condemned, then crucified. That was the blackest hour in history. Everything seemed lost. But, God had another plan.

Yes, Moses may die, but God lives on! And while we have hold on His hand whether come sorrows, losses, or temptations, we have hold on life. God alone is essential and God abides. Arise, go over this Jordan, the best hopes of your life are waiting to be realized.

Dear Father, I understand that the problems and discouragement I face are not overwhelming at all to You. In fact, the losses and sorrows that to me seem world-ending are not. Only the loss of Your presence would be so bleak, and I thank You that will never be. Thank You for Your faithfulness to me, amen.

April 28   Make Up Your Mind

Scripture Reading: Luke Chapter 6
Key Verse: "But why do you call Me 'Lord, Lord,' and not do the things which I say?" Luke 6:46

If you know where you are going, and are determined to get there, any old jalopy will serve the purpose. But if you cannot come to a decision as to your goal, then even a Rolls-Royce will be of little avail. It would wear out and fall to pieces before you would reach your goal. For the ship that is bound for no harbor, no wind can be favorable. Our Lord is constantly calling us to be decisive. "Let your yes be yes, and your no be no."

It is difficult to get people to think. It is more difficult still to get them to be decisive. Shakespeare's classic drama *Hamlet* illustrates the difficulty perfectly. Hamlet was a keen thinker, but he found action next to impossible. He did not like his situation. He rebelled at the fact that this world was out of joint and that he was born to set it right. He contemplated various courses of action with brilliant clarity, but could never quite go through with any of them.

Now, look at this question of Jesus, "But why do you call Me 'Lord, Lord,' and not do the things which I say?" Our Lord was not speaking to those who were out and out against Him. Neither is He speaking to those who are wholeheartedly for Him. He is rather speaking to those who admire Him, who honor Him to the point of calling Him "Lord," yet they are not fully surrendered to Him. They give Him intellectual assent, but have failed to give Him themselves.

Jesus is saying to us what He said to Matthew long ago, "Follow Me." And Matthew at once left all, rose up, and followed Jesus. Now, if you say that this sounds difficult, I am ready to agree. Jesus never said discipleship would be easy. But, remember, when He set out to redeem us, He did not seek an easy way. He took the way of the cross. In return, shouldn't we take our discipleship seriously?

It is only in wholehearted dedication to Him that we can please Him and fulfill His purpose for our lives and find satisfaction for ourselves. There is no peace for the undecided, beloved. The most wretched hours of our lives are those hours when we are unable to reach a decision. It is only when we are fully committed to following the will of God that we come to know the peace that abides.

If you take Jesus seriously, a thousand lesser decisions will be made in advance, for the choices you make today are born quite largely of the choices you made yesterday. Every wrong choice makes the next wrong choice easier, and even so every right choice makes the next right choice easier and surer. Thus we cultivate our right choices in the fellowship of Jesus, so they become all but spontaneous.

Years ago, I went with a number of young people to secure a Christmas tree for my father's church. Out in the woods there was a creek branch, normally two or three feet wide. Heavy rains and thaws had widened it, yet I believed we could jump it. So, I gave myself a good running start and was on my way to victory when one of the group shouted, "Stop! Stop! Stop!" The result was that I lost my decisiveness, and the further result was I landed in the middle of the creek. My failure was not due to my lack of athletic ability. It was rather due to my indecision. Do not hesitate to follow Him.

Heavenly Father, You know me so well. Please help me to resist the cry for attention from all these worldly distractions. Focus my mind on following You, Lord, that all else might fall into place. Help my yes to always be yes, Lord. Amen.

April 29   The Good and Faithful Servants

Scripture Reading: Matthew 25:20-23

Key Verse: "His lord said to him, 'Well done, good and faithful servant; you were faithful over a few things, I will make you ruler over many things. Enter into the joy of your lord.'"
Matthew 25:21

To a superficial reader the two great parables regarding stewardship may seem identical, but they are not. The parable of the pounds in Luke and the parable of the talents in Matthew have considerable difference. The parable of the pounds was given to the multitude, while the parable of the talents was given to Jesus's disciples. The Parable of the Pounds shows the same amount given to each servant while in the Parable of the Talents one receives five, the other two, the other one. The Pounds illustrates different degrees of improvement of the same opportunity with corresponding grades of reward, the story of the talents sets before us equal improvement of different opportunities with equal reward.

He that had five talents brought five more saying "I have gained five more talents." And it was the same with him of two talents. What does the Lord say and do about it? There are three great elements standing forth here. First, there is commendation. He says "Well done, good and faithful servant." How gracious and wonderful these words from the lips of his Lord. If we can see the radiance of the Lord's smile and hear those gracious accents when life on earth for us is finished, there will be glow and glory about our eternal life.

Now, note these two adjectives, "good" and "faithful." The Lord said nothing about being smart or brilliant or having ability. The only qualities that counted with Him were that His servants had been good and faithful. But there is also compensation. "You were faithful over a few things, I will make you ruler over many things." All of God's purpose toward us is to advance and bless us. "'For I know the thoughts that I have toward you,' says the Lord, 'thoughts of peace and not of evil, to give you a future and a hope.'"

But that is not all. He assures His good and faithful servants of His companionship. "Enter into the joy of your lord." You are no longer my slaves; you are my friends, heirs of God, joint heirs with Christ. A joint heir is one who shares equally with another. The redeemed of the Lord are to be the Bride of the Lamb, to be identified in all that Christ is doing.

Lastly, we see that the scope of stewardship is in three great areas. We have the stewardship of life. His life has been given to us as a mother's life is given to her babe. Our physical, mental, and spiritual lives are a gift from God. We are therefore to use these so that our Lord shall be enriched.

But the gospel is also entrusted to us. It originated from Him and we are debtors to Him until those for whom it was given have received it from us. We are debtors to these unsaved people until we pass it on to them. The heathen world is crying for that gospel that we have wrapped up in our napkin of selfishness.

Then, we have the stewardship of money. The parable is in terms of money and we have no right to think only in terms of abilities. All money belongs to God. He entrusts us with it in order that through the money which we have His kingdom may be built and His gospel may be shared. It is simply a tool, nothing more.

How will you use what the Master has entrusted to you?

Blessed Lord, how tightly I sometimes hold things, forgetting that they were never mine to hold. May I use all You place in my hands to Your glory and honor. Amen.

April 30   A Son of Shame

Scripture Reading: Judges Chapter 11
Key Verse: "I have given my word to the Lord, and I cannot go back on it." Judges 11:35

This man, Jephthah, has made a vow to the Lord and now the hour is upon him in which it is his duty to make the vow good. This vow, however, now involves much more than he ever expected. But, even though the price is big, he will not refuse to pay it. Though the promise is hard, he will keep it. "I cannot go back on it."

Let's take a look at this man who seems to have been wronged since before he was born. He has had many hard things said about him, yet perhaps he is one of the most heroic souls of the Old Testament. He lived in the morning of history, but was true to the light he had and he was true with a rugged fidelity that condemns many of us today.

Jephthah never had a fair chance in life, some would say. He was not only the son of an unfaithful man, but besides this Jephthah's mother was a woman who sold herself day by day over the counter of iniquity.

Jephthah did not have a lot of raw material from which to build a life. Yet, when Israel was in trouble, the elders remembered the great warrior, Jephthah. In astonishment he greeted them when they came to visit. They needed his help. They needed him to be the commander of their armies. And, Jephthah consented to go to their aid.

But, before he undertook the campaign against the sons of Ammon, Jephthah stood before the altar of God. He went to battle from the altar of prayer. And as he went he made a vow, the vow for which he has been severely criticized. He vowed that if God would give him the victory, he would offer up to Him whatever first came out of the door of his house to meet him upon his return.

Such a rash vow! Yet, rash as it was, I rather admire Jephthah for making it. We are so prudent today. We have such admirable possession of all our faculties that we are in danger of dying of self-control. This man, in the white heat of his enthusiasm, made a pledge to the Lord, and when we look at the outstanding stories of love in the Bible, we find that they were made possible by those who were utterly rash in their giving. The widow who gave her all, and Mary who poured a whole box of ointment on Jesus, was it not their zeal that made them immortal?

Jephthah believed that as he had put himself at God's disposal, God would put Himself at Jephthah's disposal. And God did not disappoint him. The sons of Ammon were defeated. But as he approached home, a lovely girl with dark hair and sunny face came dancing a dance of welcome to her father hero. Father and daughter, face to face, "Alas, my daughter, you have brought me very low." And the girl, with sweet resignation, understands the great sacrifice that must be made.

Do not judge Jephthah by the light of our century, but by the light of the day in which he lived. He had the sturdy courage to keep his vow, "I have given my word to the Lord and I cannot go back." Beloved, the purposes of God are furthered by those who "cannot go back," those with impossibilities in their souls. Joseph says, as he faces the temptation of his life, "I cannot do this," The Apostles, ordered to keep quiet about the gospel, proclaim, "We cannot." And Jephthah, with breaking heart and tear-wet face, cries, "I cannot go back."

Dear Lord, Oh, grant me the zeal to live wholeheartedly for You! Help me to have "impossibilities in my soul," that I may never turn back from what I have started for You. Amen.

May 1   For Christ's Sake

Scripture Reading: II Corinthians 5:12-15

Key Verses: "For if we are beside ourselves, it is for God; or if we are of sound mind, it is for you. For the love of Christ compels us." II Corinthians 5:13-14

Originally Paul wrote this statement as an apology. Paul was so enthusiastic about Christ that they said he was crazy. He wrote them to say that they didn't understand; the reason he is like he is, is that the love of Christ compels him. The world understands enthusiasm at a football game or the joyful celebration at a wedding but cannot comprehend the burning heart of a Christian who loves his God. He is called a fanatic.

Now Paul threw himself with all his heart, mind, and soul into the work of serving the Lord and the Church. He said in his letter to the Philippians, "But one thing I do, forgetting those things which are behind and reaching forward to those things which are ahead, I press toward the goal for the prize of the upward call of God in Christ Jesus." Intensity was a mark of Paul's calling. He organized churches everywhere he went. He built up the Kingdom of God with great joy and enthusiasm.

The question today is, what does the love of Christ compel us to do? First, we are called to give up our sins. They break His heart, disgrace His name, and dishonor His cause. It is not enough to play church any more than it is enough to play house. We are to release the things that are behind so that we may embrace the things which are before.

We are also to confess Him with our lives, with our tongues, and with our loyalty. Some years ago a millionaire's daughter was stricken with paralysis. Her father sent her to the best surgeon at the best hospital in America but they said her chances were nil for anything but a life confined to a wheelchair. Now a great Austrian surgeon, Dr. Lorenze was brought to the United States by the millionaire father, and was paid a princely sum to attend to the daughter. He operated on her and in six months she was walking.

Nearby, then, in one of the poorest homes there lived a widow and her fourteen-year-old son, Michael. He was also a paralytic through an accident. One day his mother came home from work and found him crying over the newspaper spread on his knees. He pointed to the picture of the cured girl of the rich man. "Mama, wouldn't it be wonderful if that doctor would operate on me and I would walk?" The heart of that poor mother rose in her throat; why she didn't have even one percent of the cost. She could stand no more and went to the outside wall of the house and wept. There, God gave her an idea. She went down to Michigan Boulevard and walked into the Blackstone Hotel. When she glimpsed the famous doctor in the lobby she threw herself on her knees and pled her case. He did operate and that boy did walk again. When the doctor came to tell the boy goodbye before he returned to Austria, the boy grasped the startled doctor's hands, "Doctor, as long as there is a tongue wagging in my head there is nobody ever going to hear the last of what you have done for me." Christ's love compels us to confess Him.

The same things that drove Paul the Apostle to the depths of his sacrificial devotion to his almost-divine love for Christ are the reins driving us, compelling us, constraining us, insisting on our going out in the name of the Lord to do the same work for Christ in our day and time that Paul did in his.

Almighty God, You have completely and totally changed my past, my present, and my future. I love You and I thank You with all my heart. May my life reflect Your great love for me and my deep love for You. Amen.

May 2 — What Time Is It?

Scripture Reading: I Thessalonians 5:1-11

Key Verses: "But you brethren are not in darkness, so that this Day should overtake you as a thief. You are all sons of light and sons of the day. We are not of the night nor of darkness. Therefore let us not sleep, as others do, but let us watch and be sober ... putting on the breastplate of faith and love, and as a helmet the hope of salvation. For God did not appoint us to wrath, but to obtain salvation through our Lord Jesus Christ, who died for us, that whether we wake or sleep, we should live together with Him." I Thessalonians 5:4-11

Among the people of God there should be great clarity as to where we stand now. What time is it then among true believers all over the world? It is a great certainty as to the fact that the Lord is coming, but uncertainty as to when He is to come.

Here is a word for you. We are not stumbling around in the dark. We are traveling toward a known goal, the coming of the Lord. No man knows the day or hour. We may look to the prophetic Scriptures and know the season, but our job is to be ready at any time.

Paul, in I Corinthians 7:29-31 says, "But this I say, brethren, the time is short, so that from now on even those who have wives should be as though they had none, those who weep as though they did not weep, those who rejoice as though they did not rejoice, those who buy as though they did not possess, and those who use this world as not misusing it. For the form of this world is passing away."

Paul certainly believed the time was short and because of it we Christians are called to unusual seriousness and special urgency. It means we are not to be too much taken up with domestic cares, nor sorrows, nor with our joys. There is no time for silly banter or small talk nor allowing our time to be taken up with possessions, but using this world and all that is ours in it with the consciousness that they are but a means to an end, for the Lord is at hand.

Let us wear the world like a loose garment, not wrapping ourselves closely with it or holding it tightly, being instantly ready to step from it and allow the wedding garment for the Wedding Supper of the Lamb to settle over us. It is time to look up with hopeful expectation, for it is a time of joyful anticipation of the coming of the Lord.

It is also time for us to invest our time and wealth in heaven. If ever there were a time for rich men to learn how to wisely invest their money for the Lord, it is now.

Lastly and most importantly, it is the acceptable time of salvation. Are you ready for the Lord's return? Are all your friends, neighbors, and family ready? If not then we still have much to do. Let us be diligent and urgent about the work of reconciliation.

I think of the story told of a woman who in view of an approaching lawsuit planned to employ an able attorney in her town. After considerable delay she asked him to take her case but it was too late. "I am very sorry," he said, "but I have just been appointed judge. I cannot plead for you now. I can only judge you."

Almighty Father God, thank You that although I can look around me and see that the day of Your Son's arrival draws near and there are many to pray for, I can take comfort that this is a day of triumph and joy and I need not be afraid. Lord, I present before your throne _____ and _____ and _____. I ask with all urgency that salvation would be theirs before it is too late and You can no longer be their Savior, but only their Judge. I ask that their hearts be softened and their eyes be opened to Your loving invitation. Amen.

May 3 — Have Faith in Eternal Life

Scripture Reading: Jude vs.16-25

Key Verse: "Keep yourselves in the love of God, looking for the mercy of our Lord Jesus Christ unto eternal life." Jude v.21

The Christian faith has always been ruthlessly honest about death. It does not sentimentalize. It says in a stab of realism, "The last enemy that will be destroyed is death." We try to persuade ourselves that death is a natural event to be accepted in due season like birth. But that is not true. Man is a creature made by God and within him God has set the stamp of His image and the love of eternity. Man is a citizen of two worlds. He is a fleshly bundle of infinity and life everlasting is inherent in his very soul. Eccl. 3:11 says that God has placed eternity in his heart.

We print the obituary columns on the back page so that we may persuade ourselves that our name will never appear. We disguise death by the embalmer's art until it seems only sleep. We spoof ourselves to say that death is only a lovely trance. We quote poetic expressions at funerals, yet they are contrary to truth. All the time our soul tells us that there is something better beyond and that although there is this enemy, there is a victor over him. For, Christ came to bring life and immortality to light by the gospel.

Who can doubt the reality of Heaven? We have the assurance that Jesus spoke of the fact when He said, "In my Father's house are many mansions, I go to prepare a place for you." Our faith is backed by the inerrant, unchangeable, eternal Word of God.

I know what kind of place Heaven is. My heart tells me, my soul whispers it. My mind loves to dwell upon it, but, most assuring of all, most satisfactory of all, the Bible describes it.

It is a planned place. God is the architect; it is a work of art and labor of love.

It is a populated place. John said he saw a great multitude that no man could number of every nation and tribe out of all the earth. Young and old, rich and poor, weak and strong, from every continent, climate, creed, country, and color; all have been bidden to the marriage feast and many will be there.

It is a perfect place. There are no disappointments in Heaven, no discouragements, no disheartenings, no sorrows, suffering, pain, or tears. None of the toil and trial of earth find entrance there.

I know I am going to Heaven. I am sealed in the eternal love, in the eternal purpose by the eternal Spirit of God. I am saved and He has promised. It's as simple and as complex as that.

Now, I urgently and kindly beseech you to go with me. You may if you will. It is altogether dependent upon your willingness. There is only one thing in your way. Not your sins, Christ can and will wash them away. Not your weaknesses, the Holy Spirit can conquer those in you. There is nothing in your way but your own will.—"That I will or I won't."

The very moment you are ready to say to God, "Lord, have mercy on me, a sinner," God stands ready to enroll you in the citizenship of Heaven. At this moment Christ leans from Heaven and beckons us to come with His pierced hands outstretched. He is longing, yearning, pleading, and calling for you. Won't you join me and this host of people on the march to the Promised Land? Jesus said, "I am the way, the truth and the life, no man comes to the Father but by me." God give you the grace to say yes.

Dearest Father, thank You for providing the way for me to have eternal life. I am so grateful! I look forward to spending eternity in Your presence. Amen.

May 4   The Sin We are Afraid to Mention

Scripture Reading: Malachi Chapter 3

Key Verses: "Will a man rob God? Yet you have robbed Me! But you say, 'In what way have we robbed You?' In tithes and offerings. You are cursed with a curse, for you have robbed Me, even this whole nation! Bring all the tithes into the storehouse, that there may be food in My house, and try Me now in this, says the Lord of hosts, if I will not open for you the windows of heaven and pour out for you such blessing that there will not be room enough to receive it." Malachi 3:8-10.

Now, I know there are those who rob the government. There are brothers who will rob brothers. There are parents who steal from their own children, and children who steal from their own parents. But, will a man rob God? When we rob each other, we feel there is some chance that our dishonesty may not be detected. But this is not, nor cannot, be the case when we rob Him in whose hand is our breath and who knows our very thoughts. But, when we face the facts, we find we are wrong. Men will rob God.

There were such in the days of Malachi. "You have robbed Me," it is charged. Yet those who were accused were indignant. Prove it, they say. Tell us wherein we have robbed God. And what was the prophet's response? Did he apologize and retract? No, he accused them of robbing God on the basis of withholding their tithes and offerings.

What excuse did the people have to plead for refusing to tithe? They could not plead ignorance, for they had known the law from infancy. So why had they failed to give to the Lord? Because they had lost all sense of God's love.

When the prophet approaches them at the opening of this prophecy with the declaration of God, "I have loved you," they answer peevishly, "In what way have You loved us?" They could see no token of His love. They were blind to His blessings. Therefore, having lost all sense of His love, they had ceased to love in return. Love delights to give. Love delights in sacrificing of itself. Believe me when I tell you, they adopted a financial system by which they were robbing God, and robbing themselves.

We ought to reevaluate our attitude in giving. We ought to enter the blood-bought privilege of life partnership with God in all the things of our lives. Tithing is a scriptural response to the fact of God's ownership. God is absolute owner of everything. As the New Testament clarifies, we are called upon to administer all of our possessions as God's stewards. Nonetheless, God has set aside the tithe as the amount of our acknowledgment of His ownership and it behooves us, indeed it blesses us, to willingly and cheerfully give. And it robs God to withhold it from Him.

Tithing, in the harsh light of examination, is a wonderful cure for a sin that we are often afraid to mention. That sin is the sin of covetousness. The more some people get, the more they want. But, think how we cheat God when we covet that which is His. Think how many people give a dollar, or two, or five, as their sole contribution in appreciation for His bounteous care and as an expression of their appreciation.

Remember that the hand and the heart that are open to give are also open to receive and God pours His blessing down. But, the hand that is fast closed against giving is also closed against receiving a blessing.

Dear God, forgive me for the times when I have withheld the token of the tithe from You. I do acknowledge that all that I have comes from You, and it is Yours. Help me to remember that to give to Your work is a blessing, and a privilege. Amen.

May 5 — The Riches Of Christ

Scripture Reading: II Corinthians 8:8-15
Key Verse: "For you know the grace of our Lord Jesus Christ, that though He was rich, yet for your sakes He became poor, that you through His poverty might become rich." II Cor. 8:9

From before the foundations of eternity Jesus was rich in station, for He was the Son of God. It staggers the human mind to comprehend the lofty height to which we must climb to see Jesus on the throne at the right hand of the Father in eternity past.

He was also rich in surroundings. Heaven was His home with its beauty, perfections, and artistry. His companions were the host of angels, and there was no sickness, no sorrow, no suffering, no misunderstanding, no heartache, no tears, and no disappointments.

Then the Lord Jesus Christ was rich in His sovereignty. He was the King of Kings and Lord of Lords. All authority which He claimed while on earth was His from the beginning in Heaven. It was not given power, but inherent power. He was rich in position, in surroundings, and in sovereignty.

But Jesus became poor. Listen, we speak a lot about the sufferings of Christ. Gethsemane, the lashings of the Roman scourge, the cross were all horrible cruelties and indignities. But the encasing of Jesus Christ in human flesh was just as much indignity to Him as was the crucifixion. What a burden for Him to wear our flesh with its shortcomings, limitations, and temptations upon His spirit. How the Son of God endured humility, submission, and subjection for you and me.

But He has made us rich in the forgiveness of sins. The poverty of the Lord Jesus Christ blots out every transgression, every iniquity, removes every stain, and washes whiter than snow.

There is the story of the young Russian soldier who got into financial trouble in the Russian army. He lost his money, then the money of the quartermaster commissary. It meant a court martial, prison, even death. One night after trying to figure out a way, he pulled out his service revolver. Laying it on top of the records he wrote on a slip of paper the words, "Who will pay my debt?" He began to cry and sobbed himself to sleep. About midnight the Czar of Russia, Nicholas II passed through the barracks. He noticed the light in yonder room, went in and seeing the revolver and the note, saw the red and black figures and understood. Carefully taking the pen, Nicholas wrote, "I, Nicholas II will pay it."

Jesus wants us to accept His riches today. It is why He came. Once, a little fellow passed a huge walled garden at a palace where beautiful grapes hung on the vines. His mother, a French widow, was dying of tuberculosis and had just that morning remembered France and said "Oh if I could just taste a grape again." As he tried to entreat the guards to allow him just a few for his mother, a tall man laid his hand on his shoulder and said, "Come with me." He picked several bunches and filled the boy's hat. The little fellow said sadly, "But I only have two pennies for the grapes you sold me." The tall man smiled at him and said, "These grapes are not for sale, I am the King of England. You may have all the grapes you want."

You cannot buy the blood of Jesus, the forgiveness of sins, or a home in Heaven. But you can take it all for nothing as the gift of God's love through Jesus Christ your Lord. He became poor that we could become rich.

Thank You, Lord, for Your sacrifice for me. Help me to not take what You've given me lightly or for granted, but to realize that a gift from the Lord of the Universe is unspeakably precious and deserves to be used wisely and usefully. Amen.

May 6   The Light That Shines In the Darkness

Scripture Reading: II Peter 1:16-21

Key Verse: "And so we have the prophetic word confirmed, which you do well to heed as a light that shines in a dark place...." II Peter 1:19

The Bible is the greatest book in the world. It was born of divine seed and planted in human soil many centuries ago and yet it speaks to our needs as if it were written particularly for our time.

It was written by some forty authors, comprising sixty-six volumes over a period of some fifteen centuries by men who ranked from shepherds and fishermen to Kings and Prophets. Yet, the golden thread of unity runs throughout its contents.

Our first acquaintance with it came when father or mother used to read it to us or when some devoted Sunday School teacher reverently disclosed its treasure to us. We have found in it words of comfort and joy so needed in the bleak moments of life. It has given strength in temptation, courage when fear was attacking, love when hate was consuming, and humility when the demon pride seemed about to conquer. It is the very word of life.

Peter speaks of the veracity of the word of God when he says, "For prophecy never came by the will of man, but holy men of God spoke as they were moved by the Holy Spirit." It is surer than a voice from heaven.

Why do people choose common rocks when pure gold is theirs for the taking? It is because they have not looked, not appropriated what is theirs. A man in New Jersey had lived for years in poverty. In the burden of old age found he would have to go to the poor farm. In packing a few things he ran across a Bible that his sister had given him on her death bed many years before. He loosened the clasp and to his surprise out dropped five crisp one-thousand dollar government notes. There amid all his poverty and want had been plenty. But the deeper tragedy of it all was the great wealth of spiritual treasure that went all those years untouched.

In the Bible we find eternal life and Christ. It is the book of the heart. It is God's revelation of Himself. It tells who He is and what He thinks and how He feels about you and me. It reveals God's mind as to sin and righteousness. It is the main book for drawing men to God.

The Bible costs little now, but it cost much in times past. Its pages are stained with the drops of Christ's blood and sifting from between its covers we see the ashes of martyred saints burned at the stake.

Certainly the Bible was a light shining in a dark place in that older time, but the Word of God is timeless. We face wars and fears, terror and cruelty, loss and despair today too. We too need its wisdom and guidance. We do well that we take heed of it, that we search it, study it diligently, thoughtfully, and systematically, for it is still a lamp shining in a dark place.

So, whoever you are, you need it. You need it in youth to combat sin, you need it in middle age to be your inspiration, and you need it in old age to be your staff. Why? Because you need God, you need His Son, and the Scriptures are His very word. "Heaven and earth will pass away, but My words will by no means pass away." It is as eternal as God Himself and in it we find a light for the pathways of our lives.

Holy Father God, thank You that you did not leave us without comfort or direction. You sent the living Holy Spirit and You left the complete book of instructions for an abundant and fruitful life. Help me to be faithful as I search the treasure of Your Word every day. Amen.

May 7 — Taking Sides

Scripture Reading: Exodus Chapter 32

Key Verse: "Then Moses stood in the entrance of the camp, and said, 'Whoever is on the Lord's side- come to me.' And all the sons of Levi gathered themselves together to him." Exodus 32:26

The question of God and our relationship to Him is the greatest question we face in the journey of life; for your relationship to God and to His Son determines every other relationship in this world. Is it any wonder this question, though asked long centuries ago, thrills us to this very hour? How did Moses come to ask such a thing?

For forty days, Moses had been in the mountain communing with God. He was seeking God's guidance for the people. Meanwhile, the people for whom Moses was praying, those to whose highest welfare he was devoting his life, drifted back into idolatry and made a calf of gold and were worshipping it. Awful indeed was the grief of Moses because of their wretched drifting. On coming down from the mount, he insisted on them showing their true colors, and taking sides for God or against Him. By his courage, Moses turned the tide of the spiritual battle. The day was saved for righteousness.

Oh, what we need today is men and women of fixed principles, steadfast, determined, and dependable; people who stand for God and His cause. Such people always are the ones to turn the tide. It was so with Moses. It was so with Daniel, Joseph, and the three friends of Daniel. It has been so all along the way and will ever continue to be so.

If we would be such men and women, we must pay the price as did Moses. We must literally seek first the Kingdom of God and openly take sides with Christ. We must follow with prompt and unfaltering obedience, wherever He leads.

This great and challenging question of Moses stirs our thoughts in several areas. First, note that it is a call to take sides. There is no neutrality on this question; there is no middle ground. All possible courses concerning Christ are reduced to two; for Christ, or against Him. Not to take the side of Christ is to side against Him.

Secondly, we see that this all important matter of taking sides calls for a prompt response. It is always and ever so with God's calls. We must give them our wholehearted attention, "If you hear His voice, do not harden your heart."

Lastly, as the Israelites who knew the One True God worshipped a statue of their own making, we should look as this scene and realize that the most perilous thing in the entire world is to have spiritual light and reject it. To know the way of duty and not travel it, to hear the call of Christ and not answer it, is disgraceful. End your hesitation.

Look at the outcome of Moses' challenge. Moses cried, "Whoever is on the Lord's side—come to me." Imagine the thrilling scene as all the sons of Levi arose and gathered themselves together with Moses! It is always a thrilling sight to see even one person stand up for the Lord. And what about you today? Because He is worthy of your love, devotion, and allegiance; come and stand with Him, and for Him today, wherever God has placed you. Help turn the tide for Christ.

Dear Heavenly Father, Please help me stand with Christ in the sphere in which You have placed me. I realize today that in whatever workplace, educational institution, neighborhood, or club that You have placed me, it is there that I must take my stand for Christ. I want to turn the tide for Christ in my little corner of the world. Please give me the strength, the wisdom and the love I will need to follow You in this journey. Amen.

May 8 — Rainbow of Grace

Scripture Reading: Genesis 8:20 to 9:19

Key Verses: "This is the sign of the covenant which I make between Me and you, and every living creature that is with you, for perpetual generations: I set My rainbow in the cloud, and it shall be for the sign of the covenant between Me and the earth." Gen. 9:12-13

It was the beginning of a new world, a fresh start. Noah's first act after he and his family descended from the ark was to build, not a house for himself, but an altar unto the Lord on which he presented burnt offerings. Then God blessed Noah, showing that the same divine favor that had been extended to Adam and Eve should now rest upon the new progenitors of the human race. The scope of this great Noahic covenant reaches even to the beasts of the field, and lasts until the end of time. God was the giver. Noah was the recipient, and had no part in the making of the covenant. It was distinctly God's covenant with Noah.

This covenant was unconditional, and inviolate. God promises that summer and winter, cold and heat, day and night shall not cease. Neither, God assures Noah, will there be another flood to destroy the entire earth. This is the merciful act of God, setting at peace the minds of His creatures. And still today, behind the so-called laws of nature, stands nature's God. The design of the covenant was to allay fear and establish man's confidence in the established order of nature.

This covenant was surely a wondrous display of grace and mercy. Man had already shown that he was utterly unworthy of the least of heaven's mercy, yet the Lord assures man of just that. It was also an affirmation of His creatorship. All the things God mentions, from the seasons and the crops to the weather and the climate, everything is beneath His control.

God also sets forth three requirements for man in this covenant. First, though all animals were to be under man's subjection, their blood was not to be eaten, for blood is the life. Secondly, whoever sheds man's blood shall have his blood shed by men, whether beast or man. And, finally, man was to be fruitful and multiply, which is a renewal of God's words to Adam in order to replenish the earth. And then God sealed the covenant with His token.

When God set His rainbow in the cloud as a token of the covenant, it speaks to us not only of assurance, but of a memorial of a new relationship which God has entered into with His creatures. In the rainbow, we see all the array of the lights of perfection in harmonious blending. Yet, the primary lights, the blue, red, and yellow, are a trinity in unity from which all the others are produced. Nature knows nothing more exquisite than the rainbow, even as heaven knows nothing that equals in loveliness the wonderful grace of our God.

The rainbow is a union of heaven and earth, spanning the sky and reaching down to the ground. So grace in the One Mediator has brought together God and men. The rainbow is a public sign hung out in the heavens, that all men might see it. So, too, "the Grace of God that brings salvation has appeared to all men," we are told in Titus 2.

Finally, as the rainbow has been displayed throughout all the past centuries, so in the ages to come, God will show forth the exceeding riches of His grace in His kindness towards us through Christ Jesus.

Dear Heavenly Father, thank You for the unmerited favor You have given man. We did not deserve it when You gave it, and we have not earned it since. The rainbow is truly a glorious, sparkling reminder of Your care over us. I am humbled and in awe of Your unceasing love and patience. Amen.

May 9   If I Were a Mother

Scripture Reading: II Corinthians 3:1-6

Key Verse: "You are our epistle written in our hearts, known and read by all men." II Corinthians 3:2

God has greatly honored motherhood. Mother is mentioned one hundred fifty times in Holy Writ. She was the last to leave the cross, and the first to get to the tomb. The first woman was named "Eve" because her husband Adam honored her as the mother of all people.

As in our text, a mother is an author, a writer with the home as the print-shop. Home is the print-shop that wields a mightier influence on the world's literature than all the publishing houses of time. Here motherhood reigns supreme.

What is more lasting, more impressionable material than the heart of a child? For what a child shall be depends in great measure on the character of the mother. The child is a copy machine taking in every impression made by the words and deeds of mother.

When Plato saw a child do wrong he went at once and rebuked the parent. Yes! How you must guard and watch the marks of your "life-pen" as it writes upon the pages of your child's heart.

There is a proverb that says: "An ounce of mother is worth a pound of clergy." Yes, the mother in her office holds the key to the soul and it is she who writes the epistle of character.

It's always easiest for a vegetarian to tell the butcher how to cut the meat, but with the example of my own dear mother to call on, this is what I'd do if I were a mother. I'd start to train my child at an early age to obey and to respect me. I'd study to win the confidence of and the respect of my child. I would seek out and strive to understand my child's concerns and problems. I would constantly remind myself that I was once young. I would also remember that the world has many more challenges and dangers than when I knew it as a child. I'd try to be a good disciplinarian not just by punishing, but by setting and teaching God's standard. And I'd endeavor by God's help to give an excellent example. This idea of shouting at a child is hurtful and accomplishes precisely nothing. The Bible says, "Children obey your parents in the Lord, for this is right. Honor your father and mother," but it also says "Fathers (and mothers) do not provoke your children to wrath, but bring them up in the training and admonition of the Lord."

We need the example of Godly parents. This counts for much. Be sincere. Don't lie to your children and expect them to respect you. They won't. Good character will not grow in an atmosphere of duplicity and hypocrisy and meanness. I'd pray for a baptism of love, sacrificial love that would hold my child to my heart. A loveless home is like a Godless Heaven.

But above all, and covering all, I'd want to be a Christian mother. That is the need of every mother because it is the need of every person. Whatever your calling, you need the salvation and the help and blessing of God. I'd bring my children to church. I'd have family devotions at home. I'd train my children to pray by praying before them. And I'd train them to live for Him who died for them.

As a pebble dropped into the harbor at Boston has its effect upon the docks of the city of Liverpool, so your child, born, trained, and nurtured by a good Christian mother will go out to bless the world.

Dearest Lord and Father, thank You for children. May I be a steadfast, true, and loving example to all who watch my life, and may they go out to bless the world. Amen.

May 10   The Difference

Scripture Reading: Matthew 5:38-48
Key Verse: "...what do you more than others?" Matthew 5:47

This is an arresting and searching question. It is obvious that Jesus expects His followers to be different from those about them. Yet, Christians are more alike as a group, than any other people in the world. Henry Van Dusen in his book *They Found the Church There* tells how the Christians of the South Seas took care of our soldiers, and he says that this tender care was the same whether those showing it were Methodists, Episcopalian, or any other denomination. They became the personality through which Christ thinks, the heart through which Christ loves, a voice through which Christ speaks and a hand through which Christ helps.

Jesus taught, "By this all will know that you are My disciples if ..." If what? Not if you belong to a certain group, not if you hold certain forms of worship, but "if you have love for one another." There is nothing as winsome as an atmosphere made warm and vital by the presence of those who love each other. Everyone longs to love and be loved, there is nothing that draws people to Christ like His unfathomable love.

Not only did these followers of Jesus love one another, not only did they love the brotherhood, but they loved those outside the brotherhood. Think of what an enormous difference this is. If you read the best-seller *Out of the Night*, you will be impressed by the author's emphasis on the devotion of one Communist to another. What a price they were willing to pay to serve and protect one another! But as impressive as was their loyalty to each other, so was their hatred of all outside their organization.

Well, not only did the early Christians love each other, they also loved strangers, foreigners and outsiders. If our world today is separated by deep and wide chasms, that ancient world was divided by chasms that were deeper and wider still. Yet, there was no chasm that separated people in that day that Christianity did not bridge. It bridged the chasm between man and woman, between race and race, between the respectable and the outcast, between master and slave. There was an eager interest in every human soul.

These early disciples of Jesus not only loved one another, strangers, and foreigners, but they loved their enemies. In the book, *Quo Vadis,* Petronis is writing a letter to his nephew who has been impressing upon his uncle the fact that if he becomes a Christian he must love everybody, even his enemies. "Must I love Nero?" writes the uncle in reply. These Christians did love their enemies. If we follow Christ we do also today.

Christian love does not mean a fondness for, or delight in ones enemies. They are not the ones we would choose as guests. We love our enemies when we exercise toward them an active and sacrificial good will. Such love Jesus taught and such love Jesus practiced.

"Bless those who curse you, and pray for those who spitefully use you," are Christ's exacting words. Jesus did that. He did that even while hanging on the cross. There He threw around the shoulders of His murderers the sheltering folds of this protecting prayer, "Father, forgive them, for they do not know what they do."

Dear Lord God, let my thoughts be Your thoughts. Let my voice be Your voice, my hands Your hands, and especially my love Your love. When I don't feel like loving those who hurt me, let me forgive and choose to act in the way You would have me act by surrendering to You. In the power of the Holy Spirit I choose today to love and forgive _____. Amen.

May 11   Windows on Motherhood

Scripture Reading: Proverbs Chapter 31

Key Verses: "Her children rise up and call her blessed; her husband also, and he praises her: 'Many daughters have done well, but you excel them all.' Charm is deceitful and beauty is passing, but a woman who fears the Lord, she shall be praised." Proverbs 31:28-30

Truly the mind of man has stored up no sweeter memories than those of a Christian mother. Her kiss soothed away more pain than all the soothing syrup she ever administered. It seems that as the years lengthen, the memories of mother just grow sweeter.

Mother, home, and heaven are not only three dear words; they are like links in a golden chain that binds us to high purposes and holy destinies. The right kind of mother can make the kind of home that is a little suburb of heaven.

Motherhood is not just a sanctuary for memory, however. It is also a repository of conscience. Mothers, it is said, are the conscience of the world for good or for evil, depending on the mold of their own souls. To be a good mother is to achieve the highest degree of success and usefulness. No one who appreciates the value of the real things in life would doubt the wisdom of a young woman's choice to devote her days to the raising of a godly family.

And, also, motherhood is a throne of power. A statue in Venice of a charming young mother with a beautiful child on each knee has these words inscribed on it, "A woman is a queen when her realm is in her lap." And, when she reigns on that throne in righteousness, far reaching is her power for good! At the knee of a godly mother is found the child's first sanctuary. It is there that the soul is set in the mold of blessed destiny. Far greater is this task of giving to the world men and women of good and lofty character than to grace the halls of congress or to sit upon a worldly throne.

But, Christian motherhood is not only a throne of power; it is a harbor of safety as well. How many young men and women have stayed the course of virtue or shunned dark temptation because of the anchor of a mother's righteous counsel. Such mothers form the mightiest bulwark of protection that can be erected by any nation. In Ponca City, Oklahoma, a statue of a woman facing west illustrates this well. She stands with a Bible firmly clasped to her breast with her right hand, and with her left hand she holds the hand of her boy as she gazes steadfastly into the future. This is surely a symbol of the motherhood that makes men, safeguards the home, builds the Church, and makes secure Christian civilization.

Somewhere there is a tombstone with the one word, "Mother" carved upon it, and above it a hand pointing heavenward. That is just what a godly mother is, a hand pointing her children to God and to heaven

A professor was lecturing to his class, propounding arguments against the Christian faith. When he had finished, he asked the students' reaction. One young man replied, "Your arguments are all but convincing, until I go back to my room and look at my mother's picture and remember her Godly life. Then your arguments fade into insignificance." Yes, Godly lives are an answer to all the skeptics of the world.

Dear Lord, let me grasp Your Word tightly. As I speak with those around me, let me be a place of sanctuary, peace, and godly influence. As I face the future, help me to be steadfast in my faith, unfailing in my love, and unwavering in my integrity. And may I always point to You. Amen.

May 12   A Love Story

Scripture Reading: Genesis Chapter 24

Key Verses: "*...And she said, 'I will go'... And Isaac went out to meditate in the field in the evening; and he lifted up his eyes and looked, and there, the camels were coming... Then Rebekah lifted her eyes, and when she saw Isaac she dismounted from her camel.... And he took Rebekah and she became his wife and he loved her.*" *Genesis 24:57-67.*

    In this place and this time, the parents did the choosing of their children's mates, and strange to say their plan seems to have worked as well as ours. Well, Abraham is getting old, and before he dies he would like to see his boy, Isaac, married. But, Abraham does not want Isaac to marry any of the Canaanites or Hittites around about him. He wants a bride for Isaac from the old country. So, he calls Eliezer, his most trusted servant, tells him of the mission, and gets ready the camels loaded down with choice gifts, for Abraham was businessman enough to know that the girl's parents would want to know something about the financial condition of the prospective husband.

    But, when the old servant approaches the bustling town of Nahor after his long journey, he found many beautiful maidens had come for water at the well. How was he to know which was the one? So, Eliezer prayed.

    God's provision, God's sovereignty, and God's blessing of those faithful to him are the primary themes in this tale of old-fashioned love. But, it is worth noting that in Rebekah's blessing are a few lessons for us all. First of all, Rebekah received this honor and blessing in the performance of her common and ordinary daily tasks. As she was carrying water for the household, Abrahams' servant Eliezer found her. She was faithful and diligent in the performance of a mundane duty of life. So it was also with Elijah, Moses, and Matthew. They were doing perfectly commonplace tasks when God called them to greater responsibilities. Be faithful, therefore, in the little things. God will make you ruler over many greater.

Rebekah also received her blessing through an act of kindness. She offered water to Eliezer, and water for his camels as well. This philosophy of kindness and service is a good philosophy for the world today as well. Kindness still wins hearts far quicker than scorn.

And, Rebekah received her blessing because she was willing to make a sacrifice. Rebekah gave up her family, her home, and her friends to go to a land that she did not know and marry a man she had never met. But in giving up much, she received a far greater blessing from God. There were trials that came her way, of course. It was not an easy life that she accepted. The Christian life today calls for sacrifice, too, but only to receive that of infinitely more value.

Finally, when Rebekah received her blessing she did not delay. Something told her it was the thing to do, and she was the more encouraged by her family. When Eliezer asked her, "Will you go," she replied, "I will go." So, too, today when God calls, He desires and expects a faithful and willing heart.

In the closing picture, Abraham is a type of God the Father. He has sent to find a fitting bride for his beloved only Son. And we are found, standing at the well. As the bride of Christ, we sacrifice the things of this world to gain the riches of His kingdom. As His bride, we are the recipients of His love, His companionship, and His presence forever. Will you go with Him?

Dearest Father, Thank You for seeking me. It is humbling to be a part of the bride of Christ. Today, in the ordinary and mundane things, help me to be faithful and true, kind and caring. And to do it all in Your name and for Your sake. Amen.

May 13   Too Many Barns

Scripture Reading: Luke 12:13-21

Key Verse: "Take heed and beware of covetousness, for one's life does not consist in the abundance of the things he possesses." Luke 12:15

    Jesus had been speaking on serious topics, but all the while one of the crowd had been thinking only of his share in his father's inheritance. This man is saying, "What do I care about being confessed before the angels, or having the Holy Spirit to teach me? All I want is my share of my father's land." Christ's answer was intentionally abrupt. He puts great emphasis into the command, "Take heed, and beware," then follows the story of the man God called a fool.

    This very successful farmer evidently knew when to plant, when to water, when to cultivate, and when to harvest. He was a good manager. There is nothing in the story to indicate he was unethical in any way in acquiring his goods. He was a prosperous citizen in his community, and his fellow citizens probably pointed with pride to the new barns and granaries he had built. Yet Jesus calls him a fool. Why? Because, there is nothing to indicate he acknowledged that he held the soil as a trust from God, or that he was dependent upon God for water and sun and germination of seed. There is no indication he realized because much was given him, much would be required. The farmer thought he was rich, but he was poor, destitute in his understanding toward God. He addressed his soul as being very prosperous, as if his soul could thrive on "much good laid up for many years." He knew not that he was impoverished toward God.

    He had forgotten God, while the first requisites for being rich toward God is a belief that He is, an assurance that He is seeking after men, and that man can find Him. This kind of faith receives from God an internal power and stability, and a capacity for growth and for daring.

    The second reason Jesus called the rich man a fool was that he had no sense of mission. He lived only for himself, compelled by his own greed. The Master calls and this calling gives adventure and fulfillment to living. A central tenet of the Christian faith is stewardship. Man is a trustee, responsible to God for the administration of the whole of life in accordance with the spirit and ideals of Christ. This is a Christian distinctive, and identifies one whose life is lived as belonging to God.

Yes, this man's foolishness lay primarily in the fact that he was a practical atheist. He had absolutely no sense of God. How do we know this? We know it when we hear him think. You can't tell a man by the way he looks, or what he says, or even what he does. But, if you could hear him think, then you would know. And the Bible says, "He thought within himself saying, 'What shall I do since I have no room to store my crops…? I will do this: I will pull down my barns, and build greater, and there I will store all my crops and my goods."

Now we see him. When he thought, he had not one single thought of God. He reckoned without God, and the man who reckons without God is a fool. The divine decree, "This night your soul will be required of you…." comes crashing down into human plans, and this rich fool was a pauper for time and eternity.

Dear Father, please prevent me from allowing accumulation of things to dull my spiritual perception. Don't allow me to become preoccupied with my own needs to the detriment of my ability to see the needs of others. And, most of all, Lord, please protect me from ever forgetting that life and all the living of it is a stewardship I owe to You. Help me to use my life, and all You have entrusted me with for Your glory! Amen.

May 14   Mother Ostrich

Scripture Reading: Lamentations 4:1-6
Key Verse: "The daughter of my people is cruel like ostriches in the wilderness." Lamentations 4:3

The text is at home in the book of Lamentations because it is a lament. It staggers under the weight of grief. But it is more than a lament. It is a sharp and cutting rebuke. It is full of hot indignation. It is spoken in the hottest anger by the prophet as a scourge for the terrible wrongs that are being perpetrated before his eyes. While breaking his heart, it also arouses his soul to battle. He cannot look upon it without a protest.

And who is this that has stirred the prophet's grief to indignation? Well beloved, here is a rebuke directed, not against the fathers of that day, but against the mothers. Surely this prophet was a daring man. It takes all the courage I can muster even to repeat, for this is the time of year we have set apart to honor her whose love has enriched the world, mothers. When we think of her, we feel deliciously sentimental. Tears are waiting just out of sight to rush eagerly upon the scene as soon as they receive their cue.

And naturally in an atmosphere like that these rude words of the prophet seem strikingly out of place. They jar and disappoint us. You feel resentful. The fact is: your resentment does you honor. It is an indication of your love and loyalty to your own mother. The mothers most of us remember are those whose efforts and sacred influence have stamped themselves indelibly upon the character of mankind.

But this prophet is daring to remind us of what we are prone to forget in a season like this. And that is that motherhood itself is not necessarily a badge of either goodness or greatness. A thoughtless, flippant, and self-centered woman is not of necessity transformed into a saint the moment she becomes a mother. It is against this type of mother that the prophet rails.

He charged them with cruelty. Listen, "The daughter of my people is cruel like ostriches in the wilderness." The Bible writers do not think highly of this bird. She is a symbol of cruelty and forgetfulness. Job describes her in this graphic fashion, "She leaves her eggs in the earth, and warms them in the dust, and forgets that the foot may crush them or that the wild beast may break them." She is hardened against her young ones as though they were not hers.

So, the cruelty of the mother that so enrages the prophet is the cruelty of neglect. These mothers failed to recognize the fact that the child was a precious, priceless gift, a blessing. The prophet was wise enough to know that the nation that fails to place great value on their children is headed for disaster.

Jesus was the supreme champion of the child. In seeing their importance He said, "Whosoever causes one of these little ones who believes in Me to sin, it would be better for him if a millstone were hung around his neck, and he were drowned in the depth of the sea."

Neglect of the physical brings disaster, but our children have other hungers. They hunger for the bread of life and thirst for the water of life. These cannot be banished by bacon and beans. Our children need us. Our children need our example. Be true to your task. Seek not to keep up with the times. Look to God and carry on.

Dearest Father, it's so easy to escape the demands of parenthood by turning aside to other interests. Help me to be true to my calling, for this time of nurture will pass so quickly. May I be diligent and joyful, remembering that these are priceless, irreplaceable years in the life of my children. May they count for You. Amen.

May 15 — The Paradox

Scripture Reading: Matthew 16:24-27

Key Verse: "If anyone desires to come after Me, let him deny himself, and take up his cross, and follow Me."
Matthew 16:24

The early Christians went out, not simply to follow Christ, but to share their blessing with the world. Their adventure was costly. They believed Christ's example of being faithful unto death. And Jesus also makes this plain to us. He declares, "Wide is the gate and broad is the way that leads to destruction." It was so hard for Jesus that it involved the cross, and He never promised that it would be easier for us.

He said, "Whoever desires to come after Me, let him deny himself, and take up his cross, and follow Me." There is no beginning the Christian life without this dying to self. There is no continuing it without daily dying to ourselves. There simply is no cheap and easy way to be a Christian. Take the heroic souls who are spoken of in the Old Testament. Read it and you will be impressed by how little God seems to care for the ease and comfort of His saints. Did He coddle or shelter them? No indeed. Here is the answer. "They were stoned, they were sawn in two, were tempted, and were slain with the sword." In the New Testament we find as Jesus kneels in prayer for the last time, He makes no plea that they might be sheltered and protected. He knew what kind of a world they were being left behind in. They were destined almost to a man to die for their loyalty to Him. Yet this is His prayer. "I do not pray that You should take them out of the world, but that You should keep them from the evil one." He is concerned, but for their character and victory. This indifference on the part of God to the comfort and ease of His saints was shared by these saints themselves. In their prayer it was not for escape that they prayed when the danger was real and threatening. Instead they prayed, "Grant to Your servants that with all boldness they may speak Your word." The early Christians dared to walk the difficult road.

But here is a lovely paradox. If these early Christians did have the hardest time of anybody, they also had the best time of anybody. When we get our first glimpse of them as a group they are so absurdly joyous that the world, as they looked on, could find no explanation. They said, "They are drunk, full of new wine." But from that intoxication they never recovered. It did not leave them with aching heads and hearts, it rather sent them joyously laughing and singing over all that hard Roman world.

"But," you say, "Christianity is a yoke." Yes, there is a yoke, but it is a yoke of a perfectly dedicated life; Jesus said, "My yoke is easy and My burden is light." Even though His yoke led Him to Calvary, Jesus was joyous and this abundant life that Jesus lived He shares with His followers. He said, "I have come that they may have life, and that they may have it more abundantly."

Look at Paul, and what a hard life he lived. He went to the whipping post many times and said he'd suffered the loss of all things, yet absolutely nothing could rob him of his radiance. But this radiance belongs to the Christians of every century, including this one. The Christian who possesses Christ possesses all that makes life supremely worth-while both in time and eternity.

Dear Lord, thank You that when life required that early Christians had to suffer, You also gave them the grace to go through it. They kept their eyes on You and not their circumstances, and You gave them the joy of their salvation. Help me to absorb this lesson and remember it when times of dificulty and trial come my way. Amen.

May 16   Pentecost

Scripture Reading: Acts Chapter 2

Key Verse: "For the promise is to you and to your children, and to all who are afar off, as many as the Lord our God will call." Acts 2:39

God's people should not lightly value Pentecost. It is one of the epochal events of spiritual history and one of the hinges on which God has swung His world into light. Pentecost was neither a passing pageant nor a religious exhibition. It was the manifestation of Jesus' promise of the gift of the Holy Spirit. We can do nothing without the Holy Spirit. Unless He guides, all will fail.

He led the believers in the day of Pentecost to pray and gave them direction for their prayers. He led them from their knees to service. He changed their timidity into courage. He was the Divine sword in their attack and each soldier had the sword. There were no camp followers, no slackers; all went to the battle. His control was perfect and absolute, He ordered and they obeyed.

Bold preaching, and simple exaltation of Christ, backed by compassionate prayer are the products of the power of the Holy Spirit seen that day. Here is the model in spirit and in action for every move of God in the world. They prayed, the gospel was preached, and multitudes came to Christ. Simple acts on the part of the believers were given the breath of life, dynamic and powerful by the promised Holy Spirit.

In the message inspired by the Spirit, the Lord and the Scriptures were magnified; Peter did not give a book review or preach on politics. He preached the Word. It was bold, clear, scriptural, pointed and pungent. It had no mincing of words, no pussyfooting, and no apologies. It climaxed in Jesus as Savior. It gave two steps to God, repentance and faith. It gave two directions for the convert, obedience and service.

Pentecost was not a day in the life of the Church; it was the day the church was born. The day the promised Holy Spirit began His work, His empowerment, and His inspiration in and through believers. Those we think of as giants of the church were weak and shepherdless after

Christ went to the Father, until the promised Holy Spirit came and transformed them.

Those same disciples who fled and hid at the moment of the crucifixion were changed into men full of power and certainty. Were they ever afraid? Probably. Times of persecution and martyrdom are not commonly agreeable times. Were they paralyzed with anxiety? No, their path was certain and their road was clear. They were unstoppable. They completed their mission. They were filled with the promised Holy Spirit and thereby fitted by God as Christian soldiers of the His Kingdom. The cares of the day did not deter them. The onslaught of the enemy did not cause them to shrink back from their heavenly assignments, even when faced with death. They were changed, filled, and empowered.

The promise of Pentecost is as needful now as 2000 years ago. Sin is 2000 years deeper and men are as much lost as ever.

But on the other hand, their God is our God. Their power is our power. Their promise is our promise. We can do nothing without the Holy Spirit of Pentecost. Until we allow His filling, we are also weak and shepherdless. We may pray, and preach and try and try and try. But if the glove has no hand its efforts are useless. The hand that guides and makes us useful is the Holy Spirit.

Dear Lord, fill me with the power and leading of Your Holy Spirit. I don't want to rush off in my own power doing useless, undirected things, as earnest as they may be. Let my life be Spirit-filled, Spirit-led, and Spirit-empowered all to Your glory and service. In the name of Christ Jesus, amen.

May 17   Speaking Faithfully

Scripture Reading: Jeremiah 23:16-29

Key Verse: "...and he who has My word, let him speak My word faithfully..." Jeremiah 23:28

This chapter of Jeremiah leaves us breathless in its rebuke of the faithless prophet and priest. We are at once aghast, and strangely acquainted with those descriptions of the prophets declaring their own words, and turning against the word of the Lord. We would be blind to not sense and see the terrifying rapidity with which apostasy is sweeping over Christendom. Instead of greater devotion to the truth, there is a growing declension that makes our hearts sick.

The Word of God is the great divider of history. Faithfulness to that Word divides men into two camps. In our day, modernism in all its hundred forms may be marked always in this one respect: it is unfaithful to the Word of God. And, fundamentalism, which likewise has its hundred forms, is marked in this one way: it is faithful to the Word of God. Now those who are unfaithful to the written word are also unfaithful to the Living Word, Jesus Christ. Contrariwise, those who are faithful to the one are also faithful to the other. You have only to think of the way modern cults distort the Bible in order to cast doubt on Christ's deity to see the link.

Truth matters. Convictions matter. And, what you do with your convictions matters. In being faithful to the Word, we must do more than believe it. Satan does that, and trembles. We must learn to proclaim it in our daily lives. We must speak the Word faithfully, as well as live it faithfully. Let us look at some important truths that we should speak, in faithfulness to God's Word.

First, let us teach that sin is real and personal. Barbarism is not behind us, nor is it creeping in upon us. It is within us. Everyone is born under its shadow. It is not popular, but it is Scriptural. "The heart is deceitful above all things and desperately wicked," Jeremiah proclaims. Then, let us teach that forgiveness of sin also is real and personal. Our

God is a God of hope and love. He forgives freely all who call upon Him.

And also, let us speak the truth of the cleansing from sin, which is real and personal. "For the wages of sin is death, but the gift of God is eternal life in Christ Jesus our Lord." God not only forgives us, but He cleanses us from every sin through the power of the blood of our dear Lord, Jesus Christ.

Next, let us tell the world that God's love is real, and personal. In creation, God's love is gloriously shown. Did He not make us in His own image? But in the cross, the love of God is supremely revealed. God gave His Son as our ransom. The Lamb of God took upon Himself the burden of man's sin.

And let us marvel at the wonder of prayer, which is real, and personal. Our God is a very present help in time of need, "Call to Me and I will answer You." Bring God everything through prayer and find a fellowship the world knows nothing about. Prayer is the gateway to peace and His presence.

Oh, beloved, be faithful to the Word, in your study, in your speech, and in your life. Be living epistles to those who read your life each day. Prove all things. Hold fast to that which is true. Walk in the light as He is in the light. Speak His Word faithfully.

Almighty Father, no matter how much I read Your Word I am always struck by how much I do not know, rather than how much I understand. Please open my eyes and my heart to the truth of Your Word. Help me to love the Scriptures. Help me to be faithful to Your Word. Help me to speak Your Word faithfully. For Your glory, and for the sake of Your Kingdom, amen.

May 18   My Presence

Scripture Reading: Exodus Chapter 33
Key Verse: "My presence will go with you, and I will give you rest." Exodus 33:14

A soul that has tasted of the sweetness of His divine presence cannot but long for more of it, as those who tasted of the grapes of Canaan longed to be in Canaan. So they who have experienced the sweetness of Divine presence cannot be satisfied with a little bit of it, but in every prayer this is the language of their souls, "Lord, more of Your presence...."

I do not know which are the more gracious and wonderful among the promises of the Bible, those addressed to seekers after God or those addressed to the redeemed who have found God in Christ. The Apostle Peter speaks of them as "Exceedingly great and precious promises." When we look back to the time we sought the Lord, we remember the promises upon which we stood. How precious to me were the words, "...the one who comes to Me I will by no means cast out." And ever since that day, the promises of our faithful God have become more and more precious as I have proved them.

Now there is one class of promises which have always had an especially tender appeal to the Lord's people. It is that large group in which we have the assurance of the Divine presence with us. If there is one thing more than another which the true servants of God have always longed to be quite sure about, it is this very thing. God has graciously responded in many assurances given to us in His word. They constitute one of the most comforting and edifying studies in the Bible.

As a specimen, let us take this promise of our text, "My presence will go with you, and I will give you rest." This promise is a benediction in itself, but when taken with its context, its fuller graciousness and glory break upon us. As with a precious stone, it is enhanced by a beautiful setting.

The promise is spoken to Moses in connection with one of the most deplorable incidents in the wilderness journeying of Israel. God raised up a deliverer to bring these people out from the bondage of Egypt into the national freedom and blessing of Canaan. He accompanied that emancipation with a mighty hand and outstretched arm. Yet, while Moses was on the mountain receiving the commandments and instructions, the people turned to idolatry and were dancing before the golden calf. Moses returned, and the sight of the idolatrous obscenity of the people kindled a righteous anger within him. Yet, the thought of it also fills him with grief. A broken-hearted man sinks down before God and sobs out a pitiful prayer. He needed the presence of God, and he said, "If Your Presence does not go with us, do not bring us up from here." Then it was in loving kindness toward His stricken servant that God gave this further assurance, "I will also do this thing."

What a difference it makes in our lives when we discover that our Lord is really with us. Jesus is Emmanuel, literally God with us, and He said, "Lo, I am with you always." God is not a respecter of persons. This wondrous consciousness of the Lord's continual presence is meant for you, too. If God foreknew us and loved us before we drew our first breath, will He fail to think upon us during our sojourn here? Assuredly, He will not fail us.

Dearest Father God, Your presence alone provides me with rest, because in Your presence I am secure. Along with Moses, I cry, "Please show me Your glory." Help me to live in full awareness of Your presence in my life. Amen.

May 19   Remember Now Thy Creator

Scripture Reading: Ecclesiastes Chapter 12
Key Verse: "Remember now your Creator in the days of your youth; before the difficult days come, and the years draw near when you say, 'I have no pleasure in them'." Eccl. 12:1

When I graduated from seminary and came as an immigrant to America, I accepted a call to a church in Northern Michigan. It was the custom to invite the newest preacher in the community to bring the Baccalaureate address, and so it fell upon me as a very young pastor to deliver the message. It was in the year 1914. And later, as the eldest preacher in another community, exactly fifty years later, I was thus honored again. Many things in life have changed since those early days, but the principles of life remain the same. The text is as sure and true today as it was in 1914, or 1000 years ago.

The first word of our text warns us against an awful sin, and at the same time points us toward real success and great blessing. Forgetfulness of God is a monster. The fabled Chimera which breathed out fire was a house cat compared to forgetfulness. On the other hand, remembering God gives us the benefit of all the experience of the ages, and in proportion to which we do it, we establish our life upon a solid foundation of safety, peace, usefulness, and joy. Remembering anything is useful. Remember the bad as a warning. Remember the good as a challenge. I want you to think seriously on the reasons we should remember God.

The first reason we should remember God in the days of our youth is that we can! Youth takes in information as a dry field takes rain. Youth can absorb facts like a well, and then, like a well, give without going dry. There is a best time for everything, and the best time to learn in order to retain, is during youth. The mind is receptive, and the soul is unbiased, unembittered by mistakes, and unhampered by prejudice.

Remember God in your youth, because youth can act. Maturity is great for holding the kingdom, but youth is bold in pushing the frontiers of the kingdom forward. Give God the "pushing power" of your youth! Remember God in your youth so that He may use your daring, alertness, and endurance.

Remember God in your youth because youth is all you may have. David Brainard, the famous missionary, wrote a diary that has inspired generations. It has been said that this diary has done more to develop the spirit of modern missions and fire the heart and spirit of the church than any writings since those of the apostles. Wesley read it, and advised Carey to read it. Carey was inspired by it to begin his own missionary journeys, and spent about 30 years in India translating the Bible into twenty-four languages and dialects and giving the Scripture to 300 million human beings. But, if Brainard had not written that diary in his youth, he never would have written it, for he died at twenty-nine.

Finally, remember your Creator in your youth because an early remembrance of God leaves you with no regrets. On the contrary, a youthful surrender leaves a lifelong remembrance that will be a perpetual delight. There are a multitude of people who cry out in remorse over a misspent youth; an untold number whose regrets over wasted time and wasted energy serve as warnings to us. God is gracious; His mercy extends to the limits of our life. But, hear me, Remember Him now. Don't waste a single day.

Dear Lord, I consecrate this day to You and to Your service. Empty me of self and fill me with Your Spirit that I may be of service to You today. Amen.

May 20   There's a Stranger at the Door

Scripture Reading: Revelation 3:14-22
Key Verse: "Behold, I stand at the door and knock."
Revelations 3:20

What tales the door of an old home would unfold if it could swing back in memory as easily as it turns back on its hinges? But a little lumber and a little hardware to the passerby, it is the sentinel of the family that lives behind it.

Past it two brave hearts moved joyously as they carried in the furniture that announced the beginning of another family. About the base of that door the little kiddies played. That door watched the crowds that gathered.

The old door, if it were human, would remember the midnight visits of the doctor, the anxious questions, and the prayers of the family solemnly offered beside it. It felt the thud of the hammer when the undertaker fastened the wreath of death to its bosom.

It heard the rumblings of that prodigal son stumbling over the sill in the early morning hours. It felt the trembling hand of age leaning heavily upon its knob. How full of pathos is the door of an old homestead.

But of all the doors I know there is none as wonderful as the door of the human heart. At that door, the Scriptures state, a stranger stands and knocks for admission. Your heart and mine are His rightful home, and this homeless one outside your heart is the saddest person in the world until He makes His home in your heart.

He is knocking at the door of your heart to which He is entitled by the best of all rights. First by creation, He made you. John's gospel says, "Without Him was not anything made that was made." And secondly, He is entitled to admission to your heart and life by the valid right of redemption, Jesus gave his life to redeem (buy back) every soul that will come unto Him.

Now what would you think of a man whose home had been bought back from a sheriff's sale by a brother, and after the sale that man refused to give his brother a room, or even worse, refused him any room at all?

This is not a common stranger at the door. This is a stranger whose heart aches as long as the door is shut against him. It hungers for admittance into all that are His own. Think of the greatness of that love as He knocks at the heart's door of millions whose doors are still closed against Him.

When Dr. Robertson, the great Scottish preacher, was a boy he went across the moor one day to play with the neighbor's children. He played and played until he lost track of time and night set in. His little heart sank as he looked out across the moor and remembered the peat bogs and the holes all along the path. How was he ever to get home? But as the tears welled up in his eyes and his spirit was lowest, he heard a knock at the door and the voice of his big older brother calling his name. He had come to take him home. Oh how wonderful to have Jesus to go with us all along the journey and take us home.

My friends give place for this stranger who knocks at your door. He offers you every blessing, rest, peace, home, and heaven. For His sake who loves you, for your sake who need Him, for eternity's sake, let Him in. Pull back the bolt, open the door, and let Jesus come into your heart.

Dear Jesus, come into my heart and live in me. I throw open the door to my life for You to enter and fellowship with me. I also pray for _____ and _____, that they may hear Your knock and also invite You in. Amen.

May 21   Beauty and the Beast

Scripture Reading: I Samuel Chapter 25

Key Verse: "She was a woman of good understanding and beautiful appearance; but the man was harsh and evil in his doings." I Samuel 25:3

Here in this masterpiece of Old Testament biography, we have the story of the beauty and the beast. Sometimes you have seen a charming, gracious lady married to a boorish, wicked man and you have wondered how it ever could have happened. But, in ancient days there is no wonder, for the woman had comparatively little to say as to whom she would marry. In the old, pagan days, men used to deck the oxen devoted for sacrifice with garlands and ribbons. But that did not keep back the gleaming knife of the priest when he slew them at the altar. Neither does wealth, station, or a great name hold back the knife of unhappiness when a woman is married to a man like Nabal.

Well, in our text passage, we find Nabal insulting David horribly, and David summoning his hundreds of men to strap on their swords. David, enraged, is going to teach Nabal a lesson. Fortunately a servant hurried to Nabal's wife, Abigail, and informed her. Abigail rushed to prepare the gifts that Nabal should have offered, gathered herself up and set off. Abigail was able to intercede with gracious generosity, and David relented. Nabal's household was spared, but "about ten days later, the Lord struck Nabal and he died."

When we sum up the truths which come to us from the story of Abigail, we are struck that she did not permit the trial and adversity of life to embitter her spirit. To have married this beast must have been a great trial, but she bore her cross with resignation. She did not become bitter, nor turn against life. As Paul would say, her affliction seemed grievous to her but it yielded the peaceful fruits of righteousness.

Another truth is the providence of God in our daily life. In Abigail's intercession with David, she reassured him that God's hand was not withdrawn from him and that however dark and forbidding the present day, he would be King over Israel. Perhaps you are discouraged, or even rebellious, and God's way seems hard. God who created you has high things in store for you. Be faithful. Hold back your hand from evil and your heart from unbelief. Wait on the Lord. Be of good courage.

The final truth we hear from the lips of Abigail herself as she pleads with David. No one ever regrets the evil he did not do. David had many things to regret in later life, but not the slaying of Nabal and his house. Through the plea of this lovely woman, and David's yielding to her plea, he was spared one regret. Oh thank God for the regrets you have missed on the scroll of yesterday because God in His grace and providence kept you back from them.

I appeal for your future. There are choices you will never regret. It will be no regret that you remembered the Creator. It will be no regret that you did not neglect God's Word and God's House of Worship. It will be no regret that you did not yield to your angry passions, nor take mean advantage. It will be no regret that when insulted, you turned away wrath with a soft answer. And, one more thing I know you will never regret. You will never regret heeding the call of God's Holy Spirit on your life every day.

Dear Heavenly Father, I, too, desire to be wise and faithful to You and the duties You have entrusted to me. Help me to bear my crosses with patience and fortitude. Help me, like David, to heed the plea of the Spirit on my heart and resist the temptation to avenge myself. Just now, I give all my burdens and hurts to You. Amen.

May 22 — Whose Neighbor Am I?

Scripture Reading: Luke 10:25-37

Key Verse: "But he, wanting to justify himself, said to Jesus, 'And who is my neighbor?'" Luke 10:29

The lawyer in the story was testing Jesus' orthodoxy and his ability. But Jesus simply replied, "Do this and you will live." Somewhat embarrassed, the lawyer seeks to justify himself. He is satisfied he has done his duty to God, but not so sure about his fellow-men, so he asks, "Who is my neighbor?"

But, you will find that Jesus turned the question around to the statement, "Whose neighbor am I?" Neighbor, in the lawyer's judgment meant nearness and he wished to know how far the boundaries of the command lay. But Christ's answer swept all such limitations aside. Said Christ, "So which of these three do you think was neighbor to him who fell among the thieves?"

"He who showed mercy on him," said the lawyer.

We are not to love, therefore, because we are neighbors in any geographical sense only, but we become neighbors to the man farthest from us when we love and help him. The word neighbor, therefore, is as wide as humanity.

What a lesson we have here as to the true manifestations of neighborliness. Compassionate sentiments are fine, but the emotions that do not drive the wheels of action and kindness of a tangible character are purposeless. It is not enough to love God, but we are to love the neighbor as ourselves also. Feelings unexpressed in action only harden the heart.

However, the various acts enumerated in the story of the Good Samaritan show the genius of true love: the Samaritan's readiness to expend his wine and oil, his willingness to do the surgeon's work, his cheerful giving up of his own beast while he plodded along by foot, his care for the wounded man at the inn, and his generosity and prudence in paying the bill.

There is a great danger here which we Christians must lay emphasis upon, that of being religious and yet unconcerned about the world's wounds. If our love to God does not find a field for its manifestation in active love to man, then our worship will be a mockery.

The poor wounded man was a victim of bad religion as revealed by the priest and the Levite. The priest was purely professional in his attitude. The Levite was purely theoretical in his attitude. Both were unwilling to help because their hearts were unaffected.

When the lawyer asked, "Teacher, what shall I do to inherit eternal life?" Jesus said, "You shall love the Lord your God with all your heart, with all your soul, with all your strength, and with all your mind, AND your neighbor as yourself." That simple word "and" which couples the two great commandments expresses their indissoluble connection. Therefore, what God has joined, let not man put asunder.

At this hour, the man with a neighborly spirit is the man of the hour. He will rise above questions of race, nationality, or religion. He will help in the material needs as well as the spiritual needs of those he would help. He will do good at the cost of self-sacrifice. Our love must be practical, unselfish, and real, as was our Savior's.

It is in Christ you will find help for your helplessness, strength for your weakness, protection from every foe, supply for every need, salvation from every sin, and healing from every wound. Now, go and do likewise.

Precious Master, help me to pour forth the love You have so generously poured into me. Help me to realize in practical ways that I have been blessed to bless others. Amen.

May 23 — Hear Him

Scripture Reading: Matthew 17:1-13

Key Verse: "While he was still speaking, behold, a bright cloud overshadowed them; and suddenly a voice came out of the cloud, saying, 'This is My beloved Son, in whom I am well pleased. Hear Him!" Matthew 17:5

Thus the Father declares and fixes in time the authority of the Son. If something is fixed, it permits progress. Two plus two equals four. It always has been and from this we can progress. In music there are eight fixed notes, no new ones, but this has not stopped musical progress.

In character also we have found a perfect ultimate in Christ. Now we know what to be like and what kind of world is ideal. We can progress. God the Father tells us to "Hear Him!" If we did hear Him and follow Him, in twenty-four hours all hunger would be banished.

There is a cloud over racial relations. Christians must hear Christ when He tells us to love one another. Our Christian love must go past the color of the face or the shape of the eyes. Christ died for all races.

There is a cloud over church relations. Why is the great power of the Christian church muffled? Because we are divided and therefore have no unity. We are divided by denominations and creeds, doctrines and philosophies. We Christians must come together on the basis of love not philosophy.

In every denomination there are saints. We worship the same Lord and Savior, experience the same glorious salvation, and upon this we must stand. As Jesus prayed, "that they may be one, as You, Father, are in Me and I in You." Out of the clouds, hear Him!

There are clouds over our individual spirits and lives. Why? Because of divided allegiance. Joshua said, "Choose you this day who you will serve." Elijah said "If God be God, serve Him." Let us release the idols of life and lay them at His feet, for the Lord of your salvation is either the Lord of all or not Lord at all.

When Elijah had yielded all, he tested God and God met his every test. When the worshippers of Baal were challenged to pray to their god for fire to light their altar without result, Elijah had water poured over the altar of God then asked God for fire. The Scriptures say, "and the fire fell." Yosemite has great falls where fire is pushed from the top of the mountain each night. Loudly it is yelled, "Let the fire fall," and magnificent glowing coals of fire eddy and twirl their way to the floor of the valley. Oh that the fire of consecration, of cleansing, of zeal and of victory might fall upon us all today.

We face war, we face untold sickness, and we face cruel tyrants who would rob us of our peace and security. God knew what we would face, and He said "This is my beloved Son. Hear Him!" When Peter tried to walk on the water to go to Jesus, he took his eyes off of Christ and looked only at the deep and swirling waters and immediately began to sink. Christ told him to come to Him but instead of hearing and obeying he focused on his circumstances. Let us not make the same mistake.

When the winds of war swirl around us, when sickness taps at our door, let us "Hear Him." Let us obey Him and let us keep our focus on Him. He is the only hope for this war-mad, fearful, and clouded world. We are in a world crisis, but it need not be a crisis of fear. Christ will supply our every need. Let the fire fall!

Dearest Father in Heaven, You have fixed forever that Jesus is Your Son and that we should listen to Him. His words are forever preserved in the Word of God, the Bible. When I am perplexed or fearful, let me always listen to His teaching for He has the answer to every question. Amen.

May 24   The Secret of Success

Scripture Reading: Proverbs Chapter 29
Key Verse: "Where there is no revelation, the people cast off restraint; but happy is he who keeps the law." Proverbs 29:18

The crucial need of the world is for vision, which is defined as revelation from God beyond our natural line of sight. Vision, decision, and deed are the beginning, advancing, and conquering points in life's progress. When Demosthenes ended his appeal, the Greeks did not applaud his eloquence. Rather, they cried, "Lead us against Philip!" His vision was presented, the decision was formed, and the deed wrought in menacing consequences to the Macedonian enemies of Greece.

Now, there are three types of vision. Physical vision deals with the visible facts and phenomena of the material universe, but knows nothing of the laws that lie back of them. Mental vision penetrates to the cause of the visible phenomena, and discovers the hidden laws that govern them. But, spiritual vision alone has that higher gift of discerning the deeper laws that govern the moral world, determining character, and regulating the conduct of men and nations. Spiritual vision sees life in its interior quality and fathoms its significance and purpose. It sees the heights of possibilities not yet visible to the realm of reality. This is the crying need of mankind today.

A bird's-eye view of life is imperative to an understanding of life, and yet that is far from our grasp. Our sidewalk view is close and narrow; things are out of proportion. As no soldier in the fight can see the battlefield, for the perspective of height is required for that vision, so it is of life. As in our text, the people who have lost the vision have also lost the purpose of life. The people who have lost their vision, their plumb line for life, have an easy philosophy of life because it is the way of the unthinking, the careless. A drifting boat always goes downstream. On the other hand, God alone has the perspective on our life that enables true vision to be formed.

There are but few fundamentals which underlie all of mankind's achievements. This is true in every realm. For instance, in mathematics there are only ten numerals with which to work all problems of addition, multiplication, subtraction, and division. The alphabet contains only twenty-six letters, yet with them the Bard of Avon fashioned *The Merchant of Venice*, and *Hamlet*. Despite the myriad of colors surrounding us, they all spring from just a few. And in music we have only eight basic notes, yet from them have sprung all song, symphony, opera, and orchestra. Just so, to succeed in life, we need only the principles God sets forth in His Holy Word. With God in your equation, you have the fundamentals for success in any arena.

Our society wrongly believes that a good education will provide for success in life. But it is not the mastering of the intricacies of a language, or of science, which lend vision to a life. No, true education must eventuate in character. To develop intellectual powers with no reference to moral values is but to increase one's potential for evil. It is only when a desire to follow God is at the heart of our ambitions that we are truly prepared for the great adventure we call life. It is only He who is Himself the way, the truth, and the life, who can give you the vision you need to find true "success" in life. He is the true "secret" to real, eternal success.

Dear Lord, so often I seek wrongly. I seek some thing, or some gain, rather than seeking You. Help me to seek You, and then to follow You whole-heartedly wherever You may lead me in this life. That is the only success I desire. Amen.

May 25   The Conqueror from Calvary

Scripture Reading: Isaiah 63:1-6
Key Verse: "Who is this who comes from Edom, with dyed garments from Bozrah?" Isaiah 63:1

The shadows of the night are beginning to lift. Toward the east, the mountains are taking shape. A watchman, standing on the wall of some town of Israel beholds in the distance a solitary warrior. The hastening day reveals him to be grand in his stature, majestic in his movements, striding forward with the carriage of a conqueror. His garments are splashed with blood and they are streaming behind him in the wind. As he nears, the watchman on the wall challenges him, "Who is this who comes?" And the answer comes, "I who speak in righteousness, mighty to save."

For ages, the Christian Church has seen in this sublime vision of the bloodstained conqueror from Edom, the prophetic sketch of the sufferings and triumph of Christ on the cross over sin and death, and the final triumph of the Kingdom of God. As we look, then, at this solitary figure there are three questions that come to mind. First, who is he? Then, what has he done? And finally, what will he yet do?

There are some who say that it makes very little difference who He is. The main thing, they say, is to obey His words and follow in His steps. Yet, those who have most fully done the will of this conqueror have been those who were most convinced as to His identity and person. Who is this? That was also the question the people of Jerusalem asked on that fair morning when Jesus rode into their Capital upon the foal of a donkey. That was the very question Paul asked at the Gate of Damascus, "Who are You, Lord?" In fact, that was the question Jesus Himself asked of His disciples, "Who do men say that I, the Son of Man, am?" Yes, that is the question that settles our faith, our service, and our future. Your answer will settle the whole question of your life, both here and hereafter.

The first answer to this question is that this One, who comes from

Edom marching down the corridors of time with the marks of passion and suffering upon Him, is God. He claimed pre-existence, "Before Abraham was, I am." He claimed omnipotence, "All authority is given unto me." He claimed sinlessness, "which of you convicts me of sin?" He claimed the right and the power to forgive men's sins. He claimed the power to judge men and allots to them their eternal destiny.

But, this conqueror who is God is also man. How can that be? How can He be both man and God at the same time? Great is the mystery of God. In all things, He who was to redeem men was made like unto man. He was complete in His understanding and sympathy with those whom He was to judge and to redeem.

He is not Deity diluted into humanity. Nor is He humanity exalted into Deity. He is God and man, the God-man, God with us, Emmanuel, our Redeemer and Savior, Jesus Christ. Because He is very God, His words and His acts have supreme authority and power. Because He is truly man, He is qualified to represent us before God, wounded for our transgressions, and bruised for our iniquities.

Who then is this that comes from Edom? He is the God-man, the Lord of Glory. He is our Elder Brother and yet the Everlasting Son of the Father. He is worshipped by angels, and loved by redeemed sinners. This is the mystery and the glory of the gospel.

Precious Lord, I worship and praise You today for your omnipotence. I praise You as the Creator-Redeemer of this world. I rejoice in Your majesty, I rest in the perfection of Your provision for me. Thank You for all You are, and all You have done for me. Amen.

May 26   The Conqueror's Conquest

Scripture Reading: Isaiah 63:3-14

Key Verse: "I have trodden the winepress alone, and from the peoples no one was with Me." Isaiah 63:3

So, we have seen Who it is that comes from the East. It is the God-man, Jesus Christ. He comes with the stride of a conqueror, and with the marks of battle upon Him. Just as in Revelation 19:13, His robe is dipped in blood. And so, we ask, what is it that this One who comes from Edom has accomplished? "I who speak in righteousness, mighty to save," is also the answer to this question. He conquered for us, on the cross, the power of sin and of death to save our souls.

Yes, He brings judgment on the nations. Yes, He wages war on the enemy at His coming. But, the great enterprise is to save—to redeem mankind. That is the only enterprise that is in keeping with that glorious conqueror, the God-man, come from Edom.

How did He save? By His sufferings and His death. This is no vacationer we see come from the East, no indeed. He comes with bloodstained garments on Him. He comes from His great conquest with the marks of suffering and death upon Him. His bloodstained vestments proclaim the price of His victory.

All great things are won with the price of suffering and death. We rejoiced at the victories won by the Allied Armies in Europe and in the Pacific at the close of the Second World War. But, not without a price were those victories won. That terrible war left behind it many crimson garments to tell the story of the price paid. In many a home on the heathered hills of Scotland, in many a lovely vale in Wales, in many an English hamlet, in many a home in America there is the indelible mark of the price paid. Marvel not at this, beloved friends, for it has been so from the beginning. Tyranny, like hell, is not easily conquered.

And so it was with our Great Conqueror from Edom. His death, His sufferings, were the price of His victory. We have been redeemed.

We have been justified. We have been reconciled. We have been washed by His blood, by Him alone.

In this great conquest, Christ was alone. "I have trodden the winepress alone, and from the peoples no one was with me… I looked, and there was no one to help, and I wondered that there was no one to uphold." No, it was not several conquerors that the watchman saw coming from Edom, the land of strife and battle. Only one, a solitary Conqueror, comes; the One who trod the winepress for us alone. "There is none righteous, no, not one."

He was alone, for He alone could do it. He looked, and there was none to help. Only He could fight this battle. See how in Gethsemane's moonlit shadows He looked and there was none to help? See how he went forward a stone's cast and alone entered into His agony? Behold His agony and loneliness on Calvary's tree, "My God, my God, why have you forsaken me?" Christ was alone, because He alone could win this victory. He alone is mighty to save.

And yet, though His great work of salvation is done, He has not passed from the stage of the world. In fact, He has yet to come as conqueror, the universally praised and worshipped Savior of the world. For that is yet to come.

Dear Father, Thank You for the provision You made from time eternal for the redemption of man. Thank You that Your patience with this lost and fallen creation is boundless. Thank You that despite the high price of our freedom from sin, despite our unworthiness, despite our ingratitude, You willingly paid that price for us. Amen.

May 27   The Coming Conqueror

Scripture Reading: Isaiah Chapter 35

Key Verse: "And the ransomed of the Lord shall return, and come to Zion with singing, with everlasting joy on their heads. They shall obtain joy and gladness, and sorrow and sighing shall flee away." Isaiah 35:10

We have seen who He is that comes in Isaiah 63:1 as the Conqueror. He is the God-man, Jesus Christ, our redeemer. We have seen what He has done. But that is not the end. We hail Him as the Conqueror of not only the past, but of tomorrow. He is not only "Alpha" the beginning, but "Omega," the end, as well. He is the first and the last Conqueror. Before Him all others fade. Their crowns tumble from their brows and their kingdoms pass and vanish. But the Kingdom of Christ is an everlasting Kingdom!

We think of this great Conqueror and this conquest of Christ as applied to each one of us. But, we want to think also of its relationship to the whole universe. Paul thought of Christ's redeeming work very personally when he wrote, "the Son of God who loved me and gave Himself for me." Me, the blasphemer; me, the persecutor; me, the chief of sinners; He gave Himself for me. But then, Paul saw Christ in relationship to the whole world, also, when he wrote, "And by Him to reconcile all things to Himself, by Him, whether things on earth or things in heaven, having made peace through the blood of His cross."

So great was that victory in Paul's eyes that he described it in the terms of a Roman triumph, saying, "Having disarmed principalities and powers, He made a public spectacle of them, triumphing over them in it." Oh, let no one imagine that this battle we see raging about us today, this conflict which has been going on ever since the fall of man, will go on forever. Oh, no, it will come to an end, for Christ who triumphed over Satan on the cross will meet him again at the end of the world.

History and prophecy tell us of two great conquerors who rode on white horses. History tells of Napoleon who when seen riding on that horse would so inspire his men that they shook the earth with their shouts and craved the privilege of dying for him. The other Conqueror on a white horse is the one John saw at Patmos, "Now I saw heaven opened, and behold a white horse. And He Who sat on him was called Faithful and True. . . . He was clothed with a robe dipped in blood and His name is called the Word of God... And He has on His robe and on His thigh a name written. 'King of Kings and Lord of Lords.'" Napoleon went down as all before him had done. Fate and death unhorsed him. Such was the fate of Napoleon, and such will be the fate of him who is called the Anti-Christ. What an abyss between him and the eternal kingdom of my Christ!

In the art gallery of Brussels, there is a great painting called, "The Triumph of Christ." In this painting, the conqueror from Calvary hangs on the cross. His body is beautiful even amid the blood and darkness of Golgotha. From every point of the crown of thorns, there streams light ineffable. Mighty angels are sounding on their trumpets while sinister figures flee into darkness. So, at length, shall it be. The Conqueror from Calvary is the last Conqueror. The Light of the World shall banish the World's darkness. Divine love shall conquer sin and hate. And, "the ransomed of the Lord shall return and come to Zion with songs and everlasting joy upon their heads. They shall obtain joy and gladness, and sorrow and sighing shall flee away."

Almighty God, I look forward with joy and anticipation to the day when the dark and sinister things of this earth are no more, and every knee bows before the true King. Even so, Lord Jesus, come. Amen.

May 28 — Decision

Scripture Reading: I Kings Chapter 18

Key Verses: "Elijah came to all the people, and said, 'How long will you falter between two opinions? If the Lord is God, follow Him; but if Baal, follow him.' But the people answered him not a word." I Kings 18:21

The picture painted by this text has a bleak background dark with unbelief, sin and indecision. Elijah stands before the people of Israel and the prophets of Baal on Mt. Carmel calling the people to decision. The confrontation is caused by apostasy. And the call to serve the Lord is accompanied by a mighty demonstration of God's power to save, to deliver, and to honor those who serve Him faithfully.

One of the greatest privileges conferred upon man is the power of decision. The human will distinguishes us from animal creation. We are free moral creatures by divine right and in everything of life it is our duty to decide. Our whole life, both here and hereafter, must be decided. We are responsible before God. Our text shows the abuse of this privilege by both professing followers of God, and by the world of unbelievers. Here we find people trying to serve two Masters—impossible!

God will not play second fiddle for you. The very first commandment is that "you shall love the Lord your God with all your heart, with all your soul, and with all your mind." "Do not love the world or the things in the world. If anyone loves the world, the love of the Father is not in him," Scripture calls out.

God calls the Christian to holiness, to right living, to honesty, to brotherly love, to separation from all that defiles. But, some of us today are halting, hesitating, hanging around the pond, wading in the muddy water by the shore, afraid or unwilling to cut the shore lines loose and go out into the deep for God.

An acquaintance once told me how he saw a drove of swine all following a man to the slaughterhouse. The man walked just ahead of the pigs, holding a bag full of beans. Lured by the tempting smell of the beans, the pigs scrambled for position all the way to their demise.

Why, those pigs never even got the beans, and the farmer had both the meat and the beans for his dinner! Just so, Satan lures us away from God with promises that will never be kept.

God wants us to follow Him only, and forsake all that will hold us back. Back at my boyhood home in Canada, I once saw an eagle descend on the carcass of a dead beast on a frozen lake and feed upon the meat until the eagle finally satiated its hunger. But, when the eagle went to rise again into the skies, he could not. He was solidly frozen to the ice.

So with the Christian who lives with unconfessed sin. Sin pulls the Christian's life and testimony down to the level of the world. No, we cannot afford to hang around the edges of Christianity. Why halt between two opinions? Why try to serve two masters? Give it up to Him. Why, if God be God, then let's walk with Him faithfully with all our might! Plunge in and find the joy of walking with God! Confess your faults and failings to God and find the freedom of His victory over sin, and His help along the way of repentance.

Dear Father, how long has it been since I stopped to think about my sin? How long since I truly asked for Your forgiveness and help? Please, God, forgive me. I am sorry that so often I fail to think like You, to love like You. Please help me to have the mind of Christ. Please help me to turn my back on temptation, and cling only to the cross. Please help me to feel the joy of Your constant companionship, and the victory of freedom from the restraining fetters of sin. In the precious name of Jesus I pray, Amen.

May 29 — What Have You to Do With Peace?

Scripture Reading: II Kings 9:1-29
Key Verse: "...What have you to do with peace...?"
II Kings 9:18

Around this Christian land today countless millions are meeting in this sacred observance of Memorial Day. In a few more hours the graves will be strewn with blossoms and flowers mingled with tears falling upon their heroic dust. It is fitting that we forget not these fallen heroes and spend time in remembering them.

You will notice the outstanding word in our text is peace. How we love it. How sweet to the ear. The very sound starts melody in our hearts. This word peace originated in Heaven and was one of the first words in the vocabulary of Eden. It is the theme of the poet, the inspiration of the artist, and the aspiration of the saint. If peace has been precious to us as individuals, how much more so as a nation.

Our prosperity, national, commercial, and spiritual, speak louder than words the blessings of peace. Our great arteries of commerce have fed the world unharmed by war. The unbounded growth educationally of our colleges, seminaries, and institutions of learning cry peace. Our mighty and influential industrial life has become powerful in the world with its arms stretching around the globe because of the peace we have had.

Now, peace was bought with a price. Peace at any price is worthless as well as dishonorable. All peace has had its price in blood. Before the morning stars sang together, God Himself saw the price of the peace of men's souls written in the letters of blood. He took from Heaven its richest treasure, His only begotten Son the Prince of Peace, and spent it on the souls of mankind.

I read of Knox, Huss, Bunyan, Judson, Livingston, who would rather die for their faith than live to be traitors and have no peace. I now hear Washington call the first American Patriots to follow him.

They spent their all in the purchase of peace. I hear the Declaration of Independence as the roar of battle ceases and the First Constitutional Convention frames the laws for the self-government of the United States.

And when we think of the 60's, we think of our Civil War Veterans and we hear them tell the story of the freedom of the slaves of the South and the preservation of the Union. They need but point to the Immortal Lincoln whose life has influenced the destiny of this country above all others. These grand Army men can answer the question of our text by pointing to the 4 million set free. And when we behold their thinning ranks, bent forms, unsteady step and think of the price they paid for our heritage; we thank God for them and pray that the God of peace might lengthen their stay here to see the consummation of their joy.

Theirs is a wonderful history. The Spanish American War, the boys under the poppy fields of France, and all the boys in dusty graves here who gave up their all in this recent war, all answer the question of the text. "What have you to do with peace?"

To the younger generation, the price paid by your forefathers is a challenge to you. You are living in a great day of the world's history. We find upon waking each morning that there is a new order. Imperial governments totter and fall; republics are born in a night. There are no greater opportunities than those that are yours in this time that was bought with so dear a price.

May that day soon come when the nations of the earth will beat their spears into ploughshares, their swords into pruning hooks, when nation will not take up the sword against nation or learn war anymore. When peace shall be had from pole to pole and Jesus will reign King of Kings and Lord of Lords. Amen.

May 30   The Secret of a Quiet Heart

Scripture Reading: John Chapter 14

Key Verse: "Let not your heart be troubled, you believe in God, believe also in me." John 14:1

Here is a picture of forlorn dejection. Eleven stupefied, dreary, and disillusioned men are gathered in the upper room facing the half-understood prospect of Christ's departure from them. They had taken part in an amazing journey with the One who has been their Teacher, Lord, and Master during three wonderful years.

Now all this is to change. They are to be left alone to face a hostile wicked world. And Christ, forgetting His own great burden of the cross less than twenty-four hours away, turns to comfort, encourage and sooth their troubled hearts. With these words of tenderness He speaks in the tone of Majesty, "Let not your heart be troubled; you believe in God, believe also in Me."

What is it Christ offers to us here? This is not a command. This is rather a merciful invitation to do what brings life and blessing. Here is a call to faith that grasps the heart of Christ, a bond that unites souls with Him, a life of committal of myself to Him in all my relations and for all my needs. An absolute confidence in Him as all-sufficient for everything I require.

Now, this is the sure derivation of what has gone before; this trust in Christ is the secret of a quiet heart. And no doubt one of the oldest and most perplexing questions of life is, how may a troubled heart be healed?

Of course, all along the way there have been various answers to this question from various quarters. There is the answer of despair. In Job's trouble, friends and family offered their suggestions and ideas and finally his wife said, "Curse God and die." Now that's no cure for a troubled heart.

Some have offered stoicism as a solution. That doctrine says steel your heart, deaden your feelings, put away your tears, and make your heart a rock. No, this will not cure a troubled heart. Epicureanism calls for you to forget your troubles, plunge into the realm of pleasure, sound its depths, and forget your grief. In the end, you will return home unhealed, still carrying a broken heart.

Denial calls for us to deny the facts and not look at them. Perhaps if we turn our gaze away long enough the problem will disappear. But a denial of the fact does not change the fact.

So where can we go to heal our hearts? Jesus distinctly says that there is no other anchor, no other reinforcement or healing, no other recovery or peace that will be sufficient for any troubled heart if you turn away from Him and reject His counsel and comfort. Have you a troubled heart? Is there in your experience that which brings a stab to your soul? Do you have burdens that crush?

Christ, when He spoke these words to the disciples, was facing the agony of the cross. Yet in the midst of His own agony, He points His disciples to trust. You see, He understood resurrection power. He trusted the Father to carry Him through the agony of the cross to the healing resurrection. God is the source of this power and it is only to Him that we can go to acquire it. Let not your heart be troubled. He will carry you through the cross and lead you to the resurrection if only you will follow the prescription of the Great Physician and trust in Him.

Dear Lord, You understand the anguish in my heart. I don't want to waste my time with false remedies. I want to follow Your instructions and go to the source of power that can truly heal. I now place sorrow, this hurt, this worry in Your precious hands and I will leave it there. I believe that You will bring Your great power to bear. Thank You for healing my troubled heart. Amen.

May 31   The Walk of Faith

Scripture Reading: Genesis Chapter 5
Key Verse: "And Enoch walked with God; and he was not, for God took him." Genesis 5:24

The Divine Writer of Genesis used the same formula for all nine men who preceded Enoch in this chapter. There were three things said about them: they were born, they reproduced, and they died; brief, commonplace biographies that don't lend much to our understanding. But, when the author comes to Enoch, He does away with the monotonous formula and adds a few very significant words. Someone said that a great painter can paint a great picture on a small canvas. Enoch's life is summed up in this one sentence, "Enoch walked with God." A lifetime in a single sentence, it is a complete biography of a faithful man.

Enoch's life was distinctive because of what he did in spite of disadvantages. He lived what we would call an "in spite-of life." Enoch walked with God in spite of the fact that he did not have a Bible. In fact, it was about 1,000 years before the world had the Ten Commandments, and Enoch was already being faithful. The Bible is a light and a lamp to us, but Enoch had no such help. The words that Enoch had were the words actually spoken by God when he talked to Him face to face.

Enoch walked with God in spite of the fact that there was no church. Yes, it seems as though no one else was walking with God, but Enoch persevered. Enoch stood true. It is also true that instead of circumstances determining the character of a Christian, his character should determine circumstances.

Enoch walked with God in spite of the fact that he did not live as long as the other nine men mentioned. He accomplished in one third the time what these others failed to do at all. So we see, it is not the length of time we stay here that counts, but the way we spend our time. The important thing is not how long we live, but how we live. Jesus was on this earth but a short thirty-three years, but in that time he remade the world.

What does it mean to walk with God? It means spiritual companionship. It means spiritual fellowship. Enoch's companionship with God was like the physical companionship that the disciples had with Christ on earth. Enoch agreed with God. To agree with God, you must change your plans and accept God's plans. We must see things God's way and make His ideals, our ideals. When you are companions with someone, you have mutual interests and mutual desires. And all of this is done not by compulsion, but out of love.

To walk with God implies responsibility. Tasks and duties will be taken seriously, if we have companionship with God. And, to walk with God implies progress. Enoch did not just sit down, Enoch moved as God moved.

What was the secret of Enoch's ability to do this? How did he walk with God? Well, this ability came from the unseen part of his life. It is said that most of an iceberg is hidden underwater, and just so most of a great life is unseen by the world. In Enoch's case, his walk with God was a walk of faith. Without such faith one cannot please God. When we are unwilling to swing out, cutting all the shorelines loose and walk with God by faith, our religion becomes a mere superstition—not a relationship. So, what was the end of Enoch's walk with God? There was no end. And, there is no end, either, for a true Christian life today.

Dear Lord, I want to be so aware of Your presence that I understand that every day is a walk with You. Please help me to be living in Your presence with my every word and deed, and may my walk with You bring glory to Your name. Amen.

June 1   How to Live the Christian Life

Scripture Reading: Colossians Chapter 2

Key Verse: "As you therefore have received Christ Jesus the Lord, so walk in Him." Colossians 2:6

Today we hear people saying "I'm serving the Lord in my weak way. I'm struggling along as best I can. I'm trying awfully hard." Poor souls, they are deluded and misguided. The Christian life is not lived by trying or struggling. Paul takes us into a new and glorious truth, a life of victory through the Spirit by complete surrender and yieldedness to God, a life of victory through sanctification in the Spirit.

What we need to know and enter into by faith today is that we have deliverance from the power of indwelling sin by union with Christ in death and resurrection. Romans 6:3-4 says "Or do you not know that as many of us as were baptized into Christ Jesus were baptized into His death? Therefore we were buried with Him through baptism into death, that just as Christ was raised from the dead by the glory of the Father, even so we also should walk in newness of life."

You see here that we are to reckon by faith. If you deposit fifty dollars in your account then draw on it, that's reckoning. It means to count it true and act accordingly. So, we reckon by faith that when Jesus died, we died; when He was buried, we were buried; when He arose, we arose—how? In newness of life.

By passing through death, resurrection, and into newness of life, the body of sin was destroyed. That means it was annulled, kept from working, rendered idle, became of no effect, that henceforth we should not serve sin. But, you ask, "How can I get victory over sin? How can I walk in deliverance over the power of sin?" The answer is "Reckon yourselves to be dead indeed to sin and alive unto God through Jesus Christ our Lord."

We must <u>know</u> that we were included in His death and resurrection. Know it by faith because God says so. Over 1900 years ago your salvation was accomplished. We must reckon ourselves to be surely, truly, certainly dead unto sin and alive unto God. Count it true and act accordingly. We must yield ourselves as instruments no longer to sin to which we died, but to God to whom we are now alive.

His Spirit dwells in us and we now have a new power, a new presence, a new personality. The Spirit takes over the conflict for me with the flesh and in Him and through Him I have victory. The Word says that if you walk in the Spirit, you shall not fulfill the lusts of the flesh.

We must have heart allegiance and remember that we are married to Jesus. Married to Christ, think of it. Ours is His name and nature. The Father has taken the hand of His only begotten Son and the hand of His newly begotten church and joined them together for time and eternity. What a glorious relationship. We will have a new center for our love, an inward presence to please. We will be occupied with Him, satisfied in pleasing Him. A single man may spend his nights out with the boys, but a married man who adores his wife will love to spend his nights pleasing her and being with her.

Remember, we have a new power in service in the Holy Spirit. It is not your living in Him so much as His living in you. It is not your victory in Him so much as His victory in you. In Him there is no condemnation, no separation. Follow His will and walk in victory and power.

Dearest Lord, I'm meditating on my position as part of the bride of Christ and how I love you. My heart is in it. Your love and sacrifice empower me and give me a triumphant outlook. I'm no longer weak, but strong. Thank You for living in me, loving me, and loving others through me. Amen.

June 2 — The Bride's Task

Scripture Reading: Acts 20:17-38

Key Verse: "But none of these things move me; nor do I count my life dear to myself, so that I may finish my race with joy, and the ministry which I received from the Lord Jesus, to testify to the gospel of the grace of God." Acts 20:24

In Jesus Christ we stand face to face with the Almighty. In Christ we see and touch the divine heart, mind, will, and purpose. And God, speaking to us through the lips of His Son, commands that we share our knowledge of Him with all mankind.

This is evangelism and it is to be done by the Church. Jesus is the builder of the Church, He died for it, and the church exists that Christ may reveal Himself unto the world through her.

Her one business is to bring the lost to God, supremely this and nothing else. The very circumstances of her beginning prove this. She was born of the Holy Spirit in the very center of world forces. Her cradle was rocked by world upheavals, bringing the whole world together to hear the first Christian sermon.

The Acts of the Apostles shows the Church embarking upon her world task as God had planned and the Holy Spirit inspired them. Everybody went everywhere to everyone. The Apostles were all missionaries and evangelists with one exception, and every one of them found death on foreign soil. The whole of our New Testament was written by foreign missionaries and the Epistles were addressed to foreign mission Churches or converts.

Now what if my earthly father should leave an inheritance to my brothers and sisters and I? There would be no moral greatness about my soul if I set about to find them and acquaint them of their heritage. That would be my privilege and duty. But, what if I should hold all for my personal enjoyment? Would I not be responsible to my father and answerable to my brethren?

Let me close with reasons why the Bride of Christ is to be about the task of winning souls. First, Because Jesus made it primary and uppermost. "Follow me and I will make you fishers of men." And He said to seek and to save that which is lost.

Then, the tragic condition of the unsaved demands we win them. Romans 3 says "There are none righteous, no not one." Yes, God believed people were lost and gave all He had to redeem and save them. Jesus believed it and gave Himself a ransom for many. The Holy Spirit believed it and came to convict the world of sin, and judgment to come. Yet, many of us do nothing about it. Some drift along from Sunday to Sunday, teaching our classes, meeting our friends, and never pointing them to God.

Suppose you had been in a fire and you knew a way to safety? And when that fire began you went that way, slammed the door and saved yourself but said nothing to anyone else. You'd be a wretch. Yet some do this very thing about salvation and about the lost. Let us overcome our pacifism and become militant rescuers. Some firemen drive the wagon, some hold the hose, some brave the flames to carry people from the inferno. Some Christians go selflessly, some pray passionately and some give openhandedly, but all are needed. It is our task.

Lord Jesus, I want to find my place in Your work of evangelism. May I always be ready to give reason for my faith and testimony of You to those You place in my path in divine appointments. May I be faithful in Jerusalem (my hometown), Judea (my country), and the uttermost parts of the world to do my part to proclaim the gospel. Amen.

June 3 God's Warnings Against Apostasy

Scripture Reading: Jude

Key Verse: "...there would be mockers in the last time who would walk according to their own ungodly lusts." Jude v.18

The warnings against apostasy recorded in the book of Jude are set before the Church for all time, but with special reference to the closing of the Church Age. In these seven examples of apostasy we will see God's overruling hand in human affairs.

First Jude relates the story of Israel. In the deliverance of Israel from Egypt, the golden calf, which they made and worshipped with pagan rites, was ground to powder and poured in their drinking water. It made a bitter dose and they were made to drink the fruit of their unholy departure from God.

Then, Jude calls attention to the angels which, under the leadership of Satan, rebelled against God and they called a civil war. Well, the judgment of God condemned them to bonds of darkness to await a greater judgment at a future day.

Then Jude cites the story of the unbridled sensuality of Sodom and Gomorrah. It is a signpost for the nations, but not the only signpost on the highway of the nations. In 1902 Mount Pelee on the Island of Martinique was destroyed by a volcanic eruption along with 40,000 inhabitants. A few days prior to the eruption during a religious feast, one of the leading citizens had a pig impaled on a cross of wood and carried it through the streets of the city bearing the inscription, "The Holy Jesus." He defiantly challenged Almighty God to declare Himself if he was alive. The whole city was involved with the merriment and not one protest was raised against his blasphemous act. As with Sodom and Gomorrah, had God sent catastrophic judgment?

Jude then relates a warning in verse nine. It is a warning against lawlessness, those who despise authority and speak evil of those vested with authority. The great need of the church today is a clear vision of

God in His authority in contrast to the prevailing despising of dominion on the part of men who cannot rule even their own spirits.

Cain was the first man to reject God's way of salvation and set up, instead, a religion more to his liking. He rebelled against God's way of providing a substitute, a lamb whose blood was shed in the guilty sinner's place. He would erect an altar that would never be stained by blood, but rather garnished with flowers and fruit as an offering to the Lord. This "way of Cain" is more popular today than ever, with appealing music, attractive ritualism, and imposing structures, having a form of Godliness but denying the power thereof. The Church or individual who substitutes ethics or ritualism for the gospel of Christ is following the way of Cain.

The sin of Balaam also claims many people in the last days. He thought he could serve God and enjoy the rewards of sin at the same time. He thought that by offering sacrifices unto God he could change the mind and purpose of the holy God. He was later responsible for actions which resulted in the plague and caused the death of 24,000 Israelites.

Korah headed a rebellion against Moses and Aaron in the wilderness. The judgment that came upon him is one to remember, for God opened the earth beneath him and swallowed Korah alive.

But you, beloved, remember the words that have been spoken. You have been warned by the apostles and the Lord, and you have been warned again today.

Almighty God, I want to submit to Your leadership and dominion in every aspect of my life. Help me Lord, to forsake any apostasy in my life. Amen

June 4 — Life

Scripture Reading: Job 33:1-5

Key Verse: "The Spirit of God has made me, and the breath of the Almighty gives me life." Job 33:4

We make a great deal of ancestry. Multitudes seek to follow their family tree back, in the hope of finding royal blood, or perhaps men or women of great honor in their line. But, there is someone grander that a Duke or a poet in your line and mine.

Your parentage, by adoption, is to the One true God and your elder brother is Jesus. We all draw lineage from the King of Kings and the Lord of Lords. Herein is the value and the dignity of human life. You are the child of the King, dear one.

Go back to the origin of the created earth. For five days, the creative hand of the Almighty is busy in fitting up the abode called earth. He adorns it. He hollows the seas for man's highways. He rears the mountains for his observations. He stores the mines for man's need. God pours the streams to give man drink, and fertilizes the field that it would give him bread. This mansion is carpeted with verdure and illuminated with the greater light by day and the lesser lights by night.

Notice that when the earth is to be fashioned, and the ocean to be poured into its bed, God simply says, "Let them be." But, when man is to be created, God seems to make a solemn pause, finding the model for this creation in Himself. And God said, "Let us make man in Our image, according to Our likeness."

Life, that subtle, mysterious thing, is God's gift to you and me. We are trustees of the Giver, unto whom at last we shall render account for every thought, word, and deed in the body. What a privilege, to live. What a sacred honor, to live for Him!

Despite the frequency of birth, and whether the event is in some obscure attic in Brooklyn or in a palatial home in Europe, to the all-seeing eye of God, it is an event of prodigious moment. A soul commences a career that shall outlast the earth on which it moves. An existence begins that will be untouched by time, continuing when the sun is extinguished like a vapor in the sky, the moon blotted out, and the heavens rolled together like a scroll.

Human life is transcendently precious. Man was not created as a piece of guess-work, flung into existence. There is purpose in the creation of every human being. God did not breathe the breath of life in you or me that we might be a sensuous or splendid animal. No, beloved, your soul was given to you for a purpose worthy of your Creator.

In that great Westminster confession of faith, the well-known phrase reads, "Man's chief end is to glorify God and enjoy Him forever." That is the double aim of life, duty first and then joy as a consequence. To honor God, to build up His Kingdom, this is the highest end and most noble aim of existence. The highest idea of life is attained by consecration to God. Such a life is infinitely valuable due to the eternal consequences flowing from it.

Life is real, momentous, a blessed opportunity. There is nothing as fine and great as the power of a well-spent life. This world, after all, is but the vestibule of eternity; this life but a precursor to that where we will know Him face to face.

Dearest Father, I desire to touch others for You. Whether through my ministry, my family, my friends or my faithfulness in another area, please bless me with this honor. All I am, all I have, is Yours to use for Your glory, Amen.

June 5 — On Trial for Your Life?

Scripture Reading: Ephesians Chapter 4

Key Verse: "...speaking the truth in love, may grow up in all things into Him who is the head—Christ" Ephesians 4:15

In the first paragraph of Howe's *World History in Our Times,* you will find these startling words, "The twentieth century has put the human race on trial for its life." This statement contains a picture that has always held my imagination: a person on trial for his life. He waits for the verdict of the jury. Shall he be free, or shall he die? Well, beloved, in this mobile, fast-paced world, we are on trial for our lives physically. Many of us are finding anymore that it is a good day's work to survive!

Stepping up another level, however, we are also on trial for our minds. Modern inventions have made it so easy to pass the time without thinking that many people get along without it very well. Someone has prophesied that if evolution were indeed true, we would in another generation all have eyes as big as cantaloupes and brains the size of a split pea. We can only win the trial for the life of our minds by employing them to find a set of stable values to live by.

Each of us is also on trial every day for the life of our soul. We are on trial to bring the soul, and keep the soul into a sustaining relationship with the life-giving presence of God. However, the task of keeping the soul near to God is not an uncertain trudge through an uncharted wilderness. Clear paths have been marked out, along which many feet have traveled to the goal.

Prayer has been, and is, a primary thoroughfare directly into the presence of the Lord. We keep the soul refreshed by keeping the person of Jesus in high visibility. Reading His Word and then meditating and acting upon it also saves our lives from being bogged down with indifference and self-satisfaction. Another well-trodden, time-proven path to soul vitality is participation in the Body of Christ.

Paul, in Hebrews 10:25 writes, "...not forsaking the assembling of yourselves together, as is the manner of some, but exhorting one another, and so much the more as you see the Day approaching." Here we are urged to hold unswervingly to the hope we profess, for it is God who made the promises and He is absolutely trustworthy. We are also urged to observe one another's good works and, above all, not forsake the assembling of ourselves, but rather exhort one another to loyalty and service.

Paul tells us the last days are to be characterized by lethargy, apostasy, form, and formality, and we are surely witnessing these in our church life today. Many things succeed in weaning God's children away from church, and spiritual life. Perhaps one reason for this is our ignorance of the importance of the church. Jesus said, "Upon this Rock I will build my church, and the gates of Hell will not prevail against it."

The greatest, most important, event that takes place in any community during the week is the church service. Here we propagate the gospel, train the saints, worship the Lord, and fellowship with the brethren. In that service God wants your talents, your presence, your praise and your prayers, all surrendered to His Glory, with the promise of His blessing. It will renew your soul with His presence.

Dearest Heavenly Father, I do long for more of Your presence, more delight in fellowship with You. I ask that You would stir me, draw me irresistibly closer to You. Help me to be a glowing coal, whose presence in my local church body glows for You, encouraging and warming the souls of those around me. In Christ's name, amen.

June 6 — Pharisees and Publicans

Scripture Reading: Luke Chapter 18
Key Verse: "...for everyone who exalts himself will be humbled, and he who humbles himself will be exalted." Luke 18:14

Here is a parable to serve as a handy directory for real prayer and worship, whether public or private. The Lord allows us to overhear two men at their devotions. The first is a Pharisee who, like so many of his class, trusted in himself that he was righteous.

The Pharisee took his position by himself in the temple, but his prayer was merely a self-complacent soliloquy. He expressed no wants. He framed no petition. He simply rehearsed the number of his religious observances and recounted his good qualities. He congratulated himself. Note well that there was no consciousness of need, no urgency for God's help and assistance, no realization of his undone condition before God. You can see and feel the hypocritical, irreverent self-satisfaction and self-sufficiency of this bold sinner in the face of God.

You can see his head up, brazen faced and formed as he stands before his God. You can hear that he is trusting in his own merits as he gloats over and despises the demerits of others. And you can feel that God was not in his thoughts or in his heart, though he called out His name.

The Pharisee's spirit is not dead today. The Psalms, or the prayer book, the deftly quoted texts and phrases, these may keep our tongues right, but what about our hearts? We can't cheat God that way, He sees our hearts. We can't even cheat our neighbors. We really only cheat ourselves. This Pharisee was condemned, for everyone who exalts himself will be humbled and he that humbles himself will be exalted.

But, wait, there was also the Publican, so abashed in the presence of God that he stood afar off and would not so much as lift his eyes to heaven. This Publican was different. His attitude was not assumed for effect, like that of the Pharisee, but was the natural expression given by the whole body to the feelings within him. A man speaks not only by his tongue, but also with his eyes, his face, his hand, and his very posture. The attitude and actions of the Publican were evidence of true humility.

Here was no playing at prayer. Out of the depths of his feelings he cries, earnestly and in one brief sentence. He cries out his whole need, as well as the conviction of his soul, "God be merciful to me a sinner." No one but a man in earnest could have done that.

One may say a great deal in prayer and yet have little real prayer in his words, and again, one may say but a few words and in those words express all his soul to God. The Pharisee's prayer is shallow, but the publican's prayer is deep. In that depth, we can see why he went down to his house justified. In the first place, his prayer sprang out of deep conviction of sin. His conscience was alive and active. Secondly, he has nothing to say about his neighbors. The sense of enormity of his guilt precludes judging any other soul. And thirdly, the publican's prayer sprang out of a sense of utter helplessness. It is a cry for mercy. He does not ask for justice, for he acknowledges the justice of his condemnation. He sues alone for mercy.

And so, we must draw near to God with humility and earnestness. We must recognize our need for God, and appeal to God's mercy. Yes, beloved, pray like the publican and wait like Abraham, whose whole life was one great patient prayerful expectation. "And he went away justified," what a directory for our daily worship before God.

Dear God, please be merciful to me, a sinner saved by grace. Amen.

June 7   The Parable of the Pearl

Scripture Reading: Matthew Chapter 13

Key Verses: "The kingdom of heaven is like a merchant seeking beautiful pearls, who, when he had found one pearl of great price, went and sold all that he had and bought it."
Matthew 13:45-46

In this parable a merchant is seeking a treasure of beautiful pearls. In this quest he is rewarded, as he finds "one pearl of great price." Let us remember that the pearl was not precious to the Hebrews. It had no place on the high priest's breastplate. But the pearl was held as a precious stone among the Gentiles. Ancient Kings of Egypt and other old dynasties used pearls lavishly on crowns and personal decorations. The most valued jewels and pearls were for use by the king only.

So the Lord took something that was outside Hebrew figures of speech and values as an emblem in this parable. Can you imagine the astonishment and surprise? Let us note some facts about the pearl. It is the direct product of a living organism. No other precious stone has this origin. It is the result of injury done to the life that produces it. A grain of sand intrudes, producing harm or injury and this is the root principle of the pearl.

But the pearl is not the injury; it is the answer of the injured to the harm done. The pearl transmutes the injury by a process of covering until the injurious thing is turned into a precious, rare, and beautiful jewel. So, the pearl is the answer of the injured life to that which injures it.

It is wholly a thing of beauty, ornamental and decorative. But in the east it is symbolic of innocence and purity, prized for its significance. So we have the pearl as the answer of an injured life and the symbol of innocence. But it is more. It stood for triumph of purity over impurity and the wearing of it meant not only innocence, but the mighty triumph of good over evil.

So what does the parable mean? This is what Paul speaks of as the definite and specific mystery of the church in Ephesians 5. That there is to be gathered out of the world and presented to God that which will be the finest, fairest, and most resplendent jewel that will ever flourish upon His bosom in all the ages of eternity. Out of the mystery of sin and evil, there is to be found and gathered the most glorious thing of God's possession. For among the treasures of this age, the Church of Jesus Christ is supreme.

The finding of the pearl is not accidental, the merchant sought it. Just so, from heaven's viewpoint Christ gave everything to purchase the church. The verse literally reads "Having gone away has sold all that he had and bought it." Not gone away from earth, but gone away from heaven to come to us. A surrender of place, possessions and honor, and all that Jesus had, that He may purchase the pearl and take it back with Him to the place He left. From Christ's viewpoint, it portrays the value God puts on the church.

And so, here is the picture. Jesus has drawn and lifted me who harmed Him and bestowed upon me His nature. Soon Christ will present me (Yes, even me!) faultless before the King. He saw the pearl when yet but a possibility. He gathered the offending thing into His own life and it wounded Him, harmed Him, and slew Him. But, praise the name of Jesus, we see that in all the apparent failure of the kingdom ideal in this age, the chief value, the chief glory, the chief business from Heaven's standpoint is the gathering of the church and its preparation for a high and holy vocation in the ages yet to come.

Almighty Lord, what a beautiful picture of Your love and the grace that covers my sin, forms me into something beautiful for God, and purchases me at great price. Thank You for Your sacrificial love. Amen.

June 8 — True Holiness

Scripture Reading: Philippians Chapter 3

Key Verse: "...I press on, that I may lay hold of that for which Christ Jesus has also laid hold of me." Philippians 3:12

Holiness is not an outward act, but an inward, constant, all-regulating principle. What exactly is it? Or, what do we mean when we say of a man that he is holy? It is not that he is virtuous alone, but that his virtue has a special and peculiar quality.

There are people who are honest and truthful, temperate, chaste, and moral, yet you would never call them holy. There is, you see, a difference between virtue and holiness. The distinction is this: the virtuous man regulates his conduct by moral principles alone, while the holy man maintains a close and constant fellowship with the living God and this is reflected in his behavior.

In the company of one you are struck by the high-minded honor which he shows. In the company of the other you are impressed with a sense of the nearness of God and the entire submissiveness of the man's soul to Him. The one gives a lofty idea of his own excellence; the other makes you feel the greatness and purity of God. The life of one may be maintained without any thought of the Lord, the other is entirely supported by the communion of his soul with God.

With one you may go days without being reminded of the Supreme, but with the other you immediately find he carries God's presence with him constantly. Immediately we see that a holy man is pre-eminently a man of God whose inward principle is the maintenance of a close relationship with God, the outward manifestation is the consecration of his life to God. It is the flower that blooms from the sprinkling of the blood of Christ. There is no flower of holiness without the covering of His blood of salvation.

How is this holiness obtained? Clearly, it is not obtained by every man. No man has it naturally. The agency of change, says the Scripture, is the Holy Spirit. In the regeneration, the Holy Spirit works. The sinner is reconciled to God by the reception of the Lord Jesus. Christ puts him into spiritual affinity with God and regeneration occurs.

Our hearts beat with His. Our aspirations are those things which He is bringing about, and thus being like-minded, I can have close relationship with Him. So, faith in Jesus Christ produces those two elements of communion with God and consecration to Him in which holiness consists. The Holy Spirit uses those means and constantly reveals Him to us, ever deepening our relationship and consecration.

If we desire to have this holiness formed within us, we need to have strong and abiding faith in the Lord Jesus Christ as our redeemer, for Christ is the source of our holiness as well as our peace. The lovely mystery is this: the source of our faith is also a gift of God. The faith, the relationship, the consecration, the holiness, and the peace is all found in Him and is from His hand.

May we cling to this view of our faith. It is not something to be worn on Sunday and cast off on Monday, for that is when we most need it. Let the love of Christ permeate your life. Desire the Holy Spirit to fill you and fit you for the consecration and holiness that leads to an abundant, peaceful, and fruitful life. He will do it to the extent you surrender to Him.

Dearest Lord, I surrender. Please fill me with Your Holy Spirit and lead me into a deep relationship with You. I want holiness and consecration to spring from my salvation and bless others as You have blessed me. In the name of Christ Jesus, amen.

June 9   All the Rivers Run Into the Sea

Suggested Reading: Revelation 22:1-21
Key Verse: "All the rivers run into the sea." Ecclesiastes 1:7

All rivers run into the sea. Whether they are great or small, ancient or modern, each one obeys the universal and irresistible law of nature that compels them eventually to lose their individuality and identity in the bosom of the mighty ocean.

We think of the old Nile, life giver to Egypt; the Mississippi, the Father of waters in its leisurely flow of thousands of miles to the gulf; the golden Hudson, the clear St. Lawrence, and thousands more of lesser size all making their way irresistibly to the sea.

And now, let us look upon these various rivers as impressive symbols and types of other rivers that run into the sea. For one, the River of Hope that runs into the Sea of Disappointment. We all at some time or the other have set afloat some cherished scheme, some hope of future good to the attainment of which we give the very cream of our years and the fine gold of our enthusiastic energies. It matters not what the coveted object may be. Despite a certain satisfaction in the moment of success or from the stimulus of pursuit, the final analysis of it all is vanity and the vexation of the spirit. Jesus said, "One's life does not consist in the abundance of the things he possesses." They are earthly and the earthly cannot meet the needs of the soul that is made in the image of God.

One beautiful stream is the River of Youth that passes into the Sea of Old Age. Beautiful in the beginning, its every ripple musical with joyous laughter and with a cadence as soft and sweet as the strains of a harp. But this river is deceptive; its progress so slumberous we hardly notice its progression only to awake to the startling fact, it has left our youth far behind.

We cannot tell how much longer the River of Time will continue to flow before it is forever lost in this great Ocean of Eternity. But this only do we know, that there is coming a crucial day. On that day when the Angel of the Lord will stand with one foot upon the sea and the other upon the earth and with uplifted hand shall declare that time shall be no longer.

And what is the vital meaning of it all? What shall we decide as to our philosophy of life? Epicurean? (Eat, drink, and be merry?) Stoic? Or shall we accept the Christian philosophy of walking with Him who is the way, the truth, and the life, and find life everlasting as our destiny?

In the light of this blessed hope, what matters if these earthly streams of our unrealized desires, our fading youth, and our vanishing time are rapidly passing away like the rivers that run to the sea? These are but drawing us nearer, nearer to that glad and seraphic moment when we shall awake in His presence.

This is the secret of life: we are only sojourning here. We are absent from our motherland. Our pilgrimage is short. Let us spend it in reverential awe of God, with haste for the King's work, for the night comes. Let us spend it in contentment, for we must not complain about the hardships on the way. Let us spend it with faithfulness to opportunities, as we pass this way but once, and must buy up all the opportunities to do all we can. Let us travel with hopefulness because we are sailing home. And let us always remember that we are only sojourning here.

Lord God, help me to count my moments and redeem them in a way that counts for eternity. Stir my heart and mind to appreciate every day, and every opportunity. Amen.

June 10   How to Find Happiness in Marriage

Scripture Reading: Mark 10:1-12

Key Verse: "Therefore what God has joined together, let not man separate." Mark 10:9

A main factor of married happiness is mutual appreciation. The deepest quality of human nature is the craving to be appreciated. Marriage is not an endless honeymoon but it must be tended and cared for by continuing expressions of appreciation on both sides.

Another important factor is mutual forbearance. Marriage is a give and take proposition. Leave no trouble unadjusted, but deal with it in the spirit of mutual consideration. Be big enough to forgive and be forgiven.

Let us not forget mutual fidelity. Marriage is not on the animal level. Christian marriage is the most sacred union of one man and one woman. To tamper with that relationship will bring heartache and sorrow. To break the marriage vow is to cause distrust and loss of faith and is the only basis for divorce.

Let us think about the factor of mutual responsibility in marriage. We need to know that behind all the thrill and glamour of marriage is a sacred contract entered into by two people for life. Marriage involves joining hands, hearts, and heads in a shared objective, that of making a home, and a happy life. It involves not living beyond our means, or independently, but each fulfilling his or her share of responsibility. In marriage we must grow up and not act like selfish, spoiled, irresponsible children. Happiness is not found in that atmosphere.

Now, there must be faith in each other and faith in God. Marriage cannot be blessed or complete if it is poisoned by a purely secular view of life. So, marriage is not only a contract, but it is a spiritual relationship. All plans and decisions should be tested and guarded by the teachings of Jesus. We need a common denominator in the home, which is Christ.

Incorporate Christ in your home. You will discover a divine blending of spirits, and build your marriage on a true foundation.

Ah yes, of course there is the element of mutual love. We don't fall in love; we climb into love. Real love that goes far beyond physical infatuation and becomes boundless, sacrificial, and holy is love that we reach out after. Love worthy of the name is touched with divine beauty and tenderness. It is thoughtful, trustful, pure, and complete. And when marriage is based on love like that it becomes a comradeship of kindred hearts that grows and glows with radiance through the years.

Let us remember that the picture of Christ and the church is the picture of a bride and groom. They are our example. He lovingly and sacrificially gives His all, even His life, for the bride. She tenderly and with great respect tends to and loves her husband. These acts are not necessarily based on feelings, but on an inner choice designed to bring great joy, fulfillment, and blessing. The feelings follow. The Word says, "Husbands love your wives." And, "Wives, respect your husbands." The Loving Father who made us understands our deepest needs.

These are the most important factors and elements in successful marriage and you can't be successful without them. Since marriage is a union by God in Heaven, you cannot leave God out of your marriage without defeat. For God is appreciation. God is forbearance. God is fidelity. God is responsibility, and God is faith. Why? Because beloved, God is love.

Holy Father who instituted marriage to demonstrate the relationship between Christ and the church, let my relationships be more appreciative, faithful, responsible, and true. Bring to my mind a way that I can start showing sacrificial love for those in my life today as You showed sacrificial love for the church. Amen.

June 11 — First Song

Scripture Reading: Exodus Chapter 15

Key Verse: "The Lord is my strength and song, and He has become my salvation; He is my God, and I will praise Him; my father's God, and I will exalt Him." Exodus 15:2

As the Red Sea crossing was the birth throes of their national existence, this is Israel's natal song. It is also Israel's emancipation song, their song of liberty. For they have had a triple deliverance: a deliverance from slavery, a deliverance from political bondage, and deliverance from religious thralldom. A triumph song, a note of joy and victory, this beautiful song is a type of all songs of redemption and salvation.

This song of Moses is inscribed and offered unto the Lord. He is the theme and the subject throughout the song, as His exaltation is sung. Singing should be the language of joy and worship before God, just as prayer is the language of holy desire before Him. The Lord is also the subject of all true praise. And, our songs should not only be to the Lord, and of the Lord, but true praise singing is for the Lord, also.

To extol and exalt the Lord was the ultimate aim and end of this and all true praise songs, and the song is the key note and the inspiration for the songs of the church is every age. Moses recounts the causes for Israel's gratitude to God, the past mercies of the Lord are acknowledged and the future mercies are anticipated. The confounding of the enemy is described and the Kingdom of God is recognized as having permanently triumphed.

What about you? Look back over your life, just now. Review the mercies the Lord has shown you. Look forward to the promise of a continued walk with Him. Look upward and praise the Lord.

It is worthy to note that up until the time of this song of Moses, there had been no praise recorded from Israel. There had been cries of deep sorrow in the brick kilns in Egypt. There had been cries of unbelief before the Red Sea. But now, for the first time, there is a cry of joy from Israel. In this, too, we see ourselves. We, too, must understand the fullness of our deliverance in the power of the resurrection before we can present clear and intelligent worship to our dear Lord.

It is also worthy to note that there is not a single word about self, its doings, its sayings, its feelings, or its fruits. Every word is about Jehovah. In all true worship, God is at once the object of worship, the subject of worship, and the power of worship.

But, the concluding verses of this chapter show us Israel in the wilderness. There is a change in the tone of the words. The notes of praise are soon exchanged for notes of discontent. "Marah," the place of bitter water, became a place of murmuring against Moses. The trials of the wilderness were plenty, but the Israelites had their "Elims" with its wells and its palm trees, as well as the bitter waters.

There were green spots in their desert wanderings, but Elim was not Canaan. No, Elim was only a foretaste of that happy land. Elim was an encouragement to press on. Just so, God's blessings in our lives here on this earth are to strengthen and encourage our hearts until we come into our eternal home with Him. Praise God for His blessings, but don't lose sight of Canaan.

Dear God, I confess that I get so tied up in this world, that I lose sight of the fact that I am not of it, nor is my destiny tied to it. I do thank You for the many blessings You have put in my path on this earthly journey. And, I praise You that when my earthly journey is done, my eternal home with You awaits. Thank You for the peace that promise brings. Amen.

June 12 The Conquest of Anxiety

Scripture Reading: John 6:1-14

Key Verses: "Then Jesus lifted up His eyes, and seeing a great multitude coming toward Him, He said to Philip, 'Where shall we buy bread, that these may eat?' But this He said to test him, for He Himself knew what He would do. Philip answered Him, 'Two hundred denarii worth of bread is not sufficient for them, that every one of them may have a little.'" John 6:5-7

There are three things that bring about anxiety in the hearts of people; the liabilities of yesterday, the possibilities of tomorrow, and the responsibilities of today. The greatest handicaps in life are the things that never happen. That we might better see ourselves as God sees us, and appropriate God's remedy for our anxiety, we take you to a familiar Bible scene.

Jesus tests Philip with a question about provision for the people. This puts Philip in a stew. He is the essence of anxiety and worry, and he is greatly disturbed. His answer was that it is impossible to feed this great company. This attitude was based upon human resources. He was limited by what he saw. He had not yet, despite seeing all the previous works of Jesus, been able to base his calculations and convictions on what Jesus could do. All anxiety is a want of faith.

Many times, it's not that we disbelieve God, but that we do not believe that God will do the practical things of life. He belongs to the spiritual and not the physical. He belongs to the unseen and not the seen.

Jesus shows Philip that He is close to life and shows him this not by unnaturally multiplying money, but by supernaturally multiplying bread. He takes the available resources and makes them meet the obligations they face. He showed Philip that the conquest of anxiety is by faith.

People carry with them the effects of their failures and they are burdened with the anticipation of their troubles. The remedy for our failures and their effect is found in Philippians 3: 13-14, "...one thing

I do, forgetting those things which are behind and reaching forward to those things which are ahead, I press toward the goal for the prize of the upward call of God in Christ Jesus." We are to forget the things which are behind. This doesn't mean that we ignore them, but deal with them in confession to God. When our spiritual obligations are settled, we are no longer to go back with regret and remorse, but rather to go on without the handicap of previous failures.

The remedy for anxiety for what lies before us is also suggested in this great book of Philippians in which we find written, "Be anxious for nothing, but in everything by prayer and supplication, with thanksgiving, let your requests be made known to God." Unless we deal with the liabilities of yesterday and the possibilities of tomorrow, we are going to be weighted with so much anxious concern that we will be unfit for the responsibilities of today.

So here is our cure for anxiety, first prayer. In nothing be anxious. Pray! Whatever causes anxiety, make it a matter of prayer and He will either remove it or give us the grace to bear it. Then, be thankful for what you have. God has promised to supply all your needs, so cultivate the spirit of thankfulness and praise Him for the little things. Then, take your troubles to the Lord and leave them there. In place of worry, take peace, the peace from trusting Jesus more. Faith is the answer.

Almighty God, sometimes I get my eyes on the problems instead of You. Help me to lift my focus to You and realize that You are the resource for whatever it is that I need. Amen.

June 13   Is it Worthwhile?

Scripture Reading: Luke Chapter 14

Key Verse: "For which of you, intending to build a tower, does not sit down first and count the cost...." Luke 14:28

Is it worthwhile to be a Christian? Is it worthwhile with all your battles, so often lost, with the disappointments that dishearten, with the sacrifices you feel called to make, with the insults the world gives?

Listen beloved, as this question comes to us today; let us face the question, "What does it cost not to be a Christian?" A young lady was being talked to about her soul. She said, "Don't talk to me that way. It makes me think and I hate to think." Think and you will thank God you are a Christian.

To not be a Christian, costs the sacrifice of peace of conscience. The Christian has peace. "Therefore, having been justified by faith, we have peace with God...." Rom. 5:1. But "'there is no peace,' says my God, 'for the wicked.'" Isaiah 57:21.

To reject Christ's claim on your life costs the sacrifice of the sense of security which the Christian has. "You will keep him in perfect peace, whose mind is stayed on You, because he trusts in You." Isaiah 26:3. "The Lord is the strength of my life; of whom shall I be afraid?" Psalm 27:1

It costs the sacrifice of the highest joy known upon earth. "Though now you do not see Him, yet believing, you rejoice with joy inexpressible and full of glory." I Peter 1:8. No one but the child of God can have that joy.

It costs the sacrifice of hope. The believer has that hope as an anchor to steady the soul. Several centuries ago, a Native American, who had pulled his canoe up to the beach, fell asleep. While he slept the pull of the water loosened it from the sand and set it adrift toward the falls. Only a few hundred feet from the precipice he was awakened by the screams of the men on shore. He sat up, glanced about him and ahead of him and seeing the futility of any effort, folded his arms and cried, "No hope, no hope!" and went over the falls to his death. But the Christian lives in hope of eternal life which God, who cannot lie, promised before the world began. The redeeming and sanctifying power will make you what you ought to be, what you were designed to be and what you can be. This priceless grace cannot be found in the colleges of the land. It is the fullness of joy to run on your highest potential, like a sleek, shiny sports car who has been harnessed to a plow in the field being opened up on the road, and meeting its intended purpose and design. What a sense of joy, purpose, and fulfillment.

To not be a Christian costs the sacrifice of God's favor. Oh to live under the smile of God's approval, not the frown of "I know you not." It costs the sacrifice of Christ's acknowledgement, "Whosoever shall confess me before men him will I confess before My Father Who is in Heaven."

Are you willing for the sake of a few short years of worldly pleasure and godless companions to sacrifice eternal peace, hope, God's favor, God's smile, and life in the world to come? After a little while you shall be a king and priest unto God. What does it matter, these petty pleasures of life? Why worry if you can't afford a Packard and have to drive your Henry? These things are fleeting. God says "Be faithful and I will give you a crown of life." The present is so brief; eternity is forever. Count the cost, beloved. Count the cost.

Father Almighty, I am so thankful that I chose You and Your way. I count the cost, and embrace it. To walk through life in Your way is worth any cost. Thank You for providing it for me and help me to walk faithfully in it. Amen.

June 14 — God's Messages from the Ocean

Scripture Reading: Psalm 93

Key Verse: "The Lord on high is mightier than the noise of many waters, than the mighty waves of the sea." Psalm 93:4

We who live close to the sea may lose sight of the messages it brings to our hearts, but to one who appreciates God's out-of-doors, the ocean is a constant marvel. Its greatness and beauty fascinate us. The great oceans are not without their lessons for mankind.

First, the Psalmist measures the power of God in two ways, first by the ear and then by the eye. He stands upon the seashore and listens to the thundering roar of many waters and proclaims His God to be mightier than them all. He watches the waves as they beat against the rocks with relentless energy and is reminded that Jehovah excels in power all forces of the universe.

The waves of the sea, however mighty, are limited in power. Jeremiah 5:22 says, "'Do you not fear me?' says the Lord, 'Will ye not tremble at My presence who have placed the sand as the bound of the sea by a perpetual decree, that it cannot pass beyond it? And though its waves toss to and fro, yet they cannot prevail; though they roar, yet they cannot pass over it.'" The attack of the sea is not mightier than the resistive power of the land. If the sea seems to conquer at one point, the land conquers at another. And so, God has also seen to it that the attack of the evil one upon us shall not be fiercer than we can resist.

I Corinthians 10:13 says "No temptation has overtaken you except such as is common to man; but God is faithful, who will not allow you to be tempted beyond what you are able, but with the temptation will also make the way of escape, that you may be able to bear it." There you are. No temptation, no attack, no obstacle, no difficulty but God will give us a corresponding grace to enable us to bear it and come out victorious. As land and sea are equalized, God sees to it that our resistive force is sufficient to match the enemies of our soul. Perhaps the first impression one takes from the ocean is its vastness. And so, the love of Christ surpasses knowledge even as the length and breadth of the sea is too great to grasp.

Another great lesson from God's great ocean comes to us from its depth. In Micah we read "He will have compassion on us, and will subdue our iniquities. You will cast all our sins into the depths of the sea." Thank God, that as Christians our sins are at the bottom of the ocean, buried in the deepest sea, unable to come up again before us. They are gone.

Surely every life must have its storms, but what a comfort to know that our Savior is Captain. The disciples were in a terrible storm, but Jesus took charge and the sea obeyed His simple command. "Peace, be still." Oh beloved, is your little boat tempest-driven? If so take Jesus on board and all will be well.

Sometimes He allows us to go through the storms to strengthen us, but when He does this He always supplies an anchor that we will not be at the mercy of the wind. God's promises are the anchor of hope that holds us secure.

No matter how long we may roam over life's sea, we look forward finally to our desired haven. To land at last upon the shores of eternity, to enter that celestial city, to greet our loved ones there and yes, best of all, to meet our Savior face to face. To finally be in the safe harbor of our Lord, this is the sweetest message of all from the sea.

Almighty God, thank You for giving us a picture of Your power, might, compassion, and promise, in the oceans around us. Amen.

June 15 — What Kind of a Dad?

Scripture Reading: Genesis Chapter 7
Key Verse: "...Come into the ark, you and all your household...."
Genesis 7:1

God had been trying to get the ear of fathers for one hundred and twenty years, but only Noah would listen to Him. A great cataclysm was near at hand, and the cup of iniquity was full. In fact, when Jesus would describe the sorry condition of the earth before His Second Coming, He would say, "As it was in the days of Noah."

To meet the emergency for the one family who had ears to hear and hearts to understand, God ordered the building of a great ship, a ship without a prow, for it sailed to no shore. God ordered Noah to build a ship without a helm, for no human hand guided it. God's plan called for just one door, one way in, and it was for just one family to embark on a strange voyage. Then, the door was shut. And the great storm swept across the hills and the valleys of the earth with thunders reverberating from mountain to mountain and winds wailing like the agonies of a dying world.

"By faith Noah... prepared an ark for the saving of his household, by which he condemned the world and became heir of righteousness which is according to faith." Hebrew 11:7. Yes, Noah entered that ark at the Lord's summons having set a godly example and having instructed his family. "And the Lord shut him in."

Note that the call of this text is to a father, not a mother. Thank God for good wives and mothers. The world would be a sadder, poorer place without them and so would the church. But, it is hard to get sons in the ark when the fathers are going in the other direction. It is the father's solemn obligation to shoulder the religious responsibility of the family. While he makes the living and provides for the education of "Ham, Shem, and Japheth," yet if he is the right kind of a father, he will have an eye on that ark of salvation for them. Why, we all would admit there is wisdom in getting our children settled for this life, but it is the far better part of wisdom to see them safely within the Savior's fold for all eternity.

There was but one door in Noah's ark, only one way in, but that was enough. Christ became the door for our salvation. Jesus said, "I am the door" and "no man cometh unto the Father but by me." There was a window in that old ark, as well, just above the door. The door was for entrance, but the window was for vision. How different things look seen through the window of grace. Do you think that Shem, Ham, and Japheth longed to get out into that flooded, doomed world? I doubt it. Once you get a look at this universe as God sees it, you never look at the world in quite the same way.

God planned for plenty of food in that mighty ship, and God has provided for us as well. Jesus is the bread of life, the living bread which came down from heaven of which if a man eats, he will hunger no more. He is the bread to satisfy the soul.

You see, there was not just something outside for Noah to lead his family away from; there was something inside that ark for Noah to lead them to. God, give us fathers—and mothers—who will lead! God today is still calling us into a place of safety.

Dear Heavenly Father, help me to know how to answer Your call in both in my home and in my extended family. Let my home, however humble, always be a place of testimony to You, I pray. And, let my life be lived in such a way as to prove the truth of the gospel. Thank You for the privileges you have given me, and for the responsibilities that accompany them. Amen.

June 16   Whose Wife Will She Be?

Scripture Reading: Matthew 22:22-33

Key Verse: "Therefore, in the resurrection, whose wife of the seven will she be?" Matthew 22:28

This question was not spoken in a spirit of honest seeking, but in a spirit of entrapment. The Sadducees were rich and cultured people, comprised of many of the leading Jewish families of the day. They constituted the political party of the Jewish Aristocracy and priesthood from the days of the Maccabees to the final fall of the Jewish state. They stood in most things directly opposed to the Pharisees. They denied the bodily resurrection of Christ, personal immortality and retribution in the future life. They also denied the existence of angels. They denied the supremacy of faith and upheld the freedom of human will. They believed that good and evil are the choice of man and that man could do one or the other at his discretion with impunity because the soul dies with the body.

Of course, there are churches and people today who hold these tenets. Their gospel maintains the outward semblance of Christianity while they deny and destroy its inner supernatural content. This gospel is like a blown egg, pricked by pinholes at both ends and the contents blown out. It looks normal to the eye, but investigation reveals it is but a shell with neither life nor substance.

Christ answered their trap simply, "You are mistaken, not knowing the Scriptures nor the power of God." Did you know that Christ answered every objection the unbeliever can produce in these few words? The answer always lies in not knowing the Word of God or His power.

Why did they not know the Scripture? Wise in their own knowledge and philosophy, they were ignorant of the Scriptures that were able to make them wise unto salvation. That great Apostle, Paul, in I Corinthians 15 declares that the Gospel of Christ was, according to the Scripture that Jesus died, that He was buried, and that He rose again on the third day. This sounds like resurrection to me.

The second reason for their error was that they did not know God's power. Once one admits the omnipotence of God, and the purposes of God for the world and life are known, there should be no difficulty in believing in a resurrection.

This story teaches glorious facts about the after-life. There is to be a resurrection. He makes plain that in the resurrected state we should live an entirely different type of life. There we shall have a body suited to the capacities of the spirit.

But Jesus taught also a blessed word concerning the intermediate state. He spoke of God as the God of Abraham, Isaac and Jacob, saying that God is not the God of the dead but of the living. The Sadducees knew that the sacred ashes of their revered fathers rested in the Holy Land. They were dead, yet God said they were living. "For dust you are and to dust you shall return," was not spoken of the soul.

The witness of the Spirit to eternal life within our hearts is our infallible password to heaven. Of course, "If any man has not the Spirit of Christ, he is none of His. But they that are Christ's have the assurance that at His coming, they too shall meet our Lord in the air where we shall be forever with the Lord." Sound like resurrection to you?

Dear Lord, You certainly reduced the matter to the basics. If there is error, either the Scripture is not known or the power of God is not known. Thank You for this insight. It encourages me as I boldly proclaim You and Your teachings. In Your name, amen.

June 17   A Full Man

Scripture Reading: Acts 6:8 to 7:60

Key Verse: "And Stephen, full of faith and power, did great wonders and signs among the people." Acts 6:8

Dr. Luke's admiration for this gifted young man is very evident, as he applies to Stephen again and again the word "full." Stephen obviously impressed Luke as being a very well-rounded, finely balanced individual.

First we see, in verse 5, that Stephen was "full of faith." He was not a man with a meager and timid faith. He did not have a sickly handful of faith. No, he was a man full of faith. That means that Stephen was on good terms with God. There was a fine intimacy between them that could exist in no other way, "For without faith it is impossible to please God."

Stephen was also full of wisdom. Jesus said, "The sons of this world are more shrewd in their generation than the sons of light." But Stephen is a lovely exception. Stephen had that faith that could see visions and dream dreams, but he was more than a dreamer. He was a man of hard-headed common sense. He was a man who brought faculties of leadership in the world of finance and politics and dedicated them fully upon the altar of his Lord. If there were hard questions about the administration of the church, they asked Stephen. Although young in years, he was wise in heart, and his answers showed keen insight and genius.

If there was a fine virtue that Stephen seemed to be more full of than any other, it would be that he was full of power. Where Stephen went, things happened. Changes took place. "They were not able to resist the Spirit and the wisdom by which he spoke." He was full of power. The word here rendered "power" is also the root from which our word dynamite comes. This young saint was full of moral dynamite. He was a spiritual tornado, sweeping things before him with an irresistible force. When folks stood in his presence, they found themselves strangely comforted and helped. But, he did not win men to himself, dear friends. No, he won them to Jesus.

Faith spoke in the tone of his voice. It looked out through his kindly eyes. It shone in every expression of his face. They "saw his face, as it had been the face of an angel." Truly, Stephen had found the secret of genuine faith.

What is the secret of Stephen? A man giving and giving as he did would exhaust himself in an hour's time, but for one fact. His fullness is fed from a hidden source. This is Stephen's secret, for he was also full of the Holy Spirit. You can only account for Stephen's faith and fine qualities by saying that he was a man in whom God dwelt in the person of the Holy Spirit.

Beloved, this fullness is just as much within your reach and mine as it was his. Stephen's fullness meant he was of the highest usefulness to God. While his position looked small, just looking after temporal needs, he administered it to the highest spiritual level. He gave out bread in such a way as to make people hunger for the bread of life. Faithful in temporal things, God made him mighty in spiritual things.

Whatever your position of service to God today, carry it out in the fullness of the Holy Spirit and you will be an abiding blessing to those around you. Be, as Stephen was, a full man for the Lord.

Dearest Lord, my service sometimes seems so meager. I am encouraged to remember Stephen. Fill me with Your Spirit, I pray, that I might be of the highest usefulness to You. Help me serve at the highest spiritual level, being faithful with that which I have been entrusted. Thank You for the privilege of serving You. Amen.

June 18   The Greatest Trial

Scripture Reading: Genesis Chapter 22:1-18

Key Verse: "Take now your son, your only son Isaac, whom you love, and go to the land of Moriah, and offer him there as a burnt offering..." Genesis 22:2

So long as men live in the world, they will turn to this story with unwavering interest. There is only one scene in history by which it is surpassed, when our Father God gave His Isaac, Jesus, to a death from which there would be no turning back. God and Abraham were friends, and here the infinite love of God stepped in to stay the hand of Abraham at the critical moment, sparing his friend what He would not spare Himself.

Abraham must have possessed no ordinary character, for early was the call of God placed on him. The God of glory called him out, "Get out of your country, from your family and from your father's house..." This call involved hardship, but each step of real advance in the spiritual life will involve an altar on which some fragment of self is offered. Nothing strengthens us so much as isolation and transplantation, and these were the first sacrifices of Abraham.

Accompanying this call, though, was a promise to make Abraham a great nation, and all the families of the earth would be blessed through him. This call, and the promise that goes with it, combine to form the key to the rest of Abraham's life. He was from first to last a separated man, separated by faith.

And so we see Abraham come to this test as a man of faith, prepared by God for this moment. Then came this startling command without reason given, and without a promise made, "Take now your son, your only son Isaac, whom you love, and go to the land of Moriah, and offer him there as a burnt offering..." Abraham's obedience to God's command threatened all the values of the past, all the promises for the future. But remember, Satan tempts us, but God tests us.

The outstanding fact of Abraham's life is that he obeyed. While Isaac was not slain, yet in the deep essential spirit of Abraham and in his intention, volition, and surrender, the thing was actually done. What was the secret of this determined obedience? "And Abraham said to his young man, 'Stay here with the donkey, the lad and I will go yonder and worship, and we will come back to you,'" verse five says. Note that he said "we" will worship, and "we" will come back. There is no greater revelation of the triumph of faith anywhere. In Hebrews 11, the writer says that what Abraham did, he did accounting that God was able to raise Isaac up from the dead.

The ultimate of faith, then, is such obedience to the call of God as brings the soul to the point of giving up. And we are not speaking of giving up something wrong, but of giving up anything and everything necessary for the accomplishment of divine purpose. How often the human heart stops just short in fellowship with God, halting just at this point.

When there fell from the lips of an apostle words telling Jesus to spare Himself, the answer of Jesus was "Get behind me, Satan." The philosophy of "spare yourself" is the philosophy of hell. Heaven's philosophy is that which carries us all the way into fellowship with God who spared not His Son, but delivered Him up for us all.

Dear Father, I am challenged by the faith of Abraham. He depended not on what he saw, but on what he understood about Your faithfulness, Your omnipotence, and Your righteousness. My heart beats faster to realize that You are preparing me as well. Help me to walk worthily, Father, I pray. Amen.

June 19   A Good Sportsman

Scripture Reading: 2 Timothy Chapter 2

Key Verse: "And also if anyone competes in athletics, he is not crowned unless he competes according to the rules." 2 Timothy 2:5

In the ancient Olympic Games, a competitor had to be of high moral character, for as the athletes were presented to the crowds the question was asked, "Has anyone anything against this man?"

Paul is saying that he runs with all the ardor and earnestness of the Grecian athlete. And so, let us think of the characteristics that go to make a good sportsman in the Christian sense. First he takes part in the game. Those who stand on the sidelines and criticize the players are like children in the market place calling to their playmates saying "We want to play wedding." But, one said, "That's too glad." "Then we want to play funeral." And one said, "Oh that's too sad." So they stood there glaring at each other instead of playing the game. Paul's team was out to win the world to the kingdom of God. Even then there were Christians who were not in the game.

Paul spoke as our coach when he said. "This one thing I do, forgetting what lays behind I press on...." He had strenuous devotion to the cause. He also called us to throw off the burdens of the world, secret sins, and the impediment of the things which clog our feet. Let us also have constancy, steadfastness in our race.

There is a famous Greek story of a race run between Hippomenes and Atalanta. Atalanta was a beautiful maiden who refused to marry anyone unless he competed with her in a race and won. The penalty for failure to win was death. Many entered, but so swift of foot was she that none could compete with her. At last there appeared Hippomenes who had been given three golden apples for the race. He was told to drop them one after another on the ground as he ran. The race began, and swift as he was, Hippomenes soon felt the breath of Atalanta upon his neck. So, taking one of the apples, he threw it before her. She gave a moment's glance at it, yet it was enough to give Hippomenes a few feet gain. Again he felt her gaining and so he threw another golden apple at her feet. This time she stopped and touched it and though it took but a moment it was enough to make her lose what she had gained. Now the goal was near, summoning all her strength she quickly made up on the panting youth and was on the point of passing him when in despair he threw the largest and most beautiful apple at her feet. This time Atalanta could not resist the temptation but stooped to pick it up and rising, made for the goal. But it was too late. Temptation had been too strong, and in yielding, she lost the race.

Satan, our adversary, would throw the golden apple of ease at our feet. "Sit down; rest a while, why so eager? Turn aside and rest, let up." So, hear me, my friend. If you have begun the race, see that you run well. Keep your eyes fixed on Jesus. Find strength where Jesus found it, in "The joy set before Him." Think much of your goal, the stimulus of the prize. Take fresh heart as you see the other witnesses who are watching and cheering you along. Take another look into the eyes of that precious Savior of yours and press for the mark more determined than ever to make this race a victorious one, and to gain an immortal crown that does not fade away, and above all to hear His "Well done," ring forth at the finish line.

Father God, to hear "Well done" at the finish line is my greatest goal. Help me avoid the golden apples of ease and temptation and with Paul, join in the game with all the strength, passion, and steadfastness I have. Amen.

June 20   The Parable of the Soil

Scripture Reading: Matthew 13:1-9

Key Verse: "He who has ears to hear, let him hear!" Matthew 13:9

This parable is commonly called the Parable of the Sower, but even a slightly thoughtful reading of it will show that it is incorrectly named. In this story Jesus is not putting the emphasis upon the sower or the seed, but upon the different kinds of soil upon which the seed falls.

That soil is the human heart, and in the parable some was hard, some was stony, some was thorny, and some was good. Naturally all did not yield the same increase and harvest. But the difference in the yield was not the fault of the sower or the seed but of the reception given by the soil of the human heart.

No wonder Jesus warns us to take heed how we hear. As Jesus faced that vast throng as he spoke that day by the sea shore, He saw four kinds of hearers.

There were those present on whom the message was utterly wasted. Perhaps they heard it with their minds wandering fruitlessly in every direction. Or perhaps they heard it with lips curled in scorn, or by proxy, regretting that so and so wasn't there, sure the message was not for them. Unmoved and unwon, they took up their drab lives as if they had been listening to the prattlings of a parrot instead of the teachings of the Son of God. What was wrong with this wayside soil? It was not wanting in fertility. It had the same capacity for a rich harvest as the best soil in the field. Only one thing was wrong. It was so hard that the seed sown on it had no chance. And that's what's wrong with the unresponsive hearer. His heart has grown hard. Therefore he locks the door in the face of the knocking Christ and goes along his Godless way.

Sometimes this hardening is the result of a definite crisis. It dates from the particular hour in which we lose some spiritual battle. But most often this hardness is the result of a long process of conscious disobedience. As we hear truth and persistently refuse to put it into practice a deadly callous steals upon us like a numbing sleep until we become "gospel hardened," until our eyes go out and our ears grow deaf.

There were also those who made a quick and ready response to the appeal of Jesus. They could hardly wait till the sermon was over to dash forward and take the preacher by the hand and say gushingly, "Lord, I'll follow You wherever You take me." They were all eagerness and enthusiasm. What was wrong with them?

Did they make too quick a decision? No, we can never respond too quickly. Was it too much enthusiasm? No, No, we all need more of it. The trouble was, they were as quick to quit as they were to begin. They were shallow, superficial, and flighty. They sought to live in the realm of their emotions instead of their convictions. They listened to the voice of inclination rather than the voice of duty. They were guided by their feelings instead of bravely doing what they knew they ought to do regardless of feeling.

Yes, they had opposition. They had to face the sun and the wind. Yet the same sun that scorched the wheat on one ground brought life and fruition to the wheat on another ground. The shallow believer's trouble is that he yielded to circumstances that might have brought only great strength and rich victory had he not surrendered to his weakness.

Tomorrow we will learn from two more types of soil. Have you found yours yet?

Lord, I confess that I have not been the best soil to bring fruit to Your Word. Please forgive me and help me to be the best soil for Your teaching that there is. Amen.

June 21   The Parable of the Soil II

Scripture Reading: Mark 4:1-20
Key Verse: "He who has ears to hear, let him hear!" Mark 4:9

Back beside the shore with the Master, He continues His lesson on the soil that represents the hearts of the hearers of the Word. As Jesus preached, there were those who heard and responded, but their response soon ceased to be wholehearted, if it was ever so. The seed sprang up and began to grow but thorns began to grow also. What was wrong with this soil?

It was not lacking in fertility. But it was not capable of growing a harvest of thorns and a harvest of wheat at the same time. Not one of us, no matter how strong or weak can serve two masters. Thorns are anything that chokes the wheat. They may be otherwise positive elements of life that have gotten out of balance or they may be glaring sins. Jesus mentions three of them in this parable. The first is worry. Poor care-filled souls cannot be fruitful. Look at Martha and how her anxious worry spoiled a dinner party for the Lord.

Another thorn is money, not money itself, but the love of it. Wealth is very absorbing. Many men and women get choked by their money making and money loving just like a bee gets strangled in its own honey.

The third thorn is pleasure. Christianity demands that we put first things first. We cannot allow the best to be crowded out by the second best. If it uses up my energies and resources and lessens my usefulness to Christ, then priorities need to be reconsidered.

I remember how we would thin out the corn on father's farm. To the ignorant it looked ruthless, but I did it in faith that the soil, by concentrating on fewer stalks would bring a greater harvest. It did. Here is a revealing poem by an unknown author which shines light on our subject:

On Monday she lunched with the housing committee.
With statistics and stew she was filled.
Then she dashed to a tea on "The crime in our city,"
And dined with the church ladies guild.
On Tuesday she went to a Babies' Week lunch
and a tea on good citizenship.
At dinner she spoke to the Trade Union bunch.
There wasn't a date she dared skip.
On Wednesday she managed two annual dinners,
One at noon, and the other at night.
On Thursday a luncheon on Bootlegging Sinners
And a dinner on "War, Is it right?"
"World problems we face," was the Friday noon date,
And a luncheon address as you guessed.
Then she wielded a fork while a man from New York
Spoke at dinner on social unrest.
On Saturday noon she fell in a swoon,
Missed a speech on "the Youth of our Land."
Poor thing, she was through for she never came to,
But died with a spoon in her hand.

Dear one, "Be still and know that I am God."
    Finally, there was present the fruitful hearer. He was fruitful because not only did he hear and receive, but having heard, he kept it by putting it into practice.
    When I was a lad, I planted a garden, and then dug it up the next day to see how it was growing. It takes patience to grow a Christ-like soul and to do a Christ-like work. Beloved, let us not be weary in well doing for in due season we shall reap, if we faint not.

Dear Lord, I notice that the good soil, the last hearer, didn't write the lesson down, he didn't memorize it, he DID it. Lord, help me to be a doer of the word and not a hearer only. I want to be good and fruitful soil for Your word. Amen

June 22   Gideon's Army

Suggested Reading: Judges Chapter 7

Key Verses: "So Gideon and the hundred men who were with him came to the outpost of the camp at the beginning of the middle watch, just as they had posted the watch; and they blew the trumpets and broke the pitchers…—they held the torches in their left hands and the trumpets in their right hands for blowing—and they cried, 'The sword of the Lord and of Gideon!' And every man stood in his place all around the camp; and the whole army ran and cried out and fled." Judges 7:19-22.

A stalwart young Hebrew, Gideon, was beating out wheat when the Angel of the Lord appeared to him and said, "The Lord is with you, you mighty man of valor!" Gideon doubted that statement and asked for a sign of the proof of his mission. God gave him three signs to prove His power and promises, and thus was Gideon convinced. Finally ready to obey God, he prepared to deliver Israel from her enemy.

But Israel was not only enslaved; she was degraded. Her condition was God's punishment upon the people for their idolatry. Before Gideon prepared to lead an army against the enemy of his country, he had first to march against the grove of idols at his father's house. Even Gideon's household had succumbed to the corruption. His own father had by his house a grove and an altar to Baal. Just so, true service for God on the part of the church must commence with reformation within the church. We must march against idols of our own hearts and put ourselves right with God and one another, then God can use us as He used Gideon.

At the first call of the trumpet, an army of 32,000 men flocked to the standard of Gideon. But God told Gideon to cut the number down. And so, the men were tested. From their mountain encampment, he let his army take one long look at the Camp of Midianites in the valley below them; their camels swarming like locusts and the morning sun reflected from thousand of brass shields. "Whoever is fearful and afraid let him return." There was no place for cowards in Gideon's army. After

22,000 accepted that invitation to go home, Gideon was left with an army of only 10,000. What was such a small number against the host of Midian? But God tells him that his army was still too large. It must be reduced by another test. This test was a test of zeal. Heated and thirsty, the men were led to a brook. Those who lay down on their bellies and drank with their mouth to the water were sent home, all 9700. The 300 who threw the water up to their mouths with their hands were the men chosen for Gideon's army.

And Gideon's army of 300, what can we learn from them? The Bible relates the story in these words, "And every man stood in his place all around the camp; and the whole army (of Midian) ran and cried out and fled." First, they stood, united in battle. Each faithfully executed the duty they were given. Lastly, they were all around the camp, just exactly where God had put them. The broken pitchers, the lighted torches, and the blowing trumpets gave way to a shout, "The sword of the Lord and of Gideon!" and God gave the victory.

Remember that in the church as well as in Gideon's army, God's divine method is quality, not quantity. God is never dependent upon numbers. Our part is to stand together, united, where God has placed us, faithfully executing the duty He has given us.

Dear Father, Grant me courage to face the battles of faith that inevitably come. Help me to be a willing, obedient soldier to the Cross. Place me, Lord, where You will, clothe me in the armor only You can give and then, having done all, help me to stand. Amen.

June 23   How Two Preachers Got In and Out of Jail

Scripture Reading: Acts 16:16-34
Key Verse: "...what must I do to be saved?" Acts 16:30

Paul and Silas were holding a revival at Philippi. Day by day a young woman, who the Scriptures say had a spirit in her, followed Paul and Silas around making slighting remarks and doing some fortune-telling. Well Paul had enough of that and decided to stop this girl in her wild career, so he rebuked the spirit and it came out of her. Her masters protested that their business was being hurt and dragged Paul and Silas off to the local magistrate. He, being a pagan, beat them and had them placed in the inner jail, charging the jailor to keep them safely. All this because they loved God and dared to preach the gospel fearlessly.

Well, the night wore on, but there was no sleep for those men with bleeding backs. They were unable to lie down or sit up, but bless God, they could sing and pray. That's spiritual victory. As they were singing and Paul was praying, God shook that old prison with an earthquake that shook it off its foundations, its doors off their hinges and the keeper out of his bed and into the kingdom of God.

He came in trembling and asking what he must do to be saved. The Scripture says, they told him to believe on the Lord Jesus Christ and he would be saved and his household. He took them the same hour of the night and washed their wounds and fed them, and he and his household were baptized. Then the jailor rejoiced, believing God.

Now, I want you to see three things in this story. First, the all-important question was asked, "... what must I do to be saved?" This question settles our destiny and our eternal future. The jailor's condition was the same as thousands around us tonight. Asleep to the need of his soul, and it took an earthquake to wake him up and bring him to God. That's conviction of the Holy Spirit. There was no coaxing, no card signing, and no pleading. There was real humility and genuine repentance.

He was an ignorant man. But God did not let him stay in ignorance long. The way is plain and simple; believe on the Lord Jesus Christ. But how was he to know if no one told him?

Because Paul and Silas told the jailor, there were blessed results. That is God's part. We may share what we know, but it is God who saves. The jailor took God at His word. How do I know? Because the Scripture says "He believed God." He was obedient. How do I know? He was baptized the same hour of the night and he made restitution. The Scripture says "he washed their stripes." He did all he could to undo the past. As he rejoiced, they enjoyed Christian fellowship. He was a child of God with the joy of salvation in his heart. And the whole family followed.

Details and times may differ, but we all come awake to the need, are told the good news and receive it with great joy. It takes an hour for some, and a lifetime for others. Are you in tune with God's divine appointments? Could you see the purpose for being unjustly thrown in jail if it happened to you? Paul and Silas just sang and prayed and watched to see what God was doing, then became part of His plans. Open your eyes to what God is doing around you, conform to His plans, and rejoice in the blessed results.

Dear Lord, how exciting to look at the circumstances of life in an entirely different way. Nothing happens to me that You don't know about, so I will try to quit complaining so much and look around to see how I can become part of what You are doing. I want to conform to Your plans and see eternal and blessed results. In Jesus's name, amen.

June 24   Lame in Both Feet

Scripture Reading: II Samuel Chapter 9

Key Verse: "Now David said, 'Is there still anyone who is left of the house of Saul, that I may show him kindness for Jonathan's sake?'" II Samuel 9:1

As king, David's life was given over as a representative of Jehovah, and so his life was filled with holiness, and joy, and humility. Instead of arrogance, David shows forth mercy and righteousness. He begins looking about to find someone on whom he might bestow kindness. He did not wait for the need to present itself, but actively searched for someone to help.

Isn't this just like God? God sought Adam, "Where are you?" and the Good Shepherd seeks the lost sheep. And, just so, we find David inquiring. And as David's mercy meets Mephibosheth's misery, it is a picture of the mercy of our Heavenly Father who is ever seeking, as well as saving, the lost. God is ever gracious to sinners, no matter how miserable and terrible their condition.

Notice three things in this picture, especially. First, look at the "sinner." Mephibosheth is a true picture of the sinner's curse. He was under the shadow of the house of Saul, born of a family whose head left an inheritance of sorrow to all his seed. Saul's sin had ruined his house and slain all but this one in consequence of his folly. This is our very condition without Christ. We are born into the world with an inherited curse. Mephibosheth inherited the curse of Saul, and the sinner inherits the curse of fallen humanity.

Further examination show that Mephibosheth was unable to help himself. We are told he was "lame in both feet." The very essence of man's fall is helplessness. In addition, Mephibosheth understands his position in relation to David, calling himself, "a dead dog." Yes, God loves us not because we deserve it, but because it is His nature to love. And finally, Mephibosheth represents the sinner's separation from God. He was hidden away from David, among strangers and far from home.

Secondly, see the Savior in this story. David here is evidencing the love of God. We have already noted his seeking someone to whom he might show God's love. Then, notice that David brought Mephibosheth all the way across the land to where he was. Beloved, that is what God does for us. He makes provision, He seeks us out, and then He brings us to Him. And David's provision for Mephibosheth was unmerited. Mephibosheth had never done anything to deserve or earn David's love. God's provision for us is also undeserved. His grace is unmerited, and unending. There is life, and plenty, and joy, and peace for Mephibosheth at David's table. All his inheritance is restored to him, and he dines as a child of the king, at his very table. We also find life, and plenty, and joy, and peace at our King's table.

Finally, look at the salvation that Mephibosheth receives. Like the prodigal, Mephibosheth would probably have been glad to simply be a servant in this great household. But, no, in David's care he is safe and satisfied. He sets a beautiful picture of true humility when he refers to himself as a "dead dog." Is there a more useless thing on earth than a "dead dog?" Mephibosheth realized the graciousness of David's offer. He had been unable to enjoy his inheritance until the king opened a way.

Beloved, we, too, have an inheritance, in Christ our King. And we, too, are safe and satisfied only in His care.

Dear Loving Father, thank You that You sought me, that You found me, and that You brought me to Yourself. Thank You for Your tender care, Your provision, and Your continued love and protection. I am so very grateful. Amen.

June 25 — Walk in Wisdom

Scripture Reading: Ephesians Chapter 5

Key Verse: "See then that you walk circumspectly, not as fools but as wise, redeeming the time, because the days are evil." Ephesians 5:15

Paul's constant appeal to us in the Book of Ephesians is to be what we are. Our walk must correspond to our position in Christ. The sinner walks as a fool, but the saint as the wise. "See then!" Paul admonishes. Take heed to your walk.

Now a walk is made up of steps taken one at a time. And all about us are the pitfalls of the world. We must not only watch our step, but know where the next step will take us. We should carefully consider our witness in each area of our conduct. What about our manner of speech? What about our fashion in clothes? What about our companions, or our habits, the magazines and books we read? What about the way we spend our money? These are all indicative of the degree of light in our lives. Consistency in common things is obligatory, for we are taught to avoid every appearance of evil.

We walk as pilgrims through an unregenerate world, and all around us is gross spiritual and moral darkness. We must not, unthinkingly, walk in the fashions or morals of the world just because they are the prevalent manner. Do not walk as an unthinking person, a fool. How does a fool walk? A fool says there is no God. A fool is unthinking, takes the way of least resistance, and has no thought of consequences. A fool goes along with the crowd.

We are to walk "as wise." It means to live with your eyes, minds, and heart opened Godward, for "the fear of the Lord is the beginning of wisdom." It means to seize upon the light Christ promises to give. Be alert and eager to follow that light whether you find yourself alone against a crowd, or in the company of other saints.

Countless Christians, people who dearly love the Lord, have taken no thought of their walk. The wise Christian has a purpose in mind, a goal in sight, and makes every step count. The wisdom of God, hidden and eternal, is revealed and taught by the Spirit. That wisdom consists of knowing the purpose of God, having the mind of Christ, and depending upon the guidance of the Spirit. It is truly only the wise who dare to take a stand for the truth and the standards of the Divine Word.

The last section of our text says, "Redeeming the time, because the days are evil." This literally means to grasp an opportunity. Picture merchants buying up a scarce commodity; this is to be our attitude towards our time. Every moment counts, each second is a link with eternity. We dare not let time slip by with no sense of the value of it in the light of our few years upon this earth.

So, beloved, here is the way to maintain a walk in wisdom. First, seek to understand God's will. Now, God has revealed His will in His Word. In God's Word He has given either principles or precepts to cover every step of our walk in wisdom. One who desires to walk "as wise" will study the Word under the prayerful tutelage of the Holy Spirit. Redeeming the time will mean that some portion of our day is set aside for this purpose.

Secondly, after systematically and prayerfully considering the lessons learned in God's Word, redeem the time by deliberately and purposefully setting out to walk in the wisdom He has given you.

Dear God, I deeply desire to walk in wisdom to be a testimony of Christ before the world. I know You are the only source for wisdom, and today I humbly come before You asking for wisdom for my daily walk. Help me to redeem the time You have so graciously given me. Amen.

June 26   That Prophetic Night

Scripture Reading: Exodus Chapter 12
Key Verse: "...at midnight... the Lord struck all the firstborn in the land of Egypt...." Exodus 12:29

Until the great night upon which Christ was born, and that other night of His betrayal, this was the most momentous night in the history of mankind. This night opened a new chapter in God's dealings with the world. When the sun set that evening, Israel was a race of slaves. When the sun rose the next morning, Israel was a nation, a nation on the march.

Over all of Egypt the April moon shed its golden light. Against the clear sky rose the mighty Pyramid of Cheops, and in front of that pyramid, the Sphinx stared out over the white moon-lit desert with its stony, mysterious gaze. Along the River Nile, a thousand villages were asleep. Pharaoh slumbered. All Egypt was asleep. But, in the homes of the Hebrew slaves, it was different.

On the doorposts and on the lintels of every Hebrew hut and home, there was the stain of blood. Within every house, the families stood by a table where a roasted lamb was ready to be eaten. Their staffs were in their hands. Their loins were girded. Not a word was spoken, but on every face there was expectation and dread. Suddenly, there arose a great cry, a long wail of woe, a tidal wave of lamentation that swept over the whole land. From Pharaoh's palace to the humblest home of Egypt, it was alike. Death reigned everywhere, and a moan of anguish went up to the skies. But, in the houses of Israel, where God's command had been obeyed, the angel of death passed over.

This is the heart of the gospel, a prophetic picture of the sacrifice to be made for you and for me. That is, Christ is the Lamb of God, slain from the foundations of the world. Christ died as a substitute for us. Christ's blood has been shed for us. This truth is the very secret of the survival of Christianity. It is Christianity's hope of victory in the ages to come. It has something more than ethics, and more than example.

It has a mighty act of God's justice and love upon which you can put your trust.

During the Civil War, a man paid a visit to the battlefield of Chickamauga, where on September 20, 1863 the army was almost destroyed by the Confederates. At one of the newly made graves, the visitor found a man planting flowers. Walking over to him, he kindly asked, "Is it a son who is buried here?" "No," the man answered. "An uncle or brother?" he questioned again. "No," the man again replied. Finally, the visitor asked whose memory he sought to honor.

The man told him that he had been drafted into the army. Just before saying goodbye to his wife and family, to report to his training camp, a young fellow came to see him and said, "You have got a wife and family depending on you, whereas I am unmarried and have no one. Let me go in your place." The offer was accepted, and the young man went off to training camp in his place. At the battle of Chickamauga, he was mortally wounded, and after hearing the news the man journeyed to mark and honor the grave of his friend. The visitor was much touched by this story, and went on his way over the battlefield. But, passing by the grave again later, he found it not only covered in flowers, but cut into a rough board at the head of the grave were these four words, "He died for me." Those four words sound the length, depth, and breadth of our faith, "He died for me."

Dear Lord, the world still slumbers unaware. Thank You so much that the blood of Jesus covers me. Thank You that it is not on my own merit, or righteousness that I rest, but on that of Your precious, spotless Son. He died for me, and I am so very grateful. Amen.

June 27   Dallying with Destiny

Scripture Reading: I Kings 20:31-43
Key Verse: "While your servant was busy here and there, he was gone." I Kings 20:40a

War raged between Ahab, King of Israel, and Ben-Hadad of Syria. With a crushing defeat, Ben-Hadad feared his life would be demanded of him. So, he sent ambassadors robed in sackcloth, covered with ashes and crawling in humility before King Ahab to know the fate of their king. Ahab, in pride of victory and thus beside himself, said, "Is he still alive? He is my brother." That meant freedom for Ben-Hadad and defeat and trouble for Ahab. Thus gloating with triumph, Ahab let his enemy slip through his hand. Retribution came quickly. A miserable dust-covered man called to him from the roadside as Ahab's chariot drove by. The poor wretch cried out that he had been told to guard a prisoner in the recent war, but, "While your servant was busy here and there, he was gone." Ahab's sense of military trust was quickened, and he immediately pronounced judgment upon such negligence. At once, the dust-covered figure revealed himself as the prophet of the Lord, and pronounced judgment on Ahab in dramatic fashion. Ahab, after all, was the one who was busy here and there, thus allowing the prisoner to escape.

How many responsibilities are shunned, how many opportunities are passed by, how many sins of omission are committed because of a wrong use of that word, "busy"? Certainly, it is right in light of eternity to be "busy." And, of all times in history, people are busy now. We cannot go fast enough for the push of industry. And certainly busy people are the ones who do things. Busy people have been the trailblazers down through the ages. They have crossed new mountains, charted new seas, discovered new worlds, ushered in new epochs.

God is busy. Ever see God work? He beautifies the hillsides with flowers, paints His sunsets and sunrises, makes the enchanting landscapes of mountains, and gorges with rivers and lakes sparkling with their diamond jewelry. His supreme concern is for man. And man, His highest creation, is endowed with the capacity to be busy for Him in this world.

Yes, today of all days we should be busy. But our text says, "Busy here and there," and it is an incriminating confession. It shows looseness of purpose, lack of fidelity, betrayal to duty. With what are you busy? Christians are the only people with a cure for earth's ills. Will we falter?

So, what is the remedy? The greatest One who ever lived said, "Seek first the Kingdom of God and His righteousness and all these things shall be added to you." What is the task He has given you? Don't allow busyness to get in the way of that task! I don't say you can do anything that you want to do, but we can do everything that God wants us to do. Yes, every one of us has the ability through grace to perform the task to which he is called. However humble a task may seem, if it is the Lord's work, it is eternally profitable.

King Ahab failed because he was not busy at his own task. He was simply busy "here and there." Oh, we can certainly see his trouble, and most of us can probably see his trouble in our own lives! He allowed secondary things to absorb him so that he neglected the primary things of life. The things he did were not necessarily vicious things. But we must put first things first. We must put the things of the Kingdom first.

Dear Father God, please forgive me for too often being busy, here and there. Help me to say 'no' to the secondary, distracting things that take my eyes off of the task You have given me. Help me rather, to be absorbed in You. Amen.

June 28   The Question of the Ages

Suggested Reading: Mark 15:1-15

Key Verse: "Pilate answered and said to them again, 'what then do you want me to do with Him whom you call the King of the Jews?'" Mark 15:12

What manner of man is this Jesus Christ? He was born in the meanest circumstances, yet the air above was filled with hallelujahs. His lodging was a cattle pen, yet He drew distinguished visitors from afar. His birth was contrary to the laws of life. His death was contrary to the laws of death. There is no miracle so inexplicable as His life. He had no cornfields or fisheries, yet He could spread a table for 5,000. He walked no beautiful carpets, but He could walk the sea and it supported Him. His crucifixion was the crime of crimes, yet no other price could pay the world's redemption. When He died, few mourned his death, but a black crepe was hung over the sun. Though men trembled not at their deeds, the earth trembled and shook. Sin never touched Him. Corruption could not get a hold on Him. The soil was red with His blood, but could not claim His body. Three years He preached the gospel, yet He wrote no book, built no church and had no money backing Him. He was born in a borrowed manger and buried in a borrowed tomb. And the question rings through the ages, "What then shall I do with Him?"

Jesus stood before Pilate, but Pilate did not know Him. He asked Christ, "Are you the King of the Jews?" And Jesus said that His kingdom was not of this world. No, the child born of the Virgin Mary in Bethlehem did not begin His career there. His advent into the world was but the manifestation of the purpose of the Godhead moving toward a kingdom of righteousness on earth as it is in heaven. Before Pilate, as He stood there in the flesh, Jesus claimed to be King. But is He? The world does not look like it. There is no place for Christ in the schemes of our world's leaders. What about us? Do we have room for Him? Do we know who He is?

Paul knew. Thomas confessed, "My Lord and My God." Yes, with all the devout, godly men of all ages, we should bring adoring worship and prostrate ourselves at His pierced feet exclaiming, "My Lord and My God." Christ is the center of creation, prophecy, history, and redemption. He is the only hope of the world.

Today, and only for a little while, the enemy of our souls—Satan—is the prince of this world. But his reign will soon be done. He is a usurper, a squatter. When I was a boy, I visited the Great Parliament Buildings of the Dominion of Canada in Ottawa. While no one was looking, and no convocation was in session, I sneaked in and sat down in the chair where the King of England and the Governor General of Canada sit. But, I soon had to get off. So, too, the devil will soon vacate the chair as the god of this world, for the Rightful King is coming!

So, what will we do, today, with this Jesus who is called Christ? Stand for your King and Savior. Stand alone, if necessary. Serve Him. And lovingly, longingly watch for His appearing. As a young man who was married in my church before a large assembly once said to me, "Pastor, I didn't really see a soul, only my lovely bride." There were many present who witnessed the appearing of the lovely bride, but there was one who not only believed and witnessed, but who loved her appearing. As the bride of Christ, let us rejoice, saying, "Even so, come, Lord Jesus."

My Lord, and My God, I thank You that You are the Rightful King! Forgive me for all the times that I don't do anything with my knowledge of You, Jesus. Rather, now, today, tomorrow and all my days let me serve You with all my heart, words and deeds. Amen. Even so, come, Lord Jesus.

June 29   In the Desert

Scripture Reading: Isaiah Chapter 35

Key Verse: "The wilderness and the wasteland will be glad for them, and the desert shall rejoice and blossom as the rose." Isaiah 35:1

In the Bible, the desert is a symbol for hardship, trial, difficulty, temptation, and testing. The nation Israel, in a sense, got its start in the desert, but they are not the only ones to have such a journey. In fact there seems to be a desert experience in the life of nearly every Christian. However painful it may be, we are led there for a reason by God, and there are deep spiritual benefits to be found. In the desert, our needs are intensified and there is no place else to turn to have them supplied but to God.

The first thing we should remember is to draw upon Israel's experience in the desert. "He...fed you with manna which you did not know...that He might make you know that man shall not live by bread alone; but man lives by every word that proceeds from the mouth of the Lord," we are told in Deut. 8. God was there in the desert, providing for Israel and teaching her. In Exodus, Scripture records that God went before them as a pillar of cloud and a pillar of fire, guiding their every step and protecting them. He will do no less for us, dear ones.

Secondly, God leads us into the desert to train us in Christian character. In Luke, we find John the Baptist living a life of self-denial before beginning his ministry. Even Christ our Savior went out to the desert places, there to pray. The loneliness of the desert will drive us to seek the companionship of the Heavenly Father in prayer.

God makes the desert a valuable place. Every year a caravan of camels stretching over seven miles crosses the Sahara to get salt. In the South American desert sulphur, borax, and nitrates are found. Gold deposits can be found in some deserts. And we, too, can find hidden spiritual valuables in the desert if we are willing to look and dig for them.

Isaiah 35:1 tells us the desert will "blossom like a rose..." Yes, on the desert one sees beautiful flowers and dramatic sunsets unlike any found elsewhere. The coloring of the rocks is gorgeous and beauty is all about, if you have eyes to see it. A spiritual desert can be a place of beauty if we look for the hand of God.

Finally, there are three kinds of people who go to the desert. First, there are those who have desert experiences unnecessarily, as a result of their own sin. Jeremiah 17:5-6 states that the man who departs from the Lord and leans upon the flesh "…shall be like a shrub in the desert and shall not see when good comes, but shall inhabit the parched places in the wilderness." Then there are those who, like Israel of old, have come to the desert because God leads them there, but they grumble on account of the hardship and do not reap the full benefit of the journey. Finally, God leads some into the desert, and instead of murmuring they rejoice and thank God for His leading, noting the beauty and the valuables they could not have otherwise found.

You may be in the desert land today, beloved, or perhaps you will soon find yourself there. It is a harsh land of trial and testing, to be sure. But rest assured, our God is able to deliver you. God is there to guide you, to teach you, and to lead you out the other side.

Dear Heavenly Father, I confess I do not relish the times of testing and trial that come into the life of every believer. Yet, I covenant with You today, Lord, that when the desert experience comes, I will look to You there. I will submit myself into Your hands to learn the lessons that only the desert in my life can provide. Thank You, Father. Amen.

June 30   The First Missionary

Scripture Reading: John Chapter 4:39-42

Key Verses: "And many of the Samaritans of that city believed in Him because of the word of the woman who testified, 'He told me all that I ever did.' So when the Samaritans had come to Him, they urged Him to stay with them; and He stayed there two days. And many more believed because of His own word." John 4:39-41.

In the fourth chapter of John, we are told of Jesus's talk with a Samaritan woman. This woman was not only a Samaritan, but a woman even the Samaritans didn't esteem. But Jesus saw her as one of those for whom He was to die. And when the woman of Samaria got a vision of Christ, look what it did for her! First, she saw herself, then she saw her Savior, and finally she saw the people around her who needed Jesus, too.

One true glimpse of Jesus, and she left her water pot and ran to the city saying, "Come, see a Man who told me all the things I ever did. Could this be the Christ?" Oh, what a thrilling testimony that is from a heart set on fire by Christ and the knowledge of sins forgiven!

But notice, before the woman of Samaria ran to the city she was convinced of some necessary things. She was first convinced of the person of Christ. She believed something, she held a great doctrine. And, she was not ashamed to tell the people she knew, "Come and see." Oh, don't be afraid of your testimony!

One night in London, during the awful bombing of World War II, a little family stood on the veranda of their cottage outside London surveying the dark terribleness of the night. The mother sobbed out, "Oh, it looks as if all the lights of London have gone out!" But their nine-year-old daughter pointed heavenward and replied, "Yes, Mamma, London's lights are out, but God's lights are still shining." The world is in desperate need of God's light, dear one.

This woman of Samaria also knew the direction in which she as going. She went straight to the people she knew needed Jesus. We also need to speed along towards the hearts of men and women. Yes, we must reach the intellect, but the path is often through the heart, for out of the heart comes the issues of life. Go where the need is. It is not necessarily China or India. It may be a neighbor, or a friend that God lays on your heart.

A father was saying goodbye to his fine Christian son, who was about to embark to fight in the Second World War, when a big burly fellow shouted out to the soldiers, "Give them hell, boys, give 'em hell." The old, saintly father leaned over and said to his Christian boy, "Son, give them Jesus, give them Jesus." Oh, it is so easy for us to criticize the lost souls all about us. But, what we must do instead is give them Jesus.

With Jesus as our theme, Jesus as our source and Jesus as our vision, we will have a sense of delight, and optimism in our work. Jesus showed that sense of optimism in the face of the Samaritan woman. He saw her face and her heart. He saw the field white unto harvest. The first missionary of the New Testament was a new convert with a lifetime of reproach working against her. But an honest testimony and a vision of Jesus made her an effective witness. What has God given you?

Dear Heavenly Father, I come to you humbly asking today that You would give me a vision of others as You see them. Help me to see Jesus, and in the rellection of that vision to see myself and others more clearly. May the gratitude for my forgiven sins, and the testimony of Christ's redeeming love make me a useful tool in Your hands. In Jesus's name, amen.

Classic Christianity invites you to visit our website for more information!

www.classicchristianity.net

**We pray for the graces of insight and blessing as you seek a more intimate walk with Jesus.
Any glory, any praise, any blessing from this work belongs to God and God alone. Any mistake or error, we humbly acknowledge to be our own, and we apologize.**

Patricia Ediger   **Cara Shelton**
and their families

www.ingramcontent.com/pod-product-compliance
Lightning Source LLC
LaVergne TN
LVHW011414080426
835512LV00005B/56